Cocktails

& JOCKSTRAPS

Paul Rimstead

PRENTICE-HALL OF CANADA, LTD., SCARBOROUGH, ONTARIO

Canadian Cataloguing in Publication Data

Rimstead, Paul, 1935-
Cocktails & jockstraps

Includes stories which appeared in the Canadian
magazine.

ISBN 0-13-139436-3

1. Athletes—Canada—Biography. 2. Athletes—
Biography. 3. Rimstead, Paul, 1935—
4. Sportswriters—Canada—Biography. I. The
Canadian magazine. II. Title.

GV697.A1R55   796'.0922   C80-094758-4

Prentice-Hall, Inc., Englewood Cliffs, New Jersey
Prentice-Hall of Australia Pty., Ltd., Sydney
Prentice-Hall of India, Pvt., Ltd., New Delhi
Prentice-Hall International, Inc., London
Prentice-Hall of Japan, Inc., Tokyo
Prentice-Hall of Southeast Asia (Pte.), Ltd., Singapore

Production Editor: Joerg Klauck
Designer: Joe Chin
Cover photograph: John Ford
Composition: CompuScreen Typesetting Ltd.
Printed and bound in Canada by John Deyell Ltd.

Grateful acknowledgment is made to the
following for permission to reprint: *Toronto
Sun* columns, pp. 14, 17, Reprinted by
permission of the *Toronto Sun* Syndicate;
Photographs, pp. 8, 18, 20, 35, Reprinted by
permission of the *Toronto Sun* Syndicate;
Photograph, p. 22, J.N. Burnett; Photograph, p. 30,
Barry Gray; Photograph, p. 33, Ed Reagan;
Canadian Magazine photographs, pp. 46, 55, 61,
67, 90, 96, 101, 102, 130, 136, 141, 160, 166, 170,
177, Courtesy of *Today* Magazine; Photographs,
pp. 80, 84, 87, 151, by Jorgen Halling, Courtesy
of *Today* Magazine; Photographs, pp. 118, 125,
by Ken Elliott, Courtesy of *Today* Magazine;
Photograph, p. 72, Courtesy of Ken Elliott;
Photographs, pp. 148, 182, John Ford; Cartoon,
p. 186, Courtesy of Karl Mueller. *Canadian
Magazine* articles reprinted by permission of
Today Magazine.

ISBN 0-13-139436-3

1   2   3   4   5   JD   84   83   82   81   80

To my bankers, mortgagees, and income tax collectors without whose constant harassment this book would have been finished in half the time.

Special thanks to Denny Harvey, my editor at The Canadian Magazine, *and the gang at Prentice-Hall who never once admitted they did not believe my excuses.*

Contents

REFLECTIONS
in an empty glass

LAHAINA, MAUI, March 3, 1980—It is rather embarrassing, lying here in the hot Hawaiian sun, knowing I am the only guy on the beach wearing a Stayfree Maxi-Pad under his bathing suit.

I should hasten to explain, I suppose, that it is for purely medical reasons. You might wonder, when I don't even know you, why I am being so personal. Well sir, we would not be together at all if it were not for the reasons behind that sanitary napkin.

I am here in Hawaii recuperating for three weeks after a quaint bit of surgery called a hemorrhoidectomy. It is the type of operation nobody really notices and not once has anybody asked to see my scar.

Actually, my condition does not really bother me other than for the fact that I have to carry around an inflated, rubber doughnut cushion to sit on. And my only real embarrassment came the other day when, as I was leaving the swimming pool area, a guy tapped me on the arm and said: " I believe you have dropped something." I looked and there, to my horror, was my Stayfree Maxi-Pad sitting on the green carpet. It had fallen out of my bathing suit. I thanked him quietly, deftly scooped it up and, eyes fixed to the ground, made my way back to my room.

I did not know a soul there but I suspect I had become a conversation piece around the pool. I never did go back to that pool and, because of the embarrassment, checked out of that hotel, the Maui Palms, and moved to the Lahaina Shores the next day.

Now the only time I feel unwell is when I am in my condominium, look in the mirror, and see myself. My eyes have become used to looking at the bronzed bodies on the beach, vibrant and healthy in their brief bathing suits and bikinis. And there I stand before my reflection—Canadian-white in March, 45 and aging, my skinny arms and legs making

◀Celebrating my 45th birthday with two friends
in Edmonton's Royal Alexandra Hospital.

me look as if I have rickets. The sun will improve my color but I am stuck with the body. If any of the other guests are in the medical profession they have already pointed me out to their friends, saying, "There goes a guy with a lousy liver."

I checked out of the Royal Alexandra Hospital in Edmonton, Alberta, the other day and, as I stepped out into the 40-below weather, the words were still echoing in my mind:

"YOU CAN NOT DRINK AGAIN FOR THE REST OF YOUR LIFE!"

The hemorrhoidectomy, you see, was secondary. My main ailment was something called cirrhosis. I had to look it up and there it was on page 149 of the huge *New Webster Encyclopedic Dictionary:* "Cirrhosis: . . . A disease consisting of diminution and deformity of the liver, often seen in drunkards." Naturally, I fired a letter off to the guy who wrote that book explaining in no uncertain terms that I had always considered myself a heavy drinker. But a drunkard? Never.

When the doctor made his pronouncement, the words struck me with the force of a piledriver. I lay in my white hospital bed, turned my head slowly to look out the window, and tried, as they do in the movies, to be very brave. It was as if I was a talented athlete who had just been told he would never play again, a dancer told he would never dance. . . .

"Never?" I said quietly, not looking at the doctor.

"Never," he said firmly.

I buried my face in my pillow and cried.

It just wasn't fair. Why me? I had been training for more than twenty years, day and night. I was just reaching my peak. Like a weightlifter who keeps adding to his weights, gradually increasing his strength, I had built myself up to maximum capacity. I had become a world-class contender for the scotch-on-the-rocks title and, although it is not a tournament event, nobody ever handled Cointreau any better. Now, suddenly, they wanted to take all of this away from me.

"Your liver," the doctor said, "is two and a half times its normal size." He said it with a hint of amazement, as if he would like to enter it in the local agricultural fair.

So here I am in Hawaii, with skinny arms, skinny legs, and very thirsty. I have been doing a lot of thinking, preparing for a new way of life and suddenly it came to me. This whole thing could be a conspiracy.

The culprit could be Gerry Halpin, vice-president of Prentice-Hall of Canada, who has been trying to get me to write a book for the last ten years. It was obvious he felt drinking was my problem when, actually, it was merely a lack of discipline. Perhaps, this time, he arranged the entire thing, worried because he had given me a cash advance. I will certainly ask him as soon as I get back to my home in Toronto.

Frankly, though, I could never believe that of Gerry Halpin. He enjoys a double scotch as much as anyone I know. Heck, for him to end my drinking career would be akin to the time my trainer told me that he would have to geld my racehorse, Marital Problem. I reluctantly agreed, but I could never look that horse in the eye again.

I guess it was The Big Guy Up There who made the decision. When it comes right down to it, He makes them all. But, between you and me, I have started to suspect His perfection. Why is it He allowed man to discover the joys of alcohol when He knew damned well that there was a flaw in the body that He had created? If He had meant man to have a drink, you'd think He would have spent more time on the design of the liver. I guess I should be thankful but, no matter which way I look at it, I feel no better than an Edsel.

They gave me the bad news the morning of February 11, 1980, my 45th birthday. Dr.

Jim Bailey, the liver specialist, explained it quite simply. If I continued drinking the way I had—in excess of 26 ounces of whisky a day for 25 years—I would die. I might live seven more years, but, no longer and quite possibly not even that long. Dr. Dick Cherry, who is perhaps the world's greatest general practitioner, had taken one look at my dissipated, yellowed condition, plopped me into a wheelchair, booked me into the hospital, and ordered ten blood transfusions. I was not too happy about this seeing as how I was supposed to go out that night.

I do not understand medical terms but they tried to explain that my hemoglobin count was five—fourteen is normal—and that I should have been dead. Then they began sticking tubes into every opening they could find on my body, trying to determine why I had lost so much blood. They did not seem to believe me when I told them it was just my hemorrhoids, a minor discomfort I had learned to live with over the past eighteen years. I suspect they could not believe that a grown man would sit on a toilet and practically bleed to death before bothering to consult a doctor.

Finally, when they couldn't find out why I was bleeding, they called in Dr. Harry Hyde, a surgeon who, when you put a mask on him and place a scalpel in his hand, really does turn into Dr. Jekyll. I have no idea what he did back there but, by golly, he certainly made it difficult for me to go to the bathroom the next day.

Oh, well, that is all, if you will pardon the pun, behind me now and I have given my word that I will at least try a life of sobriety. But, I did reserve the right to make a choice if I don't like it. I told the doctors that, if I was absolutely bored and unable to cope, I would start drinking again and enjoy two or three good years instead of twenty boring ones. They, in turn, made me promise to make a tour of a liver ward before making such a decision.

So, here I am in Hawaii, having this absolutely wonderful time, strolling to downtown Lahaina each day to buy an ice cream cone. Then I come back to my room and sit here eating jellybeans. . . .

Miserable or not, though, I did take that cash advance from Gerry Halpin and have to at least go through the motions of writing a book. Maybe it's not really a book but just a collection of magazine stories I wrote more than ten years ago while at *The Canadian Magazine* when it was carried in weekend newpapers across the country.

I used to write about sports for newspapers. It was terrible, helping to make idols of jocks, who, while signing autographs for fifteen-year-old girls, stood looking at them, wondering if they had big nipples. That's why I switched to a magazine, so that I would have space to write about athletes, like the ones in this book, who were grown up. Too often, this doesn't happen until after they retire.

T he book I kept promising Gerry Halpin was to be called: The Saga of Annabelle the Wonder Horse, A Tale of Financial Woe. My first attempt to write it was in 1971, when I sold my worldly belongings, bought a used Volkswagon camper and trundled my wife, ten-year-old daughter and Miss Sniffy Wigglebum, our boxer dog, off to Mexico. Years before, I had read an article in *Writer's Yearbook* about a little Mexican town named San Miguel de Allende which was high in the mountains, about two-thirds of the way from Laredo, Texas to Mexico City. It was a haven for writers and painters and sounded absolutely perfect. It was my dream.

I had left *The Canadian Magazine* more than a year earlier and had become a general columnist for *The Toronto Telegram*. Then one day in the fall of 1971, it was announced that *The Telegram* would fold.

"How do you like that," grumbled Ted Reeve, the legendary athlete-sportswriter, who had been there more than thirty years. "When I started here they told me this would be a steady job."

We all had to make decisions and, when I called The Missus Herself with the news she said: "Let's try it your way. We might as well go to that town in Mexico so that you can write a book."

While I still had *The Telegram* column at my disposal, I wrote that I wanted to sell my house and twelve acres near the village of Pickering, Ontario. I told everybody that I was having an open house and that they should bring their own booze. I also warned them that the setting was not exactly picturesque, seeing as the house was surrounded by barren gravel pits. Well sir, there must have been more than five hundred prospective buyers present and I closed a deal that very day. Now I had to sell the house's contents and my personal belongings so, I merely wrote another column. This time there were more than one thousand customers and I even had my own Dixieland band—with me on the drums—playing on a piano that was for sale on the front porch. We auctioned off everything, had a helluva party, and I had to pick up empty whisky and beer bottles all over the place the next day.

We had planned to roll out of town the day after *The Tely* closed, but plans sometimes go awry. I had heard of the poor medical facilities in rural Mexico and had insisted that we all undergo exhaustive checkups before leaving Canada. The checkup showed The Missus had cancer and would have to have a hysterectomy.

The Missus wasn't as afraid as I was, or, at least, she didn't show it. I will always remember, though, the night she sat quietly in the living room, looking out the picture window at the gravel pit and suddenly, tears in her eyes, looked at me and said: "Oh, Pauly, I don't want to die." Never have I felt so helpless.

I also remember driving home from the hospital the morning she was to undergo surgery. It was about 8:30 a.m. and I didn't know what to do, or where to go while I waited. All I could do was pray. I am very religious when I am in trouble. The church—that's it! I drove into Pickering village and, although I had never been inside, pulled up in front of the church. Gee whiz, I thought, I wonder if they still have me on record Up There? It had been a long time. I got out of the car, almost embarrassed, and walked up the church steps. Praying couldn't hurt. What else could I do? I tried the church door. It was locked. Dammit! I actually stood there and kicked it.

Fortunately, things worked out great. The Missus took a month or so to recuperate and, while we lived in a motel waiting, I started working with the former *Tely* employees who had decided to start a new newspaper in town. The day after *The Tely* closed, a ragtag little tabloid called *The Toronto Sun* hit the streets. There were only fifty-eight original employees and we worked on cardboard cartons in an old factory called The Eclipse Whitewear Building. The business community chuckled and the media predicted immediate disaster.

Our first day was November 1, 1971, and today *The Toronto Sun* is looked upon as a miracle of the newpaper publishing industry with a daily circulation of almost 225 000 and more than 350 000 on Sundays. Since that time, they have also opened two newpapers in Western Canada, *The Edmonton Sun* and *The Calgary Sun*. I still work for all three as a columnist.

We had fun, that first month at *The Sun* and I didn't have to go far to research my column. I just wrote about the people around me and the part each played in that madcap venture. I made public figures out of Publisher Creighton as he sipped martinis, Editor Worthington as he turned over rocks to look for communists, and General Manager Hunt, the one-time pitcher who put the squeeze play on the money.

I told the people we were easy to find, next door to Farb's Car Wash and right across the street from the King's Plate Open Kitchen. And, because all famous buildings conduct guided tours, one day I invited everyone to see our sparkling premises which, I said, had a decor resembling early Canadian factory. Traffic was stopped on King Street that afternoon when more than five thousand people showed up for free beer and hot dogs while our Dixieland band played and television cameras whirred. I think only one drunk fell down the stairs.

We struggled on. I created chaos one night, when, plugging in my electric kettle to make some coffee to go with my scotch, I blew all the fuses in the whole damned building.

Finally, The Missus was strong enough to travel and we took off, recording our little adventure each day through my column. We rolled into Detroit the first night and I planned to take an entire month driving through the U.S. before crossing the Mexican border at Laredo. All our belongings were strapped to the top of the van and, by golly, were we ever organized.

I wanted to reach the warm climate as soon as possible, so we wound our way south, stopping to visit the caves in Kentucky, the mansions along the Mississippi. . . . It was a leisurely trip. One day we travelled only fourteen miles. We stayed in motels along the way but, in case of emergency, we had a large tent, sleeping bags, a Coleman lamp, stove and oven that operated on propane and, of course, a complete bar in the back. There were two seats and a table which made into a double bed and I was absolutely in love with that little camper. I would even wash all the windows with Windex each morning and, when we started out each day, our little bus sparkled.

While driving through Kentucky, we spent a day at Churchill Downs, site of the famous Kentucky Derby and, when I mentioned my name in the publicity office, the girl obviously recognized it. She looked at me strangely and said: "Annabelle the Wonder Horse?"

"Well, uh, yes," I said, looking at the floor, "but that was years ago."

The story of Annabelle was to be my great book. Three of us, very definitely under the influence, had purchased Annabelle at a horse auction in 1967 at Woodbine Racetrack in Toronto. My partners were two old pals, Freddie (The Flashbulb) Ross and Robert Derwyn Owen. Freddie and I had worked for R.D. Owen when he was the editor of *The Kingston Whig-Standard* in Eastern Ontario and we had often frequented the races together. For the magnificent sum of $1100, we had purchased Annabelle, a lop-eared filly with a large sore on her back whom we immediately surnamed The Wonder Horse and dedicated to the losers of the world. They still talk about her coming-out party, her first race, at the track at Fort Erie, directly across the border from Buffalo, New York.

Annie never did win but we entered her in the 1968 Derby, much to the consternation of the good people of Kentucky and, if they refused us stall space, we planned to rent a parking lot in Louisville, pitch a circus tent, and spend the night with our horse before parading to the track the next day.

Unfortunately for Annabelle but, fortunately for racing, she had a training accident one week before leaving for the Derby, broke her back, and never ran again. That was quite a disappointment to me. She would have been the worst horse ever to run in the Derby but, by golly, she wouldn't have finished last. That was the year that Dancer's Image was disqualified as the winner and placed last. He would have been last even if old Annie had been lapped. But, that's enough of that. I still plan to write all about Annabelle some day.

As we rolled along the highway I kept sending back columns of our adventures, of which this was typical:

When you are traveling on the road with a 10-year-old daughter, things crop up that you didn't expect.

What I mean is, problems that you hadn't anticipated before all three of you were sleeping in one room.

"Psst . . ." I whispered to The Missus the other day as we were driving down the highway. "When are we going to do it?"

"Do what?" she said.

"You know," I said motioning to our daughter, who was listening in the back seat.

"Tonight," smiled The Missus.

"Good," I said.

"After she's asleep," whispered The Missus.

We checked into a Holiday Inn, the three of us and Miss Sniffy Wigglebum, our dog, all in the same room.

You probably know the typical Holiday Inn room, clean, bright, two double beds—side-by-side—a lamp and telephone stand between them, three-piece bathroom and a color television set.

The Kid used to go to sleep at 9 o'clock when we were at home.

But, she had a bedroom of her own then.

On this trip, we find that it is difficult for us to watch a movie without it catching her interest, too.

"Will she ever go to sleep?" I whispered that night to The Missus.

It was after 10.

"Wait," said The Missus.

We were lying on our bed, the one nearest to the television set.

You can imagine my concern as we had been waiting to do it for several days.

Finally the movie was over.

"Okay," I said to The Kid. "Roll over now, close your eyes and go to sleep. We've got a long way to go tomorrow."

I put my clothes back on, took Sniffy Wigglebum out to the parking lot to find herself a late-night relief station and then returned.

"She sleeping?" I whispered.

My Missus nodded.

Very quietly, I slipped out of my clothes, got into bed and turned out the light.

We lay there in the dark, listening.

"Sounds okay to me," The Missus said.

"Sshhh," I said. "Wait until she starts to snore."

So we waited.

"Okay?" said The Missus.

"Not yet," I said.

I wanted to be absolutely certain The Kid was sleeping. I did not want her to wake up unexpectedly.

"She can't see us," The Missus said.

"Yes," I said, "but perhaps she will hear us."

We lay there in the dark.

"Look," The Missus said. "Maybe we can go into the bathroom."

It was a thought.

"But there isn't much room in there." I said.

"Enough," said The Missus.

"What if she wakes up and has to go to the bathroom?" I said.

"Hmmm . . ." said The Missus. "Then she'd catch us."

"Right," I said. "She'd walk right in while we were doing it."

We lit cigarettes and smoked in the dark.

The Kid rolled over and sort of grunted.

Then there was a slight snore.

"Come on," said The Missus. "Let's just do it, get it over with, and get to sleep."

"Where?" I said.

It was 3 o'clock in the morning.

"The clothes closet?" The Missus said, rather hesitantly.

"That's it!" I said.

So The Missus and I got up quietly, felt our way across the dark motel room and made our way into the clothes closet.

And we finally did it.

We finally got to wrap The Kid's Christmas present without waking her up.

○ ○ ○

We spent Christmas, 1971, in the French Quarter in New Orleans, cooking our turkey in a little rented place on Chartres Street and, at night, I took The Missus and The Kid around to hear some old pals of mine playing in bars such as the Maison Bourbon, Crazy Shirley's, The Paddock, Preservation Hall, Al Hirt's, and Pete Fountain's. I have always loved jazz and, several years later, was to take a crack at playing professionally myself until I realized that I was way over my head, playing at such places as the Montreux Jazz Festival in Switzerland, the Nice Jazz Festival in France, the North Sea Festival in The Hague, and with giants such as Wild Bill Davison, Buddy Tate, Vic Dickenson, Dick Wellstood, Jimmy McPartland, Milt Buckner, Buck Clayton, Cat Anderson and others. But that is another book—I hope.

On New Year's Day, 1972, we crossed into Mexico at Laredo and, as we cruised through Neuva Laredo on the Mexican side, there was a sudden explosion. Someone had thrown a rock at the van and hit the window on the passenger's side, knocking off The Missus's glasses. Welcome to Mexico!

Three days later we pulled into the picture-book town of San Miguel de Allende, with its church spires and cobblestone streets, and peddlars selling their wares from the backs of their donkeys. As we turned off from the main plaza and went down to our rented house, neither of us noticed the two little swinging doors that would change our lives. We lived on a street called Zacateros. This was where my book would be written, up in that studio on the roof. Conditions were absolutely ideal. It was everything that I had read in *Writers' Yearbook*.

We bought our food in the outdoor market and even had a maid, The Senora, a wonderful lady who spoke no English but who remains a friend today. She lives in what is little more than a mud hut and, by herself, raised a large family, including a twenty-year-old son named Elauterio who found the house for us and became my most valuable contact in the Mexican community. The Missus, who was quite a good equestrian, began working as an instructor each morning at the Escuela Ecuestre, an internationally-known riding academy operated by an American named Harold Black. Our daughter Tracey was enrolled in the John F. Kennedy School in Queretaro, 45 kilometres south, where subjects were taught in English in the mornings and Spanish in the afternoons. I would walk her up to the plaza very early each morning to catch her school bus and, on the way back to the house, stop for a cup of coffee with sculptor Ron Crabbe who would already be working in his studio. The Senora would have prepared a breakfast of fresh fruit—papaya, grapefruit, oranges, pineapple—and, after eating, The Missus would drive up the mountain to the riding academy and I would go up to my studio to write. I had brought paper, typewriter, ribbons, carbon, three-ring binders, and even a three-hole punch.

Life should have been perfect. It wasn't. Remember those swinging doors I mentioned earlier? I went through them one day and discovered the greatest little bar in the world. It was called La Cucaracha (The Cockroach) and was known plainly as The Cuc (Kook). In no time at all, I was accepted by the inner circle and became a regular. I called it the Literary, Intellectual, Artistic, Reading Society which, when shortened, was the LIARS' Club.

Club members were people like The Judge, Tony the Painter, Deathmarch Hal, The Midnight Cowboy, Torpedo Sam, Nursey, Racetrack Sandy—characters who were known by the uppity Americans and Canadians on the hill as "those horrid people at the Cucaracha." But, they were the best conversationalists and most intriguing circle of friends I ever had. The bar was a tiny place with just a few wooden tables and chairs in the front room and a standup bar in the back where the Mexicans drank. Drinks were cheap and Chucho, the proprietor, was the guardian angel of the gringos, running bar tabs until the money came from home.

San Miguel was considered to be an artists' colony but, rather, it was a home for lost souls, widows, divorcees, and people who were trying to survive on small pensions.

They pretended they were writing, pretended they were painting. They were drinking and laughing. Drinking and talking. The bar was famous enough to have been written about in feature stories in major magazines, including a long piece in *Esquire*. Norman Mailer drank there, so did the guy who wrote *The Hustler*. Nobody got to know it better than me. I was a regular, arriving at noon each day, drinking until two or three in the afternoon or until The Missus came in, leading Miss Wigglebum on a leash, and firing me one of her patented cold looks.

I should explain that The Missus Herself never did appreciate my drinking. Inevitably, when we went to a party, I would be pouring myself a drink when she would say: "Do you really need another one?" I would, of course, then pour myself a double. I am afraid that our eleven years of marriage were not the happiest days of her life. When we were at home, I would be away half the time, on the road doing stories. There was little doubt that our marriage was somewhat rocky before we went to Mexico.

I suppose, in agreeing to go to Mexico, The Missus thought things would be better down there. At least we would be together. But, when we were together all the time, she discovered she didn't like me at all. We had been in San Miguel three months when she decided that she had had enough. She took Tracey and left me. This is how I informed my readers back home when I finally sobered up:

JUNE 6, 1972

SAN MIGUEL—Where have I been?

I have been drunk.

I have been drunk for three weeks.

I would sit, staring at the typewriter, trying to write this column and then, frustrated, stalk out to the Cucaracha Bar.

My problem was how to write that The Missus Herself had left me.

Because of the very personal nature of my column, I had to say something to explain why I would not be mentioning her anymore.

But I do not want to embarrass her by airing our problems in public.

To set the record straight, however, I should explain that there was no great blow-up. We just decided, after 11 years of marriage, that we wanted different things out of life.

We will always be very good friends.

She was my foil. I wrote about her as a dowdy, crabby housewife. I owe it to The Missus to explain that she actually is a very sexy broad.

I guess it would be impossible for anyone to put up with me indefinitely.

We both feel very badly, especially about 10-year-old Tracey Lee who has gone gack to Toronto with her.

Drinking was not the answer. I did not eat enough. It just made me sick.

I am working again.

But this is as much as I feel like writing for today.

○ ○ ○

The Missus Herself had realized that I was not going to change, I was not going to write my book, and that our marriage was not going to improve. It took guts and I admired her for leaving. Today she is still one of my best friends and, by golly, she still defends me when she hears somebody putting me down.

After she left, I threw myself into single life with a vengeance and several bottles of tequila. I closed the three-ring binder forever, kept writing my columns, and took up permanent residence at the Cucaracha. When I heard, in 1979, that the Cuc had been sold and closed, it was as if I had lost a good friend.

There followed a succession of women and I made the most of my new life until it

Members of the San Miguel LIAR's Club: l. to r., The Judge, Chucho, Deathmarch Hal, myself.

was time to go home. At that time, I knew a girl named Chipmunk, an alluring young college student from California whose blonde hair and long, tanned legs in those faded cut-off jeans turned heads all over town. Chipmunk lived across the street with her sister in a little apartment over the watchmaker's. When she awakened each day, she would put two fingers between her teeth, let out a loud whistle, and I would go up to my roof where we could talk over the street.

When it was time to leave, Chipmunk decided she would like to come along for the ride to Toronto and I had two other passengers, Torpedo Sam and a girl named Beaver (no relation to a girl by that name who will be mentioned later in this book). The four of us, along with Miss Sniffy Wigglebum, climbed into the camper and stopped at the Cucaracha on the way out of town. The gang had farewell champagne and decorated my well-known old camper with fresh roses. We finally shook hands all around and then pulled out, sputtering our way up the hill. . . .

That delightful old Volkswagon made it all the way back to Canada without so much as a flat tire. We had dropped Beaver off in Oklahoma City and stopped in Missouri where Sam was to meet his schoolteacher girlfriend who had been keeping his Lincoln Continental. Well sir, the first thing I knew, Sam had talked his girl into quitting her job and they fell in behind Chipmunk and me in the camper to follow us to Toronto.

The Sun was alive and growing when I got back and, the first thing I knew, they talked me into running for mayor of Toronto. I wore blue jeans, an old fishing hat, and made my campaign headquarters at Ye Olde Brunswick House, one of Toronto's more notorious drinking holes. Mine was a no-money campaign and straight from the shoulder.

Hell, I got almost 8 000 votes which means there are at least that many people out on the street that we should be worrying about.

My big job then was learning to be a Saturday daddy, one of the enormous number of separated parents who see their children only once a week. I admit there were tears when I saw my little girl for the first time in almost six months. About a year later, The Missus and I discussed the entire situation and she wondered if Tracey would be better off living with me. I was willing to give it a try, but I was going to have to change my lifestyle. I was sharing an apartment at that time with my pal Johnny McNamara who used to wash his underwear and socks by putting them in the bathtub, pouring powdered soap over them, and turning on the hot shower. It was no place for a thirteen-year-old girl.

I quickly rented a furnished house in Toronto's east end and became a fulltime parent again, going through a series of housekeeping and live-in babysitters which were never exactly right. Suddenly it dawned on me that a long, hot summer was coming up and, to tell you the truth, I wasn't too happy with some of the company my kid was keeping. Every time I looked at her, I saw visions of shopping centers, dope, and gangs of bored kids out looking for action. I didn't want that for her, but how could I avoid it? Hell, I was doing a daily television show, playing drums each night in a bar, writing a daily column, and doing television commercials for a beer company.

The only answer was to leave the city for the summer. I would take a leave of absence from everything but my column and rent a summer cottage on a lake. At that particular time, a young lady from Austria, whom I had met on a skiing trip to Innsbruck a year before, was in Toronto on vacation. I asked her if she would like to spend the summer at the lake as a companion for my daughter when I had to leave on business. She agreed and I went looking for a cottage. By golly, I found a dream place, a modern, expensive summer home on Stony Lake, a two-hour drive from Toronto. It was $1200 a month, but worth it. Besides, I could try to write that book about Annabelle again. . . .

That might well have been the best summer of my life. The home was so modern there was an underground sprinkler system to water the lawns, a dishwasher, freezer, two complete bathrooms, three bedrooms, and a huge electric system in the boathouse which lifted and lowered a beautiful mahogany Sheppard boat in and out of the water.

I also had a little fibreglass runabout tied to the dock which I used for fishing and there was no end to the supply of bass and pickerel. I would get up at 6:30 each morning, make a Thermos of coffee and take my cigarettes, my small battery radio, a box of worms and slowly make my way over the crystal water, through the early-morning steam, to my favorite spot. It is the most peaceful time of the day and, sitting quietly on the water, I could hear even the slightest of noises coming from the cottages—doors closing, toilets flushing, taps running. Because of the way the sound carried, I would keep my radio very quiet and be able to hear everything, the sports scores, morning news, and the music.

I would bait my hook and cast. Kerplunk! I would sit and watch the little circles expand over the mirror-like surface, open the Thermos, pour a steaming cup of coffee, light a cigarette, and sit back, totally at peace with the world. More often than not, a bass would strike and I would reel it in, unhook it and slip a fastener through its gills so that it would stay alive in the water on my chain. Sometimes I got as many as three in an hour.

I could see my cottage clearly about four hundred yards away and, when Miss Suzy Schickelgruber (the name I called my Austrian friend) awakened, she would hang a bath towel over the railing on the sundeck as a signal that they were up. I also had a towel and, if I had fresh fish for breakfast, I would just hold it up. If I didn't, I would wave the towel,

The Missus Herself, The Kid, and I in San Miguel.

the signal to start the bacon and eggs. After breakfast, I would go around the horn by boat to get more supplies or bait from Whetung's General Store and to pick up the mail.

I had made a deal with *The Sun*. I had one month coming to me as vacation and wrote six columns each week. What if I wrote only three columns a week for two months? They bought it. I would write three columns each Monday morning at one sitting, put them in an envelope and I was free for the rest of the week. We ate well, lay in the sun, swam, and waterskied in the afternoons. On weekends, more often than not, we would have visitors from the city. Once, on a long weekend, my entire band came up to play at the local regatta and it was the best time of the summer.

It should have been perfect. It wasn't. Actually, by mid-summer, I did get about five chapters of my book on Annabelle done, enough for me to phone Gerry Halpin and invite him and his wife up for a weekend. Gerry sat in my living room one evening, read the chapters, and encouraged me to continue. But, again, the book on Annabelle was never completed. It wasn't The Cucaracha Bar this time. Rather it was confirmation of something I had suspected in Mexico—I wasn't as good a writer as I thought. . . .

My life plan had always been to leave newspapers and magazines one day to become an author. The first inkling I had that I might fail to become immortal was when I suddenly realized that I could not write fiction.

Well, then, I would try non-fiction—a book on Annabelle, which, I thought, would be no more difficult than writing a long magazine story. Wrong. I couldn't handle the job.

The sudden realization that I was not a unique talent was the greatest disappointment of my life. I had actually believed that I would one day be compared to Hemingway, Steinbeck, Salinger, Twain. . . .

I am no longer saddled with dreams or great expectations.

I have learned to live with my limitations but, dammit, it was a lot easier when they would let me have a drink. Then, at least, I would forget from time to time. ●

THE GREAT MONOPOLY CAPER

prologue *I have always loved a challenge, especially if it does not require brains, brawn, or honesty to win. When Stan Fischler, a freelance writer and author from New York, first told me about the World Monopoly Championships, my reaction was immediate.*

"I love it! I love it!" I yelled, jumping up and down and waving my arms. "I want to play! I want to play!"

He said he would mention me to his friend Lee Weisenthal, a Detroit lawyer, who founded the tournament and who personally screened each player before inviting them. Sure enough, this Weisenthal fella showed up in Toronto one night. We had a couple of drinks together and, as we parted, I couldn't wait: "What do you think?" I demanded. "Will I make it?"

"I will let you know," said Weisenthal coolly.

I watched the mail for a month and, suddenly, there it was—an envelope from the U.S.M.A. (United States Monopoly Association). I was in! I had my invitation! I rushed to tell my boss! That's how I happened to find myself on a plane one day, flying to Detroit, my uniform and equipment in my bags. . . .

○ ○ ○

DECEMBER 27, 1969—Two hours before the World Monopoly Championships were to begin, photographer Terry Hancey stood up, closed our hotel room window to stop the venetian blinds from clattering, and poured two fresh drinks.

"Look," he said, attempting to flag my sagging spirits, "it's natural to be nervous. Hell, goaltender Glenn Hall was always sick to his stomach before a hockey game."

"But," I said weakly, "I've told them I'm the professional champion of Canada. And the only thing I can remember about Monopoly is that I used to be luckiest when I used the token shaped like a milk bottle."

"So," Hancey said, "get the milk bottle."

Downstairs in Detroit's Sheraton Cadillac Hotel, in the elegant English Room, the first of the 300 guests had begun to arrive. Greeting them at the door was Lee Weisenthal.

He started the championship tournament seven years ago. It has grown at a fantastic rate, and this year there were 139 challengers taking aim at the peerless Milton Manley Jr., the defending world champion.

Hancey and I—delayed while trying to figure out how to put on our rented evening dress (top hats, tails, white gloves, canes)—were late arrivals.

"Slip in quietly and maybe nobody will notice us," I whispered as we moved up to the registration desk.

Unfortunately, a photographer from the Detroit News, tipped off that the Canadian professional champion had arrived, spotted us.

"Hold it!" he yelled.

Hancey and I posed, then quickly elbowed through the crowd toward the bar.

"Double scotch," I said. "Same," said Hancey.

The News reporter came up and asked if it were true that I was the Canadian professional champion.

"Of course," I said. "Mr. Hancey and I travel from town to town giving exhibitions."

"Exhibitions?" he said, puzzled.

We were trapped.

"Well, really, they are money mangement courses for housewives told through Monopoly," I lied. "Mr. Hancey photographs each seminar and we show slides."

"They just sounded the five-minute warning whistle," Hancey broke in.

"Better hurry. You're at Table 28."

It was a relief to be rescued. The scotch disappeared in one gulp, washing around down there with the butterflies.

"Go in there and grab the milk bottle," Hancey whispered in encouragement.

"Yeah," I said weakly.

Three serious men stood waiting behind their chairs at Table 28. We shook hands and introduced ourselves but, because of my nervous condition, I still do not even know their first names. Suddenly I realized I had not been briefed on tournament rules.

"Excuse me, gentlemen," I said. "I am a professional. Is there a difference between amateur and professional rules?"

They quickly outlined the way the tournament game is played. Instead of buying properties from the bank, the properties are shuffled and dealt four ways. Each player starts with a bankroll of $1500; there is a 20-minute trading period before the game; and the game lasts 1½ hours. The player with the most money and property at the end of that time is the winner—if he has not already won by forcing his opponents into bankruptcy.

In the first round there would be 35 tables; in the quarter-finals, there would be nine; and in the semi-finals, three. The winners from those tables would play for the championship of the world.

"Has anyone claimed the milk bottle?" I asked.

"Man, how long is it since you've played this game?" one of my opponents said derisively. "That was years ago."

To my horror, I discovered that not only had the tokens changed, but my three opponents each had their own lucky tokens they'd brought along with them.

I surveyed the standard tokens quickly—a man on a horse, a wheelbarrow, a racing car, a Scotch terrier, a boot, a thimble and—a top hat.

"May I use the top hat?" I asked.

"Certainly," one of them replied. "Say, are you really a professional?"

"Of course," I said. There was no turning back.

"Gentlemen, shall we roll to see who will be the banker?" the man to my left said.

Another crisis! Please, not the banker. I am not so hot at arithmetic. But guess who won the banking job?"

"May I bank for you gentlemen?" the wife of one of my opponents asked. I forced the money box into her hands.

The properties were dealt, and the trading began. The deft moves of my opponents dazzled me. It was like a country auction. In some manner, I am still not certain how, I wound up with Pennsylvania, North Carolina and Pacific Avenues (a monopoly) and Ventnor and Atlantic Avenues, just around the corner.

"Uh, what would you like for Marvin Gardens?" I asked my opponent to the left. Combined with Ventnor and Atlantic it would give me a second monopoly.

"Nothing," he said acidly. He certainly was a serious player. Then, spotting a sucker, he said, "Well, on second thought I'll take $700 cash."

"Sold," I said, despite the fact that Marvin Gardens is listed at only $280 on the board.

Hancey in the background was perspiring and looking away. The man to my right slammed his money roll on to the table in disgust.

"You have just given him the game," he blurted. "Now he has $700 plus his $1500. Haven't you ever played before?"

"Sir, I am a professional," I said, my voice cracking. "Uh, Terry, would you mind getting me another drink at the bar—a double?"

I knew I was in trouble as soon as the man to my left rolled an 11 and moved his token directly to its proper space without having to count the spaces. They all did that. I had to count—one . . . two . . . three. . . .

A crowd had gathered around the table, and a lady's voice, a loud whisper behind me, said, "But—it's not fair. He's a professional." I began to perspire and, then, because I had forgotten to remove my white gloves, clumsily dropped my money on the floor.

"Sir, are you not going to remove your hat?" asked the man on my left.

"Uh, I never play Monopoly without my hat," I said. Actually, the truth was, I had forgotten to comb my hair.

"May I buy some houses?" I asked.

"Not until you pass Go," snapped the man directly across from me.

"Sorry."

Don't ask me to explain, but suddenly the man to my right was bankrupt. Then, gadzooks, the man to my left. And I had hotels on all of my properties. Hancey was hanging over the table, wide-eyed. I kept drinking scotch and rolling the dice. Pass GO—$200. Community Chest. Chance. I could do nothing wrong. And finally it happened, five minutes before the deadline. The opponent across from me landed on Atlantic Avenue—$1150 with a hotel. And then on North Carolina—$1275.

"I concede to the Canadian professional champion," he said, with a note of bitterness.

My three oponents begrudgingly shook my hand. Hancey walked over and whispered: "Amazing . . . absolutely amazing."

"But—it just isn't fair," one of my opponents' wives was saying as they walked away. "This is an amateur tournament."

"Ladies and gentlemen," the announcer said, "the Canadian professional champion has just advanced to the quarter-finals at Table 28. Let's have a hand for him."

Not one person clapped.

"Come on up and say a few words," he called.

"Well, uh," I said into the microphone, "they were very sportsmanlike players. Quite good for amateurs, really."

"Let's get another drink," Hancey suggested. "We have only ten minutes before the quarter-finals.There are only nine tables left. You're at Table 7."

They presented me with the Monopoly set from Table 28 to keep for my very own.

"Wouldn't it be funny if I won this whole damn thing?" I said to Hancey, the scotch beginning to take effect.

"Yeah," he said quietly. "Have you looked over at Table 7?"

There, standing as large as football great Russ Jackson, as large as hockey star Bobby Hull was . . . Milton Manley Jr.

"How do you do?" he said. "My name is Milton Manley Jr. I am the champion of the world."

He sat to my right, and across the table was Dr. James Fisch—bearded, steely-eyed—a psychologist from Winetka, Ill., just outside Chicago.

"So you're the Big Noise From Winetka," I said, making an attempt at humor.

He didn't smile. He reached into his pocket for his lucky token, a worn jewelled thing that looked as if it might be from China or India or someplace. Obviously it had seen a lot of Monopoly.

"I'm afraid," I whispered to Hancey.

"A guy just told me about Milton Manley Jr.," he replied. "They say this guy is a rich stockbroker who plays Monopoly for a living—with real money—buying and selling."

I was so upset I cannot remember the name of the opponent to my left. I don't care to, either. He cost me the game. He was a lousy trader. I could see him playing right into Manley's hands. And the doctor wouldn't give me a thing. I knew from the start who would win.

Still, I was persistent. Even Hancey said so. There was quite a crowd now. Even Lee Weisenthal came down to watch.

There is a great deal of psychology in the game, I discovered as I read the releases that had been mailed to me during the month preceding the championships. I recall the description of Tye Bixler, winner of the shortest Monopoly game on record. It was played March 14, 1949, in the Quimping Cup Qualification at Lake Borgne, La., when Bixler defeated Horace Sanchez in 7 minutes and 14 seconds.

"Bixler rattled his opponents with a whizzing blur of a token and frantically paced transactions," the report read. "Constantly drumming fingers and a grating cough were a nice touch to heighten the agitation. He also hastened the play with a trick of anxiously glancing back over his shoulder every few moments.

"By the time Bixler reached the majors, he had added a full complement of tics and his famous gasping routine. Simulating an eye-bulging gauntness, and with his uniform subtly askew, his appearance alone intimidated even the most seasoned professionals...."

So, as you can see, there is a lot to it. And here I was, completely psyched out by the world champion, fumbling with nervousness. Why, I even forgot to collect $200 once when I passed GO.

"Oh, I forgot my $200," I said as Manley rolled the dice after me.

"Too late," he snapped. "You have to ask for it while it is your turn."

So when he landed right on GO and asked for money, I protested. After all, he hadn't passed it yet.

"Referee!" called Manley.

"This is an important match," Lee Weisenthal told his referee, complete in striped shirt. "I'll handle it myself."

There was a rumble throughout the room at that precise moment as the announcer said: "Bulletin ... bulletin! Ginsberg is out! Three-time champion Bernie Ginsberg has been defeated in the quarter-finals."

Manley looked rather relieved. But, then, another announcement drew a cloud over his face.

"Ladies and gentlemen ... Karl Schaeffer, the champion two years ago, has just scored a stunning victory to move into the semi-final."

Schaeffer described his win. It seems that he had only Park Place and Boardwalk, with three houses on each, and his opponent, with most of the money, had properties almost encircling the board. The opponent landed on Park Place, paid $1100, then rolled snake-eyes, two, and landed on Boardwalk. Another $1400. Because he had rolled doubles, he needed to roll again. A seven—Chance. He drew his card. "Take a walk on Boardwalk," it said; another $1400. And he was wiped out.

But I had problems of my own. Weisenthal had ruled in Manley's favor. The player to my left had gone bankrupt long ago and now Dr. Fisch, who obviously hadn't studied Monopoly psychology, was gone. It was me against the world champion.

Manley had all four railroads, was employing what is called the Baltic-Mediterranean Blitz and had hotels on Connecticut, Vermont and Oriental Avenues. These are not particularly valuable properties, but he had one entire side of the board. I had only three houses around the corner on Virginia and States Avenues and St. Charles Place.

We rolled, one after the other, as the crowd watched. Manley went to jail, which, I learned, was the best place to be. He was there for three rolls, meaning he could not possibly land on my properties. Meanwhile, I was skipping nimbly through his properties, rolling ten from GO which got me through twice.

He, however, was even more fortunate. He landed, kerplunk, on the unowned Electric Company, right in the midst of my monopoly, on two occasions. I landed twice on Vermont Avenue and needed to sell my houses and mortgage all other properties to pay my debt.

"Concede," Hancey whispered in my ear.

"You're making a fool of yourself."

"Dammit, I will not," I said stubbornly, even though I had only $27 left. Pow—I landed in jail.

"See," I whispered to Hancey. "Now I'm safe for three more rolls and he has to play. There's only five minutes left. Maybe I can make it."

"What!" he said in disgust. "Hell, you've got everything mortgaged except St. Charles Place and if he lands on that you only get $10. Quit, I tell you, or I'm getting out of here."

He was right. The crowd was murmuring. They were disgusted also. They were seeing a stubborn, beaten man, $27 in his hand, a $10-property alive, refusing to concede to the world champion.

"And he's a professional, too," I overheard in the background. "Terrible."

"Uh, your roll," I said to Manley, afraid to look him in the eye. But I could feel his stare.

Finally the time limit was over.

"Would you like to count it up?" Manley said sarcastically.

"Naw," I said, forcing a faint grin.

"Ladies and gentlemen . . . the Canadian professional champion has been defeated!" the guy with the loudspeaker said. There was a great cheer.

"What happened?" the announcer asked, with everyone waiting to hear my excuse.

"Well, uh, I was at a terrific disadvantage," I said, trying again for a touch of humor.

"How's that?" he asked.

"Well, he charged me 10 per cent on my Canadian money," I said, laughing hilariously at my own joke. Nobody else laughed. I heard several raspberries.

"I need a drink," I said to Terry Hancey. "Let's go to a bar somewhere."

"Dressed like this," he said, "and when we get it free here?"

"Anywhere else will be better," I blurted.

That was another mistake. We went to the bar downstairs and, because we had been taught to do so by the man who rented us our formal wear, Hancey removed his top hat with a flourish, pulled off his white gloves, dropped them into the hat and set it down on a ledge. I was too disturbed to remove mine. But by the time we left, someone had stolen Hancey's hat.

The rental agency charged him $40 to replace it.

When we returned to the English Room, the final was getting underway.

Surprise! Milton Manley Jr. had been defeated in the semi-finals!

The three men remaining were Karl Schaeffer, hero of the quarter-final round; Dr. Simon Cook, a Detroit dentist who is a veteran player; and Theodore (Ted) Ploughman, a newcomer—a university counsellor—who had accomplished the seemingly impossible by reaching the final in his first year in the majors.

It was after 2 a.m. and, for some reason, Schaeffer, an insurance man from Oak Park, Mich., seemed fresher than his opponents.

"He doesn't drink, that's why," a man said.

Ted Ploughman's wife sat quietly, alone, far away from the match.

"I'm too nervous to watch," she said. "This means so much to Ted."

Three earlier competitors were asleep in chairs. The bar had been given a healthy run. Lee Weisenthal, who is far too busy, of course, to play anymore himself, was pacing nervously. The announcer was giving a play-by-play account over the loudspeaker.

But those of us who have had experience in world competition knew the outcome immediately after the 20-minute trading period. Schaeffer, that sly devil, had wound it up, and was on his way to a second title.

He dealt liberally with Dr. Cook, but Ploughman had nothing of interest to Cook, so he too had to deal with Schaeffer. That rascal Schaeffer wound up with two monopolies—Virginia, States, and St. Charles Place, and New York, Tennessee and St. James Place. Plus all four railroads. A complete side of the board!

Not only that, but Dr. Cook, once one of the fastest players in the game, had lost most of his speed now and was struggling to pass GO. He dropped out first. Ploughman hung on gamely, but couldn't manage his reserve cash or hotels. It was only a matter of time.

At 3:15 a.m., Schaeffer was declared the winner.

The presentation of the Stein-Fishbub

Trophy was made on the platform by Lee Weisenthal, and Schaeffer finally revealed his strategy.

"First," he said, clutching the huge cup under his arm, his face flushed with victory, "I have to explain that my biggest problem is getting past the first round. This was my sixth year. Four times I was knocked out in the first round, and twice, when I got through, I won the title."

"But—how did you do it this year?" called a reporter from the back row.

"Well, I have to give credit to my wife," said Schaeffer, sounding every bit the gentleman athlete. "Before I came tonight, she told me to use psychology. 'They'll all go for the masculine tokens,' she said. 'You choose the iron.' Gentlemen, that is exactly what I did—I put the heat on with the iron. And—ha-ha—you know what they say about ironing out your problems."

Later Schaeffer revealed that he has four more potential champions in training at home—his sons, Neil, 13, Lyle, 11, Paul, 8, and Todd, 6.

"I feel just like Marciano, after he put Louis away," he said quietly. "No, I haven't had any direct offers to travel the banquet circuit yet, but I'll listen. Imagine, that other fella couldn't make a deal with Cook. Sure was a break for me."

He left then, a host of new-found camp-followers with him, the large cup swinging from his talented, dice-throwing arm. Then he paused, turned to his fans who had stayed behind, and waved his arm slowly, a shy smile on his face. A true champion.

Hancey and I went back up to our room where we had three bottles of pink champagne chilling underwater in our bathtub, just in case there was reason to celebrate victory.

He popped the first cork, filled two glasses, then leaned back and unloosened his white bow tie. He was most unhappy at having his top hat stolen.

"Imagine," I said, "Schaeffer doesn't drink."

"You're a lousy Monopoly player," he said.

"Well," I said, ignoring his remark, "one consolation is that they work this the same as they work the Masters Tournament in golf. If you finish high enough up the ladder, you're automatically invited back the following year. In Monopoly, the quarter-final is high enough."

"You're a lousy player," he repeated.

"See here ..." I said, standing as I spoke.

"You're such a lousy player," he said, "that you forgot to collect $200 when you passed GO."

Dammit, you know, he was right. ●

ᗡᖴᓰᒪᐤᖾᑌᖴ *Looking back, I still think I would have done better if I hadn't had so much to drink. Mind you, I had the same trouble when I went back the next year and was blasted out in the opening round.*

Usually I don't create much of a stir when I write anything but my story on the Monopoly championships certainly had an effect. Suddenly, similar tournaments sprang up across the country. Karl Schaeffer became a minor celebrity. His first offer was from Victoria, British Columbia, an expenses-paid trip for him and his wife if he would consent to be the official referee at that city's first Monopoly tournament.

Schaeffer's biggest opportunity, though, was an invitation to appear on the popular television show To Tell the Truth *which was viewed by millions of North Americans. You remember the show. Three people would come out and, in answer to the question: "What is your name, please?" would say, one after the other, "My name is Karl Schaeffer and I am the Monopoly champion of the world!" A panel of four celebrities would then try to determine, through their questions, which two contestants were imposters and which was the real*

Karl Schaeffer. That appearance really made Monopoly tournaments boom and Schaeffer suddenly became known to millions.

It is the only favor I ever did for a non-drinker.

Monopoly is the world's most popular game and was invented by a man in Atlantic City who sold the rights to Parker Brothers. The original game, the one still sold throughout North America, is based on the streets of Atlantic City—Pacific Avenue, Oriental Avenue, Marvin Gardens, etc. But Monopoly is sold internationally, in most languages and, to make it more familiar to people who have never been to Atlantic City, the streets are sometimes localized. In England, for instance, the game is based on the streets of London—Bond Street, Oxford Street, Trafalgar Square, and so on.

It did not take Parker Brothers long to notice the sudden popularity of Monopoly tournaments and, realizing a good thing, they decided to get into the act. They now sponsor a genuine world-wide Monopoly championship, with champions from various countries competing against one another for the over-all title. And, as far as I know, it was all started by Lee Weisenthal and his pals in Detroit.

I finally visited Atlantic City in 1978 on the weekend its first legalized gambling casino opened. It was cold and raining and the sky was lit up by huge searchlights. Thousands lined up, shivering as they waited to get in. Police were everywhere, by the thousands. The only guy who was a bigger loser than me on that first night was the youth who robbed a grocery store a block away. He raced from the scene of his crime, the loot in a paper bag, a gun in his other hand, around the corner, and into the arms of hundreds of startled policemen right in front of the television cameras. He had to be the only person in the country who did not know that it was the first night of legalized gambling in New Jersey.

The only room I could get was in a tacky motel across the street from the casino for which I was paying an exorbitant $45 a night. I suspect, before gambling came to town, that the rooms went for about $18. Two nights after I checked in, I overheard the room clerk tell a prospective customer that their rates were now $85 a night, with a two-night minimum, and cash up front. The man paid it gladly.

I started thinking about it when I got up to my room, how the gambling boom has effected real estate values in Atlantic City. The next morning I tried to telephone the mayor, whose name I did not know, and, of course, could not get an audience with him. All I wanted was to suggest a sure-fire publicity gimmick to him, one that was certain to make him known throughout the country.

I was going to advise him to sue Parker Brothers for falsely representing his city and to force them to recall every Monopoly set sold in North America to be replaced by an updated version. For instance, Park Place, second most expensive property on the board at $350, is no longer a fashionable street in Atlantic City. And, Mediterranean Avenue, priced at only $60 in Monopoly, now is one of the most expensive properties in the city, thanks to the location of the casinos and redevelopment. The entire board should be reviewed and properties re-assessed according to current market values.

Maybe that mayor of Atlantic City would have seen me if he had known who I was—the Professional Monopoly Champion of Canada for crying out loud!

Top Hats
& Tales of Woe

N O ONE has ever accused me of being sartorially elegant. Not in my own clothes, anyway. For some reason, because I thought it was funny I suppose, I took to renting outlandish formal wear for special occasions, such as the time I entered the World Monopoly Championships. Perhaps I kept dressing that way because it was sort of a disguise that would allow me to act outrageously when I happened to be in that particular mood. Unfortunately, I was too often outrageous. Back in the days when the doctors would let me drink, I took full advantage of the opportunity and, well, one thing usually led to another.

I have always had this great passion for parties. Not little parties—great big parties. And, I enjoyed being the host. It surprises no one that I have no money in the bank today. I would just shrug and say that my love for excesses was merely the result of the constant pressure of being a magazine writer. Hell, I just liked a good time.

Sometimes, though, my parties were part of my work. Take the time, in 1971, when I camped on the doorstep of Ontario Place for six days and nights in order to be the first paying customer inside. Ontario Place is a recreation and entertainment complex built on Toronto's waterfront, directly across from the grounds of the Canadian National Exhibition. Millions of people pass through its gates each summer to hear world-class artists perform in the outdoor Forum, watch thrilling, experimental movies in the Cinesphere, eat in one of the many sidewalk cafes, or just stroll along the yacht basin.

When Ontario Place first opened in May, 1971, I had left *The Canadian* and was a daily columnist with the old Toronto *Telegram*. Everybody was writing about this gigantic new Ontario government project and, well, I wanted to be a little different. It was bitterly

◀Arriving at the Royal York in a coach with my date, Miss Canada.

cold but, I remembered reading stories of kids camping out to be the first ones inside various events and decided that is what I would do at Ontario Place.

I went around town, gathering my equipment. A sporting goods store provided a tent, about 12 feet by 12 feet, and I had a sleeping bag, air mattress, and canvas bunk along with a propane lamp, stove, and a large cooler. I shopped for groceries, loaded up with booze, and drove down to the main entrance of Ontario Place which was to be opened to a curious public six days later.

It was the beginning of a week-long circus. I established squatter's rights at the edge of a huge, asphalt parking lot, right behind Exhibition Stadium, home of baseball's Toronto Blue Jays and football's Toronto Argonauts, at the opening of a footbridge that crossed over to Ontario Place. I had my typewriter, a small table and chair, and had talked Bell Telephone into running a line to my tent so that I could have a private phone. Private? Well, it was until I published my phone number, told my readers I was lonely down there, and then it never stopped ringing.

I had one hell of a time setting the tent up on the hard ground and my only heat came from that propane lamp. But, shortly after I had taken up residence, my tent became crowded, almost twenty-four hours a day. Guys dropped in with wine, whisky, and beer. Restaurants sent food and a radio or television interviewer was almost always dropping by. The Missus Herself drove in from our farm on the third day, took one look at the shambles, turned her back, and stalked away. She was starting to worry about the guy she had married.

Whenever things got out of hand, I merely had another drink, stood back, and watched. Once, I counted thirty-three people drinking inside that little tent while a pouring rain bounced off of the parking lot. I was damp, cold, dirty, and very tired. There was no time to sleep, no time to sober up.

As my story became known, more and more gifts and cards arrived. Mike Rogers of Rogers and Williams Tailors provided me with a new outfit to wear as I stepped up to that gate on Saturday morning. He had made an elegant set of white trousers and a bright red, double-breasted sports jacket which must have cost a fortune. He even included a shirt and an appropriate tie. Unfortunately, I hung the jacket from the top of my tent, next to the lantern, and burned a huge hole right through the front of it. Mike later had it mended and I wore it for years.

Actually, I was starting to feel rather silly, sitting there in a tent waiting for Ontario Place to open. Teenagers started camping behind me in little pup tents and my area was starting to resemble a gypsy camp. They were good kids though, and not one of them tried to get ahead of the old guy with the telephone.

I finally had a quiet night, a chance to sleep and, just after falling into it deeply, I was suddenly awakened by the sound of rock music right outside my tent. It was 3 a.m. and a group called Jalopy had driven up in the antique roadster that was their trademark and sat there, playing a private concert in the dark. . . . One more day and one more night to go.

The government then announced that it had arranged a special VIP party for the Friday evening before Saturday morning's official public opening. Well, how do you like that? All those stuffed shirts, wearing black ties and long dresses, would be wined and dined at the public's expense and would get to see Ontario Place before us plain folk camped outside. This would never do. By golly, we would have a party of our own.

Camping at the Ontario Place opening, 1971 ▶

This called for a change into my official party uniform—top hat, tails, white tie, white gloves, and cane. Unfortunately, I didn't have any dress shoes so I wore sneakers. When they got word of my party, all hell broke loose. I had an official visit to discourage me, almost a plea on bended knee as it turned out.

I guess I can understand why they were worried. I had decided to throw a party for the entire city, for the thousands of people not invited to that big party inside, right in my own backyard. The drinking law in Ontario stated you could drink on your own property—specifically, that part which was judged to be your regular living area. Well sir, the way I figured it, my backyard included the entire parking lot, right up to the stadium, an area consisting of some four or five acres. I reasoned it qualified as my living area because I had to use the stadium's toilet facilities, which meant I had to walk right across that parking lot every day. And, having spent six days living in that tent, this made it my temporary but fulltime place of residence.

I planned to write a column inviting the general public to bring their own drinks to my backyard and I would provide the music. We would have a huge party and dance. By my reasoning, it would all be within the law and one hell of a night. Because we were on, uh, private property, we wouldn't even have to worry what time we closed. I was rather excited by the whole idea.

Jim McHarg, an old friend and jazz bassist, heard about my plan and offered to bring his band, The Midnight Special, to play beside my tent. We set up microphones, drums, electric bass, guitar, a front line, and produced some blaring, red-hot Dixieland jazz. They even let me sit in on the drums. Finally, however, I had had to bow to the pressure. There had been calls from liquor board lawyers, Ontario Place officials, and government legal advisers.

"You know, it could just be legal," one lawyer from the liquor board smiled. "Really, you have created quite a sticky problem for us. We cannot stop you. But, I'm asking for your understanding. Do you know what could happen down here tonight? There could be more than 20 000 people there. More than 50 000 maybe. Can you just imagine 50 000 drunks, drinking openly in a public place, and the police unable to do anything about it?"

I thought about it and didn't write the public invitation in my column. But, even without an invitation, there were still more than 1000 people there that night. To prepare for the evening, I dressed in my tent and called John Anastakis, my pal who was the maitre 'd at Hy's, one of the fanciest steak houses in the city, and ordered my dinner.

Johnny A. had helped me once before, when I was playing in the semi-finals of the press club pool tournament, again, of course, wearing top hat and tails. He showed up with his charming hostess, imported champagne cooling in a bucket and, with a flourish, I broke the balls with my cane. My opponent had no chance.

Johnny A. arrived at my tent in a limousine and, formally attired himself, spread out a fancy cloth on my card table, had a fresh rose in a small vase, and served his best steak along with the finest of imported wines and liqueurs.

The VIPs were starting to arrive as I began my dinner and they looked down their noses at the scene as they passed. Some chuckled and, when I saw one I knew, I'd invite him and his lady for a cocktail. Our party was in full swing by the time they started to leave their party, the band was cooking, and my tent was as well stocked as the best cocktail bar in the city. I think we wound up with all of the VIPs, too.

I tried to hide as one of the guests approached me. It was Colonel Sanders of Kentucky Fried Chicken fame, resplendent, as usual, in his familiar white suit. I had

written a column after attending his 80th birthday party, saying the six speakers were the most boring I had ever heard.

"Paul," he said, putting a hand on my shoulder, "I want you to know I agree with you."

"Gee, about what?" I asked.

"They were the six most boring speeches I ever heard, too," he winked. Fortunately, he had a sense of humor.

Our parking lot party ended about 3 a.m. and I looked at the mess around me. The official opening was set for 10 a.m. and I would have to pack up and clean the area before that time. But, all I wanted to do was lie down and sleep. That's when Tiny appeared. He must have been at least six and a half feet tall. He was a young guy, who, while rather loud and full of what seemed to be nervous energy, was eager to help.

"You go to sleep," he said. "I'll organize it and we'll clean the place up."

I slept about three hours and, when awakened, saw that Tiny had enlisted the kids in the smaller tents and, together, they had done a remarkable clean-up job. We got my tent down and I was still dressed in my rumpled top hat and tails and sneakers. We hadn't even washed our faces and the crowd was starting to form at the gate.

The photographers were there, awaiting the arrival of the first paying customer at the turnstiles and all the kids lined up behind me. They cheered as we bought our tickets and Tiny was right beside me, larger than life, his long black hair blowing in the wind. I started thinking. Because I was a member of the media, other papers couldn't very well use my picture the next day as I entered the grounds. And I thought about the work Tiny and his gang had done overnight.

"Go ahead," I said, shoving Tiny in front of me. I was number two. Tiny's picture was in all of the papers the next day and on television that night. For a very short time, he was somewhat of a celebrity.

Later that day, I sat in the warm sun among the thousands at the outdoor Forum, still wearing my rumpled top hat and tails, and listened to the opening ceremony speeches by the politicians. Carefully, I unscrewed the cap on my hollow cane which was filled with little containers of scotch, had a drink, and promptly fell asleep.

The Missus Herself was not at all impressed by the time I got home, especially after learning I had also quit my job at *The Telegram*. On my final day in the tent, I had called the office to ask if they would send fifty bucks down to my tent because I was broke and couldn't leave my position to go to the bank. Doug Creighton, the managing editor at *The Tely,* and still my boss today as publisher of *The Toronto Sun,* said no. He was angry with me for not having filed my expense account for over six months and had ruled that I was to receive no more cash advances until my bookwork was cleaned up. I said bluntly that if I didn't get fifty bucks, after all the publicity the paper had received from my stunt, that I wouldn't be back to work. He did not send the money.

The next day I left for Detroit to see Gordie Howe, the hockey legend, who had asked me to write his memoirs. We had already done some work on it and I planned to spend a week at his home with my tape recorder. The hell with *The Telegram.* That is another book I never completed, but this time it was because of legal complications. Gordie was bound to an earlier commitment. Anyway, Creighton then told The Missus he wanted to talk to me and I called him from Gordie's. I went back to my old job a week later. I was never certain who was madder at me, my boss or my wife.

*　　*　　*

The old top hat and tails came out again that same summer when, for a column, I decided to try and visit 42 different pavilions in one night during the annual event called Caravan. This is a festival with an international flavor that lasts ten days and features pavilions from more than 50 different ethnic communities each of which serves specialties from its home land, offers authentic entertainment, and sells souvenirs and produce. A pavilion may be in a hockey arena, the basement of a church, a community hall, or the clubroom of an ethnic organization. They are spread throughout Toronto and revellers can buy passports which are stamped at each pavilion and are used as admission tickets.

Anyway, I had visited about nine of the pavilions and announced that I would visit the rest, more than 40, in one night and set myself a rule. I would have at least one drink at each pavilion and sample the food in several. Naturally, I had to dress for the occasion, especially since the owner of Addison Cadillac donated his private chauffeur-driven limousine to take me around that night.

It was one of those hot and humid summer nights when the air stands still—one of the most uncomfortable of the year. Realizing my outfit would be rather warm, I did the only thing possible. I cut off the trousers at the knees and dressed formally, complete with formal Bermuda shorts.

I was the epitome of elegance as we started picking our way around the city. I would run into a pavilion, rush up to the bar, tip my top hat, down one of the international drinks and rush out to my limousine. Actually, I cheated. If the drink was exceptional, I might have a second. I remember having four in one place. Well sir, we set a world record that night even though I failed to reach my goal. We hit a total of 37 pavilions! I guess I was getting a little tipsy. The last pavilion I remember was the Russian one, where I downed straight vodka and watched the energetic dancers through rather bleary eyes. We didn't run out of energy, we ran out of time. I bid my chauffeur good evening and went off to a house party with some Irish friends I had met along the way. I burped the next morning and tasted almost as many varieties of drinks as Heinz has tomatoes in its ketchup. To breathe on someone would have been to create an international incident.

*   *   *

My most famous parties involved Annabelle The Wonder Horse. Everything dealing with Annabelle was strictly a formal affair, from beginning to end. My partners, Freddie the Flashbulb and R.D. Owen, and I decided that this forlorn horse should travel first class, from obscurity to the Kentucky Derby. We didn't quite reach our goal but, by golly, we had a lot of fun trying.

We had two tremendous parties about a year apart and just ordinary, gigantic parties about every two weeks in between. Take the day in 1967 our trusty horse was to make its first start at Fort Erie, Ontario, just across the Peace Bridge from Buffalo, New York. Because of Annabelle's publicity, you couldn't get a hotel room anywhere on the Canadian side and, a track record for attendance was set that day as the curious turned out to see her run.

On the eve of the race, we held The Annabelle Wonder Ball, the highlight of which was when Gerry Cheevers, the outstanding goaltender for the Boston Bruins who was working at the track that summer, pulled a pair of lady's panties over the head of John J. Mooney, the director of racing. What made this a highlight was that Mooney, now general manager of Laurel Racetrack in Maryland, just smiled. Music was provided by Annabelle's Wonder Band whose drummer had a piece of the horse and, by golly, I can honestly say that everybody got drunk.

The next morning, as advertised, the doors were opened at a local hockey rink, the Fort Erie Arena, and the general public was invited to sip drinks from three large feed buckets which were marked Win, Place, and Show. Win, as I remember, was a rather potent screwdriver, vodka and orange juice, Place was vodka and Wink, and Show was vodka and tomato juice. The men in Annabelle's party were dressed in top hats and morning coats, and the ladies wore dresses designed in our stable's colors, white with black splotches, like ink spots. We called ourselves The Byline Stable and the entire affair was filmed by CFTO-TV from Toronto with Johnny Esaw and Tom McKee doing the commentary and interviews. It was produced and directed by John Spaulding.

"Best damned half-hour I ever produced," Spaulding lamented years later, "and it was never shown. The management said there was too much drinking for it to be on the air." I just happen to have that film at home and, when people do not believe The Saga of Annabelle the Wonder Horse, I subject them to a showing. Anyway, we finally finished at the arena that morning, traipsed along to the track and then, rather unsure on our feet, led our hapless filly to the post with an 85-piece marching band.

That evening, back at the motel, one guy was almost killed when, in full formal wear he went off the diving board, narrowly missed hitting his head on the edge of the pool and then almost drowned, having forgotten that he did not know how to swim. Meanwhile, at the motel next door, they had a canoe in the pool. One guy, showing his expertise as an athlete by using his bed as a trampoline, went up in the air, put a hole through the ceiling and knocked himself cold. They tried to make me pay for motel repairs all over town.

We chose the following April 1, a very appropriate day, to announce that old Annie was going to run in the 1968 Kentucky Derby. We were selling shares for one dollar apiece, 5000 of them, which promised 1/5000th of whatever she earned in purse money. It was an elegant affair and, instead of wearing top hats and tails, Freddie the Flashbulb and I dressed in dinner jackets and wore derbies. The party was held in the Manitoba Room of the Royal York, Toronto's most fashionable and prestigious hotel. It is on the mezzanine floor, and was used the previous night by Pierre Trudeau who was seeking election as Canada's prime minister and had been booked the night after us by Arthur Hailey who was publicizing his new book, *Hotel,* which was based partly on the Royal York.

We were still going first class even though neither of us could afford to take a room there overnight and we had fresh mint flown in from Kentucky so that we could serve mint juleps. The room was filled with television cameras, writers, broadcasters, politicians, and show business personalities who all looked up in alarm when, bouncing through the door and wearing her familiar sunglasses and flowered straw hat, came Annabelle the Wonder Horse herself. We had arranged with Angus McKinnon, who was retiring that very day as the longtime hotel manager, to bring Annie up the service elevator and down the hall. Mind you, we gave her a sedative just in case she decided to kick up her heels at the party and hit one of the unsuspecting guests. We convinced Mr. McKinnon that he should have a horse as a registered guest just once to make his long and colorful career complete.

"Okay, okay," he finally relented, "but, get one of those bags to tie under her tail in case something happens."

I looked in the yellow pages but couldn't find a company that sold poop catchers for horses. Instead, we painted a washtub in her colors and Freddie and me were supposed to carry it behind her wherever she went. We forgot it in the van downstairs.

I was talking to comedian Shelley Berman, who was playing at the hotel, when I first noticed it. Annabelle slowly started to arch her back and spread her feet. "No! No! Not here!" I cried. One thing about old Annabelle is that she always had a mind of her own. She didn't care where she was—she had to go. And right there, recorded by television cameras and news photographers, Annabelle the Wonder Horse committed a most unladylike act—Kerplunk! Kerplunk!—right on the rug. I wasn't fast enough. I whipped off my derby but caught only the last half of it.

"Where was the bag? Where was the bag?" cried Angus McKinnon, looking at the pile on his plush rug and wringing his hands.

They tell me they had to lift the whole rug off the floor overnight and have it steam cleaned. All I know is that we sold $857 worth of shares and the bill for the party was more than $1200. When I went to sell my farm five years later, the deal almost didn't go through.

There was a lien against my property for $500 by the Royal York Hotel. I still owed that for Annie's party.

This horse named Annabelle had quite an effect on my life. For one thing, she ended my four and a half year job with *The Canadian Magazine*. I had decided to spend my time promoting her instead of going to work and, when I hadn't shown up for more than three months, Mike Hanlon, then the editor, had no alternative but to write me a letter saying I was fired. It really wasn't much of a surprise.

*   *   *

On the subject of parties, I would like to tell you about my biggest date—the night I took Miss Canada to the Musicians' Ball. This unlikely story began one cold day when I had a rather disturbing hangover and remembered, to my disappointment, that I had agreed to take part in a charity parade. I made it just in time as the parade was about to leave Toronto's City Hall and one of the parade marshalls hurriedly shoved me into the front seat of an antique roadster. There was a pretty young thing in the back seat.

"Who are you?" I asked.

"My name is Sylvia McGuire," she smiled.

"How come you got stuck in this parade?" I asked.

"Well, I guess because I'm Miss Canada," she said.

"You can't be," I said. "You have a pimple on your chin."

I was always really smooth around women.

"Is that thing still showing?" she said. "I thought I covered it up with makeup."

She was a good kid, this Miss Canada and, as our parade wound up University Avenue, I spotted a man selling roses on the corner, had the driver stop, and presented some to her. Unfortunately, this disrupted the parade somewhat. When the light changed they waited for our car and, because we were stopped, other traffic started to go through again. They gave me hell for that. We all had lunch together at the University of Toronto and, while we were eating, I had this terrific idea.

On the following Sunday night, Local 149 of the American Federation of Musicians was holding its Ladies' Night, when Toronto's musicians would honor the ladies who do without them on almost every other night of the year. I was a member of that local and leader of a jazz group that played nightly at a joint called the Saphire Tavern, which didn't even know how to spell its name. To thank the guys who played with me, I had invited them and their wives to be my guests for the gala evening.

My problem was, I didn't have a date myself. This was after a marriage, between affairs, and during a lengthy run of short-term relationships with cocktail waitresses. Quite frankly, I did not know a girl with enough class to take to an affair like that.

"This is going to sound awfully silly," I said to Miss Canada, "but, what are you doing Sunday night? Wait, before you answer, let me explain."

An explanation was rather necessary seeing as how I was 41, short, dumpy, and balding and Sylvia McGuire was 22, rather short, but not dumpy, had all of her hair, and was Miss Canada. I did not want her to get the wrong idea. I told her all about the Musicians' Ball and how I had invited a bunch of people, planned to rent a small suite for cocktails and a place where the ladies could freshen up, and how I did not have a date.

"I was wondering if you would go along with a joke," I said. "You know, something I could write about in my column, how an old guy like me was going to have his last fling— 41 years old and going to a fancy ball with Miss Canada."

"I'd love to," she said, surprising me very much.

This Sylvia McGuire was certainly not a typical beauty queen. She was an athletic girl from Halifax, Nova Scotia, sort of short, somewhat chunky and, really, more attractive because of her personality than her actual looks. I found out later that she didn't want to be either a beauty queen or Miss Canada. She entered the Miss Halifax contest on a dare from her university pals and unexpectedly won. She hadn't read the fine print which said she was expected to go on to the next level if she won. She became Miss Nova Scotia and then went to the Miss Canada pageant.

"When it started to look as if I might win the Miss Canada title," she said, "I tried to blow it in the interview. I won anyway and I laughed when somebody wrote about the tears of happiness in my eyes as I was crowned. Actually, I was crying because I didn't want the job. It meant I would have to take a year off from university."

She really enjoyed the experience, though, and liked the people she worked with and met, and fell in love with Japan when she was sent there on a promotional tour. I also met some of the pageant organizers later and they told me that she was one of their best and most popular Miss Canadas. When I met her, she had only three weeks left in her reign.

A date with Miss Canada! Whoopee! This just had to be a first-class event. Instead of a small suite, I booked the Royal Suite at the Royal York Hotel, the same one that the Royal Family used when they came to Toronto. Movie stars and other VIPs also stayed there.

The date just kept growing. I increased my guest list, hired a butler to announce incoming guests, a bartender to handle the bar, and a strolling violinist to circulate through the crowd. I bought the best French champagnes, top-line whiskies of every kind, expensive liqueurs and took them up to my suite. What a suite! There was a magnificent living room complete with fireplace, the elegant master bedroom, a second bedroom, two complete bathrooms with gold-plated fixtures, and a dining room with a long, long table. The rooms are huge and, as you enter through the large double doors, you step into an ornate foyer.

I decided that in this setting, we would require the best in canapes that the hotel could provide and, by golly, there should be an orchid for each lady guest and fine cigars for the men. This was all getting to be a very expensive joke. Naturally, it called for my top hat and tails—serious this time, not with sneakers. Next came my mode of transportation. I might as well go all the way. So, I rented a carriage, two matched ponies, and a formal driver and coachman.

I had not spoken to Miss Canada since confirming our date and so she didn't know about my elaborate preparations. I arrived in mid-afternoon (my invitations were for 4 p.m.) at her apartment building and had my carriage wait in the circular driveway. She looked impressive, indeed, in her long dress and the mink coat she had won in the pageant. I tipped my cap and tapped the marble floor with my hollow cane. It gurgled.

She was quite impressed, I think, by my carriage, horses, and driver and coachman, also wearing top hats.The only problem was that there was a light drizzle of rain but, our coachman wrapped us in a heavy blanket and there was a roof on the carriage.

"Would you like to take any particular route?" asked my driver.

"Right down Yonge Street, please," I said.

We clippety-clopped down Toronto's main street, past the body-rub joints, the porno theatres, and the young people who hang around The Strip.

"This," I said, sitting back to enjoy it, "is not a bad way to live."

"You're absolutely crazy," said Miss Canada sweetly.

We made one brief stop at the headquarters of Big Brothers where publicist Charlene

Roycht was holding open house, had our horses wait, and went inside. It was a lucky thing. My pants were falling down and one of the nice ladies who was working there fixed them up.

When we arrived at the Royal York, right across the street from Union Station, there were people waiting under the huge canopy, standing on the bright red carpet on the sidewalk. Pictures were taken again as we stepped out of our carriage and, there to officially greet us were the hotel manager and singer Frankie Laine, the headliner that week in the Imperial Room. We were whisked into the luxurious hotel lobby, went to the elevators while lobby-sitters gawked, and made our way to the Royal Suite.

I had taken to calling Miss Canada "Beaver" because I couldn't remember Sylvia and I couldn't go around calling her Miss Canada all evening. Besides, I explained to her, nothing is more Canadian than the beaver and, after all, she wouldn't be Miss Canada for much longer.

"Well Beaver," I said, "what do you think of it."

We were met by our butler and the violinist was busily fiddling away. The orchids had arrived and we pinned one on her. Other guests started to arrive and, by golly, it wasn't at all difficult to be a host in that setting. People were wandering from room to room, absorbing the feeling of royalty, each carrying a glass of champagne. The bartender walked around with a tray of them, just like in the movies.

"Absolutely crazy," said Beaver. "But, I love it."

One of the first guests to arrive was my oldest sister, Diane, who is four years younger than me but, many years ahead in maturity.

"What is all of this?" she asked in a corner. "Are you making a fool of yourself over a 22-year-old girl? She is only 22, brother."

I hastily explained that it was all a joke, fodder for my column, the last fling of a middle-aged man.

"I certainly hope so," she said, smiling through gritted teeth.

All my guests had now arrived and, within the first hour, every woman had gone into the Queen's bathroom to use the royal toilet. That, to me, was the most amusing part of the entire evening.

"Imagine that," I overheard many of them say, "a heated toilet seat."

Hell, that toilet seat wasn't heated. It was just continually warm from the play it was getting.

I watched as the violinist strolled from room to room, filling the air with romantic strains and noticed, with some pride, that all the ladies were smiling, proudly wearing their orchids and sipping champagne. You should understand that this was a rather unusual setting for a bunch of musicians. They make us eat in the kitchen on some jobs so the guests can't see us between sets. Finally it was time to go down to the main ballroom for cocktails and dinner, followed by dancing.

The huge Canadian Room was filled and, that particular year, the executive of the Toronto local was playing host to their counterparts from New York and several members of the International Board, all of whom were sitting at the head table. I think we danced twice, which was certainly enough for Miss Canada because of my rather quaint and old-fashioned approach to the job, and then it was everybody upstairs—the Royal Suite was still open.

When the dance was over, I discovered my open invitation to other musician friends and the executive board had not been taken lightly. We must have had more than 200 guests in the Royal Suite. If you ever fear that nobody will come to your party, go out and rent the Royal Suite, buy imported champagne, hire a strolling violinist and warm up your toilet seat. I guarantee that everybody will come.

However, I was not spending much time with Miss Canada. I was mingling, talking to people, and I noticed that my sister Diane was sitting with her, in deep discussion. Beaver had won my sister's approval early in the evening when, as we were walking to the elevators to take us to the ballroom, she spied the huge, shiny table in the middle of the lobby. Without saying a word, Miss Canada, her long gown flowing behind her, had taken a run, jumped, and slid the length of the table on her stomach.

"I've always wanted to do that," she said.

I noticed the sudden acceptance on Diane's face. Now, as she passed me in our crowded suite, she leaned towards me and whispered: "You know, I quite like her. She is amazingly mature for her age."

The party finally broke up about 3:30 a.m. and I remember that the last two guests were tailor-booker Dave Caplan and his companion, a blonde singer named Melanie. As I left to take Miss Canada home in a taxi, I recall that Melanie was standing at one end of the dining room in the Royal Suite and, at Mr. Caplan's urging, was struggling to hit a high C.

"Thanks very much," I said to Miss Canada. "I had one of the best times of my life. We didn't spend much time together but you were the perfect date for an old guy."

"I really enjoyed myself," she said, yawning. "But, I'm not used to these hours."

"You know," I suddenly said. "We should do something absolutely different tomorrow afternoon just to unwind."

"Well," she said, "I'm clear in the afternoon. What did you have in mind?"

Sharing a drink with Beaver
in the Royal Suite.

"Let's go fishing," I said.

"Okay," she said.

I went back to the Royal Suite and crawled into the royal bed. I lay back on the elegant bed, my top hat and tails thrown over a chair in the corner and smiled. It had been a perfect evening. As the last couple left and went down the hall, I remember eavesdropping on their conversation:

"Do you know," she said to her husband, "that the toilet seat is heated in the Queen's bathroom?"

"You're kidding," he said.

"No," she said. "It really surprised me. I've never heard of that before."

*　　*　　*

My coach hadn't exactly turned into a pumpkin, but it did change into my old white car, Rusty Rita, and I picked up Miss Canada the next day at noon wearing an old pair of blue jeans.

"This is more like it," she smiled as we drove north to Orillia.

I had made arrangements with Cliff Snache, one of the best Indian fishing guides on the Rama Reserve, and we were to meet him at Fern Resort which is about 100 miles from Toronto. After we arrived at the resort, we played a game of one-on-one basketball on the outdoor court and, while Beaver ran circles around me, I puffed and coughed befitting a man of my 41 years.

Cliff arrived and we made our way to his little boat on Lake Simcoe. It was very cold, bitterly cold in fact, and the rough water was black under the overcast skies. Cliff must have thought I was crazy. There weren't no fish out there that day.

The three of us sat quietly, trying hard not to be first to complain, each of us freezing, wondering what in the hell we were doing out on the water on a day like that. Finally, feeling responsible for our predicament, I casually mentioned that I was ready to go in anytime seeing as how I had to go to the bathroom. They fairly flew into action as Cliff began tugging on the starting rope of the outboard.

As we drove back to Toronto, I started figuring out what my big date had cost me. There was the rental of the Royal Suite, the horses and carriage, the driver and coachman, the violinist, the booze, the canapes, the bartender, tickets for my original 12 guests to the ball, the butler, the orchids. . . . As near as I could figure, it had cost about $2000! We were nearing Toronto and Beaver was saying how sorry she was that I had spent so much money.

"Well," I said. "If you're serious, you could help me to get it back."

"How?" she asked.

"See that, over there?" I said, pointing to a large grandstand on the outskirts of the city. "Well, that is what they call Woodbine Racetrack. The horses run there every afternoon and, if you have the time, we could go there tomorrow and they will give me my money back."

"You know you are just kidding yourself," she said. "But, I guess I'm willing to try."

"There is absolutely no doubt in my mind," I said, "that we will win $2000 and I will come out of this experience even."

I kept up that tune even as we were walking to our table in the Etobicoke Dining Room the next day. I had told Beaver to bring a large bag to carry the money home in and, as I met the betting girls and waitresses I knew, I told them bluntly that I had come to win $2000. They snickered, knowing I was probably the worst bettor who ever went to the races and that I never, ever won money.

I had $600 in my pocket and, as I lost bet after bet, Miss Canada looked across the table sadly. She knew I was a fool and that the story had to end somewhere.

"Please, Paul," she said quietly. "You've already blown enough money. Let's just go. It would have been nice, but. . . ."

"I came here," I said stubbornly, "to make $2000."

I knew she was right, of course and, when the last race came up, I had only $100 left. I had not cashed a single ticket. I looked across at Sylvia McGuire, the 22-year-old Miss Canada from Halifax and thought how much fun the entire operation had been. It was over now, of course, but, hell, it was a great memory. I let my eyes go down the list of horses and one name at the end made me smile—Foolish Ambition. That was an appropriate name for me alright.

"Miss," I said to the betting girl as she came up to the table, "$100 on Foolish Ambition to win, please."

Beaver looked at me with something resembling disgust.

"What the hell, might as well go all the way," I shrugged. "But, there's no sense in even watching it. Let's go down to Bruce Walker's publicity office to say hello before we go."

We sat in Bruce's office, telling him about our big date and I forgot all about the last race. It came on the closed circuit television set in his office and suddenly I remembered my bet.

"Say, I've got some horse in here," I said.

"Which one?" Bruce asked.

"Something called Foolish Ambition," I said.

"Oh no," he said, shaking his head. "You didn't bet on that horse."

They came into the stretch and Daryl Wells, calling the race, suddenly said, "And here comes Foolish Ambition!" We all perked up as we watched the stretch drive.

"How much have you got on it?" Walker asked.

"A hundred bucks to win," I said.

"You're kidding," he said.

Dammit, but it was close. Foolish Ambition came up to the leader and they ran head-to-head towards the wire, close enough for it to be a photo finish, but we all knew that my horse had lost by almost a head.

"Too bad," said Walker.

"Well, it was close," I said to Beaver. She was still flushed with excitement and absolutely downhearted when they posted the results showing my horse second.

"Hold it!" said Bruce. "There's an inquiry!"

We sat quietly, watching the TV set in silence as the numbers of the two top horses flashed off and on while the stewards examined the films. If the flashing stopped and the numbers stayed where they were, the result would be official. If, when they stopped flashing, the numbers disappeared, it meant that they were changing the order of the finish and Foolish Ambition would be the winner.

"How much do you want for that ticket, Rimmer?" a guy joked.

"Ten bucks," I said. "I've never won anything."

"No sale," snapped Miss Canada, clutching the ticket for luck, her eyes riveted on the flashing numbers.

The investigation lasted an agonizing fourteen minutes and suddenly they stopped flashing. They disappeared! A cheer went up from the office. I sat, dumbfounded. Beaver looked as if a miracle had been performed. Dammit, we had won!

"That, Mr. Rimstead," said Walker, "will pay you $2600!"

"Certainly," I said. "That's my original $600 and the $2000 I came here to win."

We had to go back to the dining room to cash the ticket and Beaver was fairly bubbling along the way.

"I can't believe this," she said, shaking her head. "It's just like in the movies."

All the betting girls and waitresses had waited to see our faces, knowing we would be back and knowing of my boast to win $2000. They had the twenty-six $100 bills lined up on a table in the empty dining room and they applauded as we walked in. Hell, Foolish Ambition indeed.

Two weeks later, with her reign over, Beaver couldn't wait to get out of Toronto and back to her beloved Halifax. She claims that her Halifax is the only sensible place in the world for a person to live and, I suspect, she wants to own the city some day. She drops a note periodically to tell me what she has been doing and she now is sales manager of a large hotel, the television hostess for the Atlantic Lottery show, and plays a lot of racquetball. Beaver does not own Halifax yet, but, by golly, she does own two little houses.

I don't know about her, but our date was certainly the biggest I ever had and, it was all paid for by a horse. It was too bad, looking back, that we did not catch any fish. ●

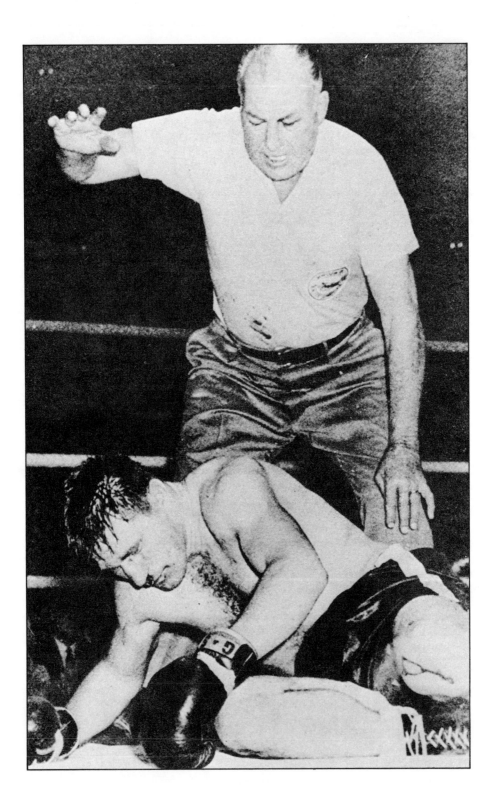

Canada's Fighting Fisherman

One night in 1958
Yvon Durelle had champion Archie Moore
on the floor four times.

prologue *Few athletes anywhere have been as colorful as Yvon Durelle, Canada's fighting fisherman.*

He was larger than life, a sportswriter's dream, and there will never be another like him. I was so fascinated by stories I had read of his exploits and lifestyle that I knew I had to meet him some day, talk to him and write my own version of his story.

Frankly, I can't think of a better subject for a movie script than Yvon. Mind you, his story was sometimes stranger than fiction. Movie-goers might not believe it.

o o o

MARCH 23, 1968—Yvon Durelle was a fighter, a big, raw fisherman from New Brunswick who didn't give a damn for anybody or anything.

He was crude, hewn from the hardy stock of the desolate fishing village of Baie Ste. Anne, where 500 souls fight for survival on the south shore of Miramichi Bay.

He drank whisky, stayed up late at night, gambled and cheated at cards. He was profane. He ruined fast cars and he hated to train.

His haircut was homemade, his fisherman hands calloused and his Acadian accent as thick as pea soup.

The big city boys may never see the likes of him again.

New York, London, Berlin, Miami, Boston, Montreal, Toronto. . . . He was "Ee-von from de Nort' Countree."

He would be in a gym, supposedly training for an important fight and, instead, would gather the sportswriters around him and tell them stories. He would tell them about the big fish of the Miramichi, about his five brothers at home who could beat him with one hand tied behind their backs. He would tell them lies.

And he would laugh—a deep guttural laugh that resounded off the walls.

◀ Yvon Durelle knocked out by Archie Moore in their 1958 championship bout.

47

Meanwhile, a nervous bespectacled little man with a large, pulpy nose would be pacing the floor. It was Chris Shaban, who ran a little grocery store back home in Moncton. It was Shaban's impossible task to try to manage Durelle.

"What can I do with him?" he would moan, throwing up his hands. "He won't train. He won't train."

His fighting style was best described, perhaps, after a fight late in his career against Canadian heavyweight champion George Chuvalo, when Chuvalo had knocked him out in the 12th round.

"Durelle," wrote Milt Dunnell of the Toronto Star, "was like a drunken sailor on roller skates."

Incredibly, this is the same man who once was within a whisker of winning the light heavyweight championship of the world.

On the night of Dec. 10, 1958, in the Montreal Forum, big Yvon knocked champion Archie Moore down three times in the first round, again in the fifth, and finally was knocked out himself in the eleventh.

It was picked as the best fight in the world that year, and people still wonder how Moore managed to get up after the first knockdown.

After several retirement announcements. Durelle finally quit fighting in 1961. He turned to wrestling and his name still pops up occasionally as a wrestler or referee in the Maritimes.

His best year was 1958, when his earnings, after expenses, were $39 000. It's all gone, of course. Yvon blew it long ago.

He's a utility forester now in Baie Ste. Anne—take-home pay $133 twice a month. That's with the income tax taken off. (He and the tax people have finally reached an agreement after years of difficulties. They decided to deduct $15 a month from his salary for 20 years, a little reminder of his fighting days. He has only 19 years to go.)

"You want to do a story 'bout me?" Durelle had said on the telephone. "Dat's a funny t'ing. Why do the sportswriters still want to write 'bout an old man who don't fight anymore?

"You come anyway. Fly in the plane to Moncton, then drive 100 miles nort'. I take a day off work for you. I do everyt'ing for you."

Then he laughed, the raspy, raucous laugh.

"Everyt'ing," he said, "'cept lend you money. I got no money."

Chris Shaban is *the* living expert on Yvon Durelle, so I stopped in Moncton to talk to Chris, who just got out of the hospital.

"Ulcers, Paul," he said, recuperating in his modest bungalow. "Ulcers. And Ee-von, he gave them to me. He's a terrible man, Paul. A terrible man. I couldn't do a thing with him.

"Mind you, I love him like a son. I really mean that. I really do."

Chris sold the little grocery store several years ago and opened the Chris-Rock Tavern with his friend Rocky Stone. Naturally, the walls are adorned with pictures of Durelle's fights. Two summers ago, Yvon worked there for a few days as a waiter.

"I'll never forget that night when he fought Moore the first time, Paul," he said. "I was sick, Paul, sick. Ever since I was a boy, I dreamed of being a second in a main event fight at Madison Square Garden. But I never dreamed I would have a fighter going for a world championship.

"I can remember every minute. Every minute. I didn't sleep for two nights. And I've never been as nervous, Paul, as I was when I was putting on Ee-von's gloves in the ring. My hands shook."

Chris was reliving the night, how he went to Moore's dressing room and saw old Archie putting a piece of tape over the knuckles of his left hand.

"Do you want to kill Ee-von?" Chris asked Moore. "I didn't think you were that kind of a man. You'll have to take the tape off."

Chris was laughing now as he remembered being in the ring, trying to put on Durelle's gloves with his shaking hands.

"Do you know what Ee-von did? He looked down at me and said, 'Mac,' (he always called me Mac) 'Mac, please stop shakin'. Geez, Mac, that don't look good.'"

After the fight, as they were on their way to the interview room, Moore's wife ran up to Archie and said, "My God, that man Durelle is awful!"

"The Lord was with me tonight," Moore replied quietly.

"Humph," said Durelle, standing nearby, "he didn't use *me* too good."

Shaban looked thoughtful for a few

moments, then leaned forward.

"Paul," he said, "I've never told anyone this before, but you can write it if you want. You know, they postponed the rematch twice. Ee-von should never have been in there when it was finally held. He wasn't in shape. He got knocked out in the third round. And Moore hurt him, Paul, he really hurt him.

"But if Ee-von had fought him when it was originally scheduled, he would have knocked him out. I've never seen him in such shape. He told me, 'Mac—I'll train for this one, you'll see.'

"You see, Paul, he wouldn't do any road work. A fighter's legs are important, and I tried to tell Ee-von that. But when I'd wake him up in the morning, he'd look at me and say, 'Mac, I know how my legs feel better than you do. Now go 'way and let me sleep.'

"He was just too lazy to get up, Paul. A terrible man. Anyway, he was in good shape for the rematch. He even ran a bit. And the Moore people knew it.

"You've heard of Doc Kearns—he had Dempsey, Mickey Walker, Jake Lamotta, and he had Moore. Well, Kearns asked me up to his hotel room just before the second fight. Charlie Goldman, he was trainin' Ee-von, he said 'Beware of him, Chris.'"

Kearns, says Chris, tried to make a deal. "He said that when he had Lamotta, he made a deal with the Moore people. If Moore took away Lamotta's title, Kearns would get 25 per cent of Moore. Now he had Moore and he wanted 25 per cent of Ee-von if Ee-von won. I wouldn't go for it, Paul. I wouldn't.

"And he said to me, 'It's too damn bad you won't listen to reason.'

"Paul, seven days before the fight, they called it off. I went to see Moore and all he had on was a Band-aid on his heel, Paul. Just a little Band-aid on his heel, Paul. They're just a damn bunch of crooks anyway, Paul.

"They said his heel was festered. Maybe I made a mistake. Maybe I should have made the deal. Ee-von would have won that time. He would have been the champion."

Nobody knows for certain how many fights Durelle had in his career. But few fighters had as many. Yvon never had an amateur fight.

The first time he put on gloves, in Chatham, N.B.—35 miles west of Baie Ste. Anne—17-year-old Durelle was matched against a fellow named Sonny Ramsey who had been in 17 pro bouts. Yvon, who hadn't even trained, knocked him out in the first round.

In 1956, with 10 years of fighting behind him—most of it in the Maritimes—he decided to quit. That's when Chris took him over.

They went to Miami for their first fight, against tough Clarence Hinnant, and Durelle was stopped with a cut eye. Hinnant was furious after the fight. He said, and Yvon confirmed it with a crooked grin, that Durelle had been spitting blood in his face all night.

After the loss to Hinnant, Durelle won 14 in succession. Finally, Chris—without telling Durelle—matched him against top-ranked Tony Anthony in Detroit.

"He wasn't going to get any better, Paul," says Chris, "so I thought we might as well go for the best. It was a draw, Paul, and that's what got him the Moore fight."

It also put some money in Yvon's pockets, money to buy big, fast cars. Shaban shook his head in disbelief as he remembered the cars.

"Paul, he was a very fast driver. Very, very fast—just terrible altogether. Ee-von couldn't stand to see somebody ahead of him on the road. Nobody would give him any insurance. He'd wreck the cars one after the other. Paul, he had three new cars in one summer and spent $17 000 or $18 000 on them.

"I remember one night, Paul, when he was coming down from Baie Ste. Anne, he was going so fast, he couldn't make the left turn at Buctouche. So he just drove it straight into the river."

It didn't take long for people to realize that Yvon and money were not good for each other, so an arrangement was made whereby Theresa, Yvon's wife, signed all the cheques.

"I was up there once, Paul," said Shaban, "and Theresa, who's as nice a woman as you'll meet, wanted Ee-von to go to Chatham and buy a television antenna. She gave him a blank cheque and signed it.

"Paul, he came home with a new convertible. It cost him $6300. And his other car had only been seven or eight months old. He was afraid to go into the house. He didn't get the antenna."

Only three years ago, an RCMP officer, hearing that Yvon planned driving to Halifax, took Chris aside.

"Chris, you can't let him drive," said the officer.

"Oh, Paul," said Chris, who was holding his head more and more as the afternoon wore on, "do you know what the officer said? He said, 'Ee-von's got no more points left. As a matter of fact, he's three in the hole.'

"Paul! How can a man, even Ee-von, be three driving points in the hole!"

While on the subject of cars and money, it was inevitable that income tax enter the discussion.

"The tax people used to come to me about him, Paul," said Chris. "They couldn't get anything from him. One day I went up there to help him figure it out. He pulled out a big jar and poured crumpled bits of paper all over the table. It was impossible."

Yvon had trouble sticking to facts. If the true story wasn't doing the job, he'd jazz it up a little. It got so that Chris was afraid to send reporters to Yvon's home.

"His father listened while Yvon was being interviewed up there one day on the boat and he called me after," said Chris. "He said, 'Chris, you got to stop Yvon telling lies.'

"I said, 'Look Mister Durelle, you couldn't stop him. What do you expect me to do?'"

One of the situations Chris was able to prevent happened in New York, where Yvon was training for a big fight. A man came to Chris to ask if he could go and see Yvon to sign their contract.

"What contract?" asked Chris.

"For the salmon deal," said the man. "Yvon's going to ship me 50 cases of one-pound tins of Miramichi salmon and 50 cases of half-pound tins. I'll distribute it in New York."

"Oh, Paul, Paul, Paul," moaned Chris. "I told the fella, 'Look, you'd better not depend on this too much.'

"Miramichi salmon is the finest salmon in the world. They wouldn't get that much in two years. I got mad at Ee-von over that. I said, 'Ee-von, what's the matter with you? This isn't

good. You can't tell a man you'll do something like that.'"

"Aw, Mac," said Durelle, "what the hell's the difference. I don't even know the guy."

And then there were the social functions. . . .

"Paul, he wouldn't chew his food," said Chris. "You'd sit down to eat a meal with him and it would be gone. Even steak. He would swallow it without chewing—swallow it whole."

But the biggest problem was when Yvon got his hands on a microphone.

"I remember once, Paul, in Thunder Bay," said Chris. "They had invited us there and we were in this fine, magnificent ballroom. The mayor was there, and his wife. All the ladies, you know, wearing furs and long white gloves.

"Paul, I was worried sick," said Chris. "Oh, the jokes he told. My God, I thought I was going to die, Paul. It was terrible, just terrible. Sometimes, though, he was really a good speaker, you know, when he didn't cuss and swear. But I could never tell, from one place to the next."

Once, in Ottawa, they attended a function with former fighters Jimmy McLarnin and Barney Ross. McLarnin was demonstrating how to throw a left hook to someone in one corner and Ross was showing some other people how he used to defend himself.

"Ee-von called me into the washroom," says Chris. "And inside was this old guy, shadow-boxing around the urinals. Ee-von looked at me and said, 'Please, Mac, make me stop fighting before I get like this? I don' wanna be that way, Mac. Promise me! Promise me you'll make me quit!'"

Chris tried to make him quit in 1959, after the Chuvalo fight, but Durelle continued on his own until he was barred from the ring for his own protection.

"Ee-von has this very good friend in Fredericton," said Chris. "His name is Dr. B. L. Jewett. He called me one day a few years ago and asked me if I thought Ee-von could handle a job with the youth and welfare department. You know, Paul, going around and working with the kids.

"I told him I'd speak to Ee-von and tell him what it would be like—that he'd have to stop swearing and cussing around the young people.

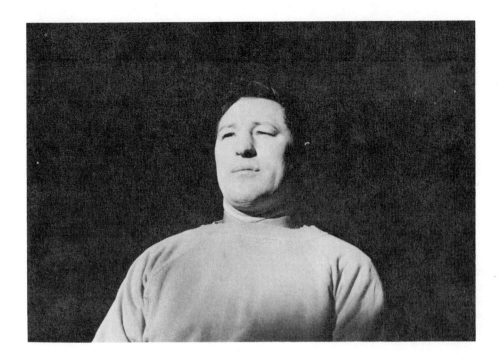

"Oh, it would have been good for Ee-von, Paul. He wanted it, too.

"But, Paul, the very next morning, I read a story on the front page of the newspaper. Ee-von was charged with shooting a cow moose out of season. Oh, Paul—the job was gone.

"I phoned Ee-von and asked him what he was doing up there. 'Aw, Mac,' said Yvon. 'I didn't shoot no moose. I set a trap last night and I caught it.'"

"Now isn't that quite a thing, Paul? To set a trap and catch a moose? I don't know about you, but I never heard of a trap that would catch a moose. He said something about it hanging from its back legs in a tree, or something. Paul, I don't know. . . ."

The snowbanks were higher than the car and the road narrowed considerably after I turned at Black River on the way to Baie Ste. Anne.

Finally, up ahead, squatted some bleak, unpainted houses. Some were boarded up; others had greyish-white fishing boats up on blocks in the yard.

And, just as it had been all along the coast, the largest building—magnificent stone with a towering steeple—was the Roman Catholic church.

There was only one business of note, the government store which sells liquor, wine and beer. It was the only new building in the village and a group of men stood talking in front of it.

"Yvon Durelle?" said one old man, rather suspiciously. "Over there, across the road from the church."

It was a square frame house, the paint peeling. The driveway had drifted over with snow.

"Paul," Chris had said when I left, "I think it was wrestling that hurt him. I think it was in Brockville one night, when he fell from the ring and hit his head on the concrete floor. He had a concussion, Paul. Moore hurt him, too, in that second fight. I think Ee-von'll tell you that. And he had a bad accident with a boat and hurt his head.

"Some people think it was Chuvalo that hurt him. I wanted to stop it in the eighth round. But Ee-von, he came to the corner and said, 'Hell,

Chris, if that guy could fight, I would've been dead four rounds ago.'

"But, you'll notice, Paul, that his balance is no good. He walks as if he's drunk sometimes. You know what I mean, Paul?"

A huge figure appeared at the door.

"Hah!" said Yvon Durelle, engulfing my hand with his.

He led the way through the large country kitchen into the living room and plunked himself down on the sofa.

He introduced his wife, Theresa, a polite, pretty woman who seemed rather shy, almost uncomfortable.

"I call her M'am," he grunted. "Dat means Mother in French."

Then Yvon, who's 38, introduced the kids: Geneva, 16, a striking young girl; Yvon Jr., 14, whom they call Beau; Paul, a smiling little fellow who is 10; and Francine, a mischievous young lady of 9 who is known in the family as Poulette, "little chicken."

"M'am!" Yvon roared suddenly. "Get my suits."

Mrs. Durelle went upstairs and returned with two tuxedos on hangers.

"See!" grunted Yvon as he slipped on one of the jackets. "It fits. An' I got two of them."

They explained that a Montreal reporter had written last summer that Durelle had appeared somewhere in an ill-fitting, rented tuxedo and that his other clothes had stains on them.

"It hurt Yvon," explained Mrs. Durelle. "We may be poor, but we're clean. I try very hard to look after our clothes. I didn't know what to think when I heard you were coming; our furniture isn't very good. We had nice furniture once, when Yvon was fighting."

"M'am!" grunted Yvon again. "Put on the record."

She reached down behind a box and pulled out a small record.

"I always hide this," she explained. "Yvon plays it too much and it hurts him. It was hurting too much."

She placed it on the record player and the living room filled with the noise of a roaring crowd.

Yvon sat there silently and motioned to her to increase the volume.

A ring announcer was introducing Yvon Durelle, who was about to fight Archie Moore for the light heavyweight championship of the world.

It was a record of the broadcast that had gone to the armed forces, the blow-by-blow description of the highlights of their first fight.

Poulette walked over to ask her father something.

"Not now!" he barked. "Not during the record."

He sat there, leaning forward on the sofa, wearing the green shirt of his forester uniform, too short in the sleeves, too small around that massive neck.

The crowd roared again and again as Durelle knocked Archie Moore down—once, twice, three times.

There was a far-away look in Yvon's eyes, a misty look.

Now it was the fifth round and Durelle knocked him down again.

The big man sat motionless on the sofa, his huge fists clenched.

Now the abbreviated broadcast would switch to the eleventh round, when Moore would knock him out.

"Shut it off!" he barked at his wife, who had been standing over the record.

"I never listen to the end," he said, his voice suddenly soft. "Sometimes it make me cry. I miss it so much it hurts inside. I only knew about boxing."

He sat there quietly for a few minutes. Nobody said anything.

"You know," he said. "I t'ink I'm gonna box again.

"Next summer . . . at the fairs."

The folks in Baie Ste. Anne have noticed a change in Yvon Durelle.

David Savoie was talking about it one night over a hot cup of coffee in the kitchen of his boarding house. He had been out on the bay all day, fishing for smelt, and his wife, who runs the boarding house, was finishing up the dishes.

"I don't know why Yvon stopped fishing,"

he said. "He wasn't the best fisherman, but he was a good one. He don't go on the water no more, though—not since he quit the fighting. He's got that job with the foresters, but that don't make him much money."

They all remember when Yvon had money. He drove big, fast cars—too fast, usually. And he spent a lot. He was a huge man, the hero of their village and, because of him, Baie Ste. Anne became known throughout the world.

"Some of the people is mad at Yvon," said Savoie, "because he had his chance and didn't save any money. But most everybody likes him. He's a good man. He has a good wife. Yvon, he would give you anything."

"Humph," interjected Mrs. Savoie. "He had too many friends. He's too good. That's his trouble."

Now Savoie, suddenly serious, leaned forward.

"Tell me," he said, "what's the matter with Yvon? He didn't use to act like that, before the fighting. Now he has trouble saying his words. He didn't use to have trouble saying his words."

Chris Shaban, Durelle's former manager, had tipped me off in Moncton, before I went to Baie Ste. Anne, when he said; "Paul, his balance is no good. You know, he walks as if he's drunk."

The most blunt, however, had been fast-talking little Vince Moar, the postmaster at Chatham, 35 miles away, where Yvon started fighting.

"Doesn't Yvon look good now?" Moar had said, with Yvon standing there grinning. "You know what I mean, when he first came back home he was punchy. Well, you know, he didn't walk very good. But just look at him now. He looks good, doesn't he? And he's walking better every day."

Yvon stood there proudly, wearing the green dress uniform of the forester. And though it was clean and neatly pressed, his thick build made him look somewhat like a big country boy in his first scout uniform.

He had dropped around to introduce me to Vince because Vince was the man who put him in a ring for the first time.

"Dode Dealey—he promoted the fights here—and I, we decided to go up the shore to see if we could find some new talent," said Moar. "They put up a ring in a field at Baie Ste. Anne and we were really interested in seeing Yvon's brother, Placide.

"But they got Yvon to go into the ring and, even though he'd never fought, we decided to give him a chance. We brought him in against a fellow who had had 17 pro fights and Yvon knocked him out in the first round. He never did lose a fight here."

"And I got eight bucks that first time," said Durelle.

Later, he was asked about his slurred speech and lack of balance.

"Haw, haw, haw," he had laughed, very loudly. "T'ree times now the cops pick me up and think I'm drunk. I swear at them.

"It's getting better now. Before it was real bad. Now, only if I have a couple drinks. Then I can't talk and I can't walk."

He went on to list the number of times he has been hurt in the head—fighting, the boat accident (he crashed into another boat at 60 m.p.h.), and the wrestling fall when he suffered a fractured skull.

"I started to get headaches so I eat a lot of aspirin," he said. "A whole box at once."

"That's right," Chris Shaban said later. "I couldn't keep him away from them. I'd tell him, 'Ee-von, that isn't good for you.' But he wouldn't listen."

Yvon still doesn't listen. He had a bad cold that day, so after the visit with Moar, he picked up a prescription from the drugstore in Chatham—pills and cough medicine.

On the way back to Baie Ste. Anne late that afternoon, Yvon looked over from the driver's seat and said: "Hey, gimme that medicine. Hmmm—it says two teaspoons four times a day."

He lifted the bottle to his lips as he drove and drank half of it.

"Haw, that's two teaspoons, huh?"

Later that night, after a few belts of scotch, Durelle's face broke out in brilliant red splotches—on his chin, both cheeks, the end of his nose and on his forehead. He looked in the mirror and was surprisingly concerned. He phoned his doctor to ask him about it.

When his wife came home from a school meeting, she scolded him for drinking when he was taking medicine.

"What did the doctor say?"

"Aw, he said to don't drink any whisky tomorrow," Yvon told her.

Walter Gibbs was visiting that night. Walter has been a close friend since they were kids, and his wife Rita teaches at the high school. He is a full-fledged forester and works with Yvon.

"Hey, c'mon," barked Yvon suddenly, "I got to see my little boy before he sleeps. He always wants to see Yvon. I got to give him his pop and candy. I give it to him every night."

Durelle led the way outside, across the dark highway to the small home owned by his brother, Ernie. Inside, an old man was doing a step dance for three children and their mother.

It was Yvon's father, but they haven't spoken to each other for several years. Yvon says his father sold a piece of land that belonged to him.

"It had to stop somewhere," he said.

Now they ignored each other, even though the room was very small, and Mr. Durelle, a small man with bristling grey hair, talked to Walter Gibbs.

The boy Yvon wanted to see was Allain, his brother's six-year-old son.

"Hah!" roared Yvon, presenting the youngster with a chocolate bar and a soft drink. The other children looked on hungrily.

"How does Uncle Yvon's car go?" he asked in French.

"Brrmmm . . ." said the little boy, making a smooth sound.

"And your daddy's?"

"Putt-putt-putt. . . ."

"Hah!" said Yvon.

As he was walking back home, he turned and said: "See—my feet's no good. I can't walk good because I had a drink." He stumbled in the snow, lurching forward with each step.

Inside, he was asked if his father had gone to all of Yvon's big fights.

"He went, but he didn't *see* them," said Yvon.

"He saw most of them," objected Walter. "Yvon, you're too hard on him. He was asking me over there, 'How's Yvon doing?' I told him good. He doesn't like it now, when you don't talk to each other."

Durelle was upset.

"How do you think I feel?" he demanded. "He's my own father. I love him. But it had to stop somewhere. But I love him. He's my father."

His eyes were misty and there was an embarrassing silence. Yvon's eyes get that way often.

Chris Shaban had told about how difficult it was for Durelle to visit sick children in hospitals. Finally he had to stop.

"Once, at a school for the blind," Chris said, "the kids were running their hands over Eevons face to see what he looked like. And Eevon burst into tears. He couldn't stand it, Paul. He has a big heart, that Ee-von."

Walter Gibbs changed the subject now, recalling the time Yvon fought a fellow named Arnold Flegeir (who's now married to one of Yvon's sisters), in Chatham.

"Yvon knocked him out and all of us from Baie Ste. Anne were there," he said. "After the fight, we were sitting in a restaurant in Chatham when some guys came up to our booth.

"'You guys from Baie Ste. Anne?' one guy asked. 'Well, you better leave now. Get the hell outta here.'"

Yvon laughed as Walter told about the ensuing brawl—Flegeir fans from Chatham versus Durelle fans from Baie Ste. Anne.

"Ripped my pants right up the leg," said Walter. "We were going to a dance on the way home and I had to wear my overcoat on the dance floor so my bare leg wouldn't show."

Durelle fought some of the best of his time—Moore twice, Floyd Patterson twice, George Chuvalo, Tony Anthony. But when he talks about fighting he talks about the early ones, the big ones at Chatham and Moncton when town was pitted against town.

"One time I fight a guy in Charlottetown," said Yvon. "We hate each other. Finally, he throws off his gloves. Mine are too tight, they

won't come off.

"The referee, he runs away and we go at it for maybe half an hour, him with bare fists. Finally, I catch him down on the floor and I sit on his chest and hit his head into the cement until I knock him out."

"Oh, I remember that," said his wife, Theresa. "That was just before we were married."

"Anyway," Yvon continued, "we fight again in Moncton. Hah! Now we're in my city. I hate that man. I tell the referee—'Look, don't stop this fight. I gonna cut this man up so he bleed to death.'

"I want this man to bleed all night . . . I'm gonna cut him until he die."

Yvon sat there, a glow in his eyes.

"We go out for the first round. I swing and just touch him. You know what he done? He fall down flat on his back. I was mad. I yell at him, I scream at him: 'You get up! I didn't touch you! Get up and fight!'

"But he knows what happens so he stays down. I was so mad I ran over and jumped on his arm and broke it. Haw, haw . . . he think I'm a tough customer."

Durelle was one of the most crude of all fighters, in and out of the ring, but popular because he didn't give a damn.

"The worst time was when I won with my teeth," Yvon grinned. "They asked me to carry this fella four rounds.

"But then I can't catch him. He runs away. I can't stand that. I wait until we get in a clinch, then I put my head down and put my teeth right here." He reached over and squeezed the large muscle that connects the neck and shoulder.

"I bite and bite until I taste the warm blood in my mouth. I look up at him and his face is like this—'Arghhhh!' Then I step back and let him have it. Broke his jaw on both sides, haw, haw."

A quiet woman, rather shy, dropped in to visit M'am, and Yvon, in his booming voice, started to kid her.

"Y'know, she's got 16 kids," he said. "Yeah— she's workin' for the country. Haw, haw."

The woman smiled shyly. It was Seline Martin and the fact was she had only 11 children. Exiline Martin dropped in later that night. She got the same treatment, but she did have 16 children.

"Look," said Yvon. "Tomorrow morning we go to the moose country."

"Be careful," warned David Savoie, back at the boarding house. "Make sure you got two pairs of snowshoes. The snow is deep back there."

Yvon arrived early the next morning.

"Yesterday," he said, "I like you should go to hell. I was sick with that cold. Today I feel good."

He drove to the forestry office a few miles away where he, Walter and two other men work. Yvon, however, is only a utility forester because he didn't take a course.

"But I got full power," he said proudly. "I can catch people breakin' the law and I have full power. Look here, we got files and records of everything. See, I just pull out this drawer and we know right where to look." He pulled out a file folder and jammed it back in, off centre so that it bent when he closed the drawer again.

Yvon put the department's Ski-Doo on a half-ton pickup truck, drove it to the moose country, and started it up.

There were many moose tracks in the moose country, but no moose. Yvon sat there, his parka done up tightly, and looked at the blue sky, white snow and dark green pines.

"Who needs anyt'ing else?" he said softly. "Look at this. Look how healthy it is. My kids will never fight. It's no good."

Chris Shaban had told me to ask Yvon about the time he fought Floyd Patterson for $1.00 at Newcastle, N.B.

Was it true?

"Hah! But it was an American dollar," laughed Yvon. "That made it worth $1.10.

Haw, haw. . . ."

He said he found out that the promoter was paying Patterson so much that night that he, Durelle, was certain to lose money. So Yvon told the man to pay everybody and not worry about him.

"Lotsa times I fight for nothin'," he said, "lotsa times."

It was back to Chatham that afternoon and, while manoeuvring his little car down one of the city streets, Durelle got behind another car that was travelling too slow for his liking. He was enraged. He leaned on the horn and screamed at the other driver. Then, for the third time in two days, he cut up a one-way street the wrong way.

"It's okay," he roared. "I know all the cops in Boston."

"Tell him he isn't in Boston," said Renee Martin, M'am's brother, who was also in the car.

"We'll go and see Cassidy, he used to be a fighter, too," said Yvon.

Cline Cassidy, a consumer service representative for 20 years with the New Brunswick Electrical Power Company Commission, smiled patiently as he led the way into his fresh, new office.

Yvon started reminiscing. He always had trouble making the 175-pound weight as a light heavy and they talked about the time, when he was fighting in Chatham, that they had to take him down and put him in somebody's dry kiln for the afternoon.

Vince Moar, the postmaster, had remembered it well. "Yvon lost six pounds," he said, "but he passed out when we got him outta there to drive him up to the arena. He knocked the guy out, though."

Yvon knocked a lot of guys out.

"Remember the first one?" Walter Gibbs had asked. "You were about 14 and we were at the school putting a show on. This big guy, a really big man, came along lookin' for trouble. Yvon weighed about 145 pounds then and he hit the guy right in the mouth and broke his jaw."

"I remember them talking about it," M'am said. "They said Yvon was pretty wild."

Yes, Yvon was pretty wild, indeed.

But he didn't look wild now, driving his car home.

"Funny thing," he said. "I had lotsa friends when I was a fighter, but they don't come around any more. My best friends now are the ones I had before I was a fighter."

"Did you ever think about a book? Your life might make a good book."

"Naw," he said. "No books. I have to tell the truth in a book and it would be bad. I was too bad when I was a kid. I couldn't talk about how bad. You know, I was a gangster. People don't know that."

As he drove along, a dog started chasing his car. Yvon steered the car right at the dog, but missed it.

Driving through Baie Ste. Anne, Durelle points out each house along the way and says who drinks and who doesn't.

"Him," he would say, "he drinks everything he makes."

Then, as his own frame home appeared: "They say a crazy guy lives in that one there."

Renee, his brother-in-law, had been at the house two nights before and Yvon had reached behind the sofa and pulled out a large cribbage board. He loves games and he has to win. He beat Renee and kept kidding him.

Walter was there now and Yvon told him how easily he had beaten Renee. He was trying to force Walter into a game but Walter didn't want to play.

"Look, quit your braggin'," Walter said.

Yvon made him play. When he won, he talked about it. When he lost he was silent.

"I'll never play cards with him again," Chris Shaban had said. "He cheats. He really does."

"Haw, haw—did Chris say that?" laughed Yvon. "Y'know, when I was in a hotel room, I'd walk around with no clothes on—nothing. Well, one day, me and Chris and Placide, my brother, was playing cards. Me and Placide, we were holding cards under the table, between our toes.

"We always cheat like that. One night, Chris dropped a card on the floor and when he bent down to pick it up, he sees all these cards. Was he mad!"

"I remember that," said Shaban.

"But the thing I remember most was once when Yvon was in a big money game. There musta been $1200 in the pot. I looked at his hand and he's got four kings. But—six cards instead of five. Oh, I was so scared. But, the next time I looked, he had only five. I never figured out what he did with that other card."

"Hah! Chris was mad," says Yvon. "I never told him either. He stopped the game and got me outta there. Was he mad—whew!"

Yvon fought too long and then he wrestled. Finally, as he says, "They barred me all over the world."

But, if it hadn't been for M'am, he would have continued to fight at fairs. "He gave me a nervous breakdown," she said. "I just couldn't carry on, raising the children alone and worrying about him. So I told him, Yvon, quit before you wind up in a mental hospital. Do you want the kids to ask, 'Where's Daddy?' and me to say, 'Your daddy's in a mental hospital?'

"I told him, quit, Yvon, or I'm leaving you."

"So I quit," said Yvon. "I love my wife and my kids. And it got so I could see a punch coming from 'way back but I couldn't duck in time.

"An' there was the headaches. Here, feel this, on my nose. That bone you feel there, that was a bad one.

"But," he said as an afterthought, "if she had told me when I was at the top to quit, I guess I would have let her leave. Because when I did quit I wasn't much good. Fighting had been the most important thing to me. More important than anything."

When you know about Yvon Durelle's exploits and the way he is, you might wonder about his four children and how they are being brought up. All I can say is that I'd hate to be the man who tried to harm them in any way. Yvon gloats over them—they are his whole life.

He's been a wild kind of a guy and he'll continue to be wilder than most. But his kids are first-class. He insists that they keep up their marks at school and that they show respect.

"You know," he said quietly, "you've got to have some of the devil in you to be a fighter. I was born with that.

"And, if I'm crazy, it wasn't fighting that made me that way. That's the way I was born."

epilogue *Theresa Durelle answered my call twelve years later and said Yvon was in the back yard, working on his fishing boat, but that she would get him. I was worried that Yvon would not remember me. We had not seen each other since I had written the stories in 1968. I wasn't even sure that he had ever read them. That is not what I should have worried about. Yvon certainly remembered my name. He also remembered the stories. He hated them. They had been embarrassing to him.*

"I treated you good when you came to visit me," he said on the phone. "But, you didn't treat me good. You came and ate our food, stayed at my house, and didn't pay nothing. I didn't ask for nothing. An' I was one of the poorest guys in the country then. Sometimes I didn't know where the food was coming for the next day."

I fumbled for an appropriate apology. "You said I was an alcoholic," Yvon said. "You called me roly-poly. . . ."

I tried to explain that I had never used either term to describe him but, it was no use.

"I learned a lesson from you," Yvon said. "Now I am careful when I talk and who I talk to. I'm gonna do a book soon and I'll tell you what I think of you then. You caused me lots of trouble. Police would stop me when I was driving my car after those stories and ask me if I was drunk. You caused me a lotta trouble. You know I told you I can't drink because of my legs."

That is true. His unsteadiness on his feet when he retired became even worse if he drank, which was mentioned in the stories, and, while I wrote about Yvon's drinking when he was younger, I did not intend to give the impression that he was drunk all the time. Mind you, we did have a few social drinks while we were doing the story but nothing excessive.

I called Yvon only two weeks after they buried likeable, little Chris Shaban, his manager. Chris died of cancer after a lengthy illness and Yvon, of course, was at his funeral.

"That hurt me a lot," he said quietly. "Chris, he was like a father. We were closer than father and son."

Yvon's fortunes, I was happy to hear, had taken a turn for the better.

"I'm retired now," he said. "I am fishing again. I fish for herring, codfish, flounders, and mackerel. I sold my Fishermen's Club, my taxes are paid. I'm not rich, but, both me and my wife are working and we're happy."

He opened his own bar, Yvon Durelle's Fishermen's Club, on a lot next door to his house in Baie Ste. Anne a few years after I had interviewed him. I read about it in the newspapers, especially the night of May 20, 1977, the night of what he still calls "the accident." Yvon became involved in an altercation with Albain Poirier, 32, in the parking lot of his club, fired five shots from a .38-calibre revolver and killed him. Yvon claimed that Poirier had repeatedly threatened his life and, when charged with second-degree murder, entered a plea of self-defence.

There was a five-day trial and Yvon was on the witness stand for two and a half hours. The jury deliberated for only fifty minutes before bringing back a verdict of not guilty.

It bothered me that Yvon had been embarrassed by my stories because I liked him when I met him and I am very grateful for the time he spent with me, his honesty, and his hospitality. But, I wrote about him as I found him, a gregarious big guy, tough on the outside, soft on the inside, and obviously from a mold that had a shape of its own.

If an apology will make him feel better, I offer it now, publicly. He is too big and strong to have walking around mad at me.

From the Bush to the Big Leagues

PROLOGUE   *I have always been more interested in the people who play sports than in the results of their games.*

This interest, I suspect, came from listening to my father spin stories about sports and athletes in the old days. We lived on a small farm in Beatrice, a tiny community nine miles north of the town of Bracebridge in the heart of the Muskoka tourist area in Ontario. Dad would tell me stories while we worked, sometimes as we drew a crosscut saw back and forth in the bush, while we hand-milked our cows, while we were doing the haying each summer, and even while we walked one of our cows five miles to the nearest bull for servicing. My favorite time was each spring while we sat next to the fire in our sugar bush overnight, boiling the sap from our maple trees to make syrup.

My father had been a good athlete as a young man in the Kenora area in north-western Ontario. He was a tough defenceman for hockey's Kenora Thistles and told me about his teammates, including Tweet Bird who I was to meet years later. He also played baseball and, because we had lived in Sudbury before moving to Beatrice, he told me all about a pitcher named Phil Marchildon who pitched up there with the Creighton Indians.

I had watched the Nickel Belt Baseball League as a youngster, after Marchildon left, and my heroes were guys like Gerry Wallace, Herb Perigoe, Spike Boal, Rollie McLenahan, Lefty Barbeau, Spike Wormington, Andy Barbe, and the irascible Boogie Signoretti. . . .

If I could have become a professional athlete, I would have wanted to play baseball.

Most Canadians who made the majors were pitchers who were blessed with natural ability. Very few made it at positions that required fielding or hitting skills because of a lack of coaching and competition.

When a Canadian went to a pro camp in the United States, he was as raw as the rawest rookie. There could never be a Phil Marchildon today. Nobody comes from as far back as he did. I always remembered my father's stories about him and, when I became a magazine writer, I just had to find him to get the full story. If he played today, his name would be known by every sports fan on the continent.

The incredible story of
Phil Marchildon, the fabulous pitcher
from Penetanguishene, Ontario,
who made it into the American League
as the star of the Philadelphia Athletics.

JULY 12, 1969—They still call him the Babe
when he walks down the main street in Penetanguishene, Ontario.

Not because he was a baseball player, but
because that's what they've always called Phil
Marchildon in Penetang. His mother started
it years ago, when he was just a kid.

He doesn't get back to Penetang very often,
though. The Babe, 55 now, lives a quiet life
on a quiet street in the Toronto suburb of
Etobicoke. He leaves the house each morning
at 6:30 to go to his job at Dominion Metalwear
in Port Credit, Ontario, where he helps make
hospital beds. He gets home at five.

"C'mon in," he said one evening this summer. "I been in the back, puttin' in some tomato
plants."

Life has changed. The Philadelphia Athletics are in his past. But the Babe is still
surprisingly trim. Not big, mind you. He never
was. He extends a large, knotty hand, the first
knuckle of the thumb permanently enlarged.
He gave a guy a straight arm once when he
played football and the thumb bent back.

His hands are very strong. He likes to
squeeze your arm or knee in a playful gesture
leaving bruises or finger marks.

"Some of our friends don't like it when he
does that," said his wife, Irene. "He doesn't
know how strong he is."

Irene works as a switchboard operator.
Together—and with the baseball pension he

gets—they had just bought a new Chevrolet Malibu.

"Good lookin', huh?" Phil said as he looked at the car in his driveway. "You just have to touch that gas pedal and—zoom!"

He has his two scrapbooks out on the coffee table and two autographed baseballs, coated with shellac. "Look," he said, handing over a ball. "Frank Baker—Homerun Baker."

Fourteen-year-old Dawna, tall like her mother, sat wide-eyed, listening while her father paced the living room floor and talked. Carol, 22, had moved into a downtown Toronto apartment a couple of weeks earlier to be nearer to her job.

The Babe, neat in brown slacks and a plaid sportshirt, was stalking the floor, puffing endlessly on a White Owl cigar. He got a beer from the basement. He has an incredible story to tell, more than even his next-door neighbors might believe. He was a great one—a busher in the truest sense who made it big.

"Do the people on the street know how great a pitcher you were?"

"Oh, they know I was a ball player," the Babe said. "But they're not ball fans. You know what I mean? I can't talk ball with them."

His movements are still quick, a nervousness that carries over from his war days and finally forced him to quit.

Bushers come from unlikely places and this one had come from Penetanguishene, (popularly known as Penetang), a town of 3500 at that time, near Midland in the Georgian Bay area. His father, Oliver, was a tinsmith, a poor man who raised seven children.

The Babe likes to tell people that he was a catcher on the high school team and, when he was throwing the ball back to the pitcher faster than the pitcher was throwing, they asked him to pitch.

He threw hard all right—hard enough to make the ball take a crazy hop at the plate. Soon he was pitching for the Penetang intermediate team against teams from Barrie, Orillia and Midland in the Georgian Bay league.

He could hit, too. "Once a team come in from St. Mary's, a senior team," he said. "They were going to beat us hicks from Penetang. Well, it turns out they got beat, 2-0. I pitched and I hit two home runs."

Penetang played a series against North Bay in Northern Ontario and some people saw this kid Marchildon pitch. They were from Sudbury, from the Creighton Mine Indians of the Nickel Belt League.

That was 1936 and Phil was 23. He moved north with the promise of a good job. "They gave me a job workin' out in the sun—handling timber they used to stope the mines. Then I ran the cage for awhile, taking the guys underground. On game days, they'd let you off at three in the afternoon."

Marchildon was big in the Sudbury area for three years. Meanwhile, back in Penetang, Jim Shaw, who had been Phil's manager there, kept telling Dan Howley, manager of the Toronto Maple Leafs, about the kid who had gone up north.

The thing is, Phil Marchildon was no longer a kid. Still, Howley told his fishing buddy Shaw to bring the Babe to a baseball school he was conducting in Barrie.

"I pitched a playoff game one night, drove all night and got to Barrie the next day," said the Babe. "They told me to pitch. I was still hot from the night before. I went four innings in this game."

Then, when nobody said anything to him, Phil got back in the car, drove to Penetang, and then returned to Creighton. He hadn't wanted to go in the first place.

"Howley and Shaw come up there to see me," he said. "They asked me to go to training camp the next year."

To fully appreciate this, remember that the Leafs were in the International League, one step away from the majors. Marchildon was 26 and had never given professional baseball a thought. In fact, he not only had never seen a professional game, he had never talked to anyone who had.

"But what the heck," said the Babe. "I thought I might as well go."

The Leafs sent him a train ticket to Avon Park, Florida, site of their spring training camp, and the Babe, after spending the winter skiing in Penetang, rode a day coach all the way—the first time he had ever been across the U.S. border.

The thing that had impressed Dan Howley was the crazy hop this black-haired, dark-eyed busher had on his fastball. Howley couldn't keep the Babe off the team, despite his lack of experience. Mind you, Howley didn't have much of a team. The Leafs were destined to lose 101 games that season.

The Babe developed a sore arm shortly after the season opened and was sent down to Cornwall of the old Canadian-American League.

"It was my tooth," he said now. "I had broken it playing football and the poison had gone into my arm. The dentist pulled my tooth in Cornwall and I won six games in six starts. The Leafs called me up again. How could they leave me down?"

The Leafs in those days had a working agreement with Connie Mack's Philadelphia Athletics and, late in his second season at Toronto—in 1940, when the Babe was 27 years old—Mack asked for him in Philadelphia.

"I was makin' $350 or $400 a month at Toronto, I can't remember which," said Phil, pausing to light another cigar. "I still think the Leafs owe me $500, you know. They promised me a bonus and I never got it. Boy, if I ever had a clue, if I knew what I knew years later, I'd'a never signed that contract with them.

"I can't remember a gol'darn thing about that first season in Toronto, but the second year—with that lousy club we had—I won 10 games and lost 15 before going to the A's."

Mack wanted to take a look at him. Philadelphia was a hopeless last anyway, but Toronto put up a fight. They had wanted to sell Marchildon and the A's were taking him away for nothing—exercising their option.

That's when the Babe met a guy named Earle Brucker, the pitching coach who was to change the course of his life.

"I didn't know how to pitch, not even with Toronto," said Phil. "I wasn't smooth and I didn't know what to do about it. There was nobody at Toronto to help me."

"I know your trouble," Brucker told the Babe after seeing him pitch a few innings at Philadelphia. "Go home to Penetang and we'll work it out at spring training."

Phil opened a new beer and stopped in the center of the living room to demonstrate. He stood on an imaginary mound, checked his baserunners and then delivered an imaginary pitch. "I was throwing like that," he said, "across my body."

He explained that his hip had been locked when he delivered the ball, throwing his left foot off line and resulting in wildness.

"There were mounds all over the place," Phil recalled. "Brucker took me to one and drew a straight line from it, toward the plate. He told me to throw so that my left foot landed on that line and it would give me better control."

While the rest of the A's worked at various training camp exercises, the 28-year-old rookie from Penetang was left out in a corner with a rookie catcher, practicing his new delivery. He played catch every day for two months.

Finally, Brucker gave him a start in an exhibition game against the Chicago Cubs. The Babe, his fastball hopping and his control vastly improved, won it, 2-1.

The season was 1½ months old when the A's allowed their old rookie to make his first official start. It was in Detroit's Briggs Stadium, against the Tigers.

"We're expecting big things from you," Connie Mack had told him when he signed his contract for $4500.

During his first major league season, Marchildon won 10 games and lost 14 for one of the weakest teams ever assembled in the majors.

"Ted Williams use'ta hit me pretty good," the Babe recalled. "He had the greatest eyes in the game, claimed he could actually see the ball hit his bat.

"Anyway, one day he was at the batting cage before a game in Boston and he calls me over. 'Hey, what's that pitch you're throwin'?' he asks me. 'I don't know what you mean,' I says. 'Well,' he says, 'it comes up to the plate and, when I start swingin', it breaks in on me, toward the handle. I can't get power on it.'

"That was a slider—the origination of the slider, I think, and I was pitchin' it natural. But, here's a guy, tellin' me how to pitch him. That's how much confidence he had.

"And you know what? I got him out after that—not always, but more."

It is doubtful if Canadians ever really appreciated what happened in the Babe's second year at Philadelphia.

Suddenly, Phil Marchildon from Penetanguishene, who had been pitching for the Creighton Indians when most successful players are already in the majors, had became a star.

Connie Mack took his ball club to training camp that year, moaning about his pitching staff. It, like the rest of the club, promised to be little better than terrible.

The Babe pitched the opener against the Washington Senators and won it, 5-1. He didn't stop. Before the season was over, Marchildon had 17 victories.

Sample a few quotes from that era:

"That kid Marchildon," said the great Jimmy Foxx, after the Babe had beaten the Red Sox, "what a pitcher he is. I reckon Dizzy Trout of Detroit is the fastest pitcher in our league since Bob Feller's gone, but Marchildon this afternoon was faster than Trout and had more stuff. He was great. He's got the darndest fastball I ever saw. Ordinarily he's about as fast as Johnny Rigney of the White Sox.

"But none of the other fastball pitchers can make a ball twitch the way Phil does. It comes down the middle then sails away from a right hand batter. What makes his curve more effective is that you never know what he's throwing, fastball or a hook."

The Yankees:

"He's the kind of pitcher who's tough even before he throws the ball," said outfielder Tom Henrich.

"He pitches as though he knows he can get you out," said Joe Gordon.

"When Marchildon is pitching, I might just as well leave my bat in the dugout," said Phil Rizzuto.

A column written by Franklin Lewis on Wednesday, Sept. 9, 1942, in Cleveland, when Phil had 16 wins:

"I telephoned Phil Marchildon for an appointment. Phil pitches for the Athletics, which is not a distinction or even a career. But he's won 16 games for the worst team in the American League. That is not only a distinction, it's a miracle."

Writers compared him to the great Walter Johnson. Baseball men agreed that, with any other team, the Babe's 17 victories would have been 25, perhaps 30. He needed a shutout to win.

"He fought every batter in every inning in every game as if the World Series was at stake," wrote Hub Miller.

Everything Phil Marchildon did that season made headlines. People talked about him hunting timber wolves at home in Canada, and about him carrying his glove around with him, even into hotel dining rooms, to practice his pitches.

"Did you know all of these things about your father?" Dawna was asked.

"Not everything," she said, still listening to every word.

"I shoulda pitched today," said the Babe. "I was born too soon."

He opened another beer, lit another cigar and started reliving the past again. You could see the excitement build within him. He remembers every minute of every game. But nobody else does, so he hadn't thought about it much in the last few years.

A New York newspaper, in naming him man of the week for becoming the first American League pitcher to win 13 games, wrote:

"With the Athletics you not only have to win a game as a pitcher, but you must also drive in runs if you are to have any runs scored behind you."

And Marchildon drove in runs. The scrapbooks are studded with headlines: "Marchildon Wins Own Game in 11th! ... Marchildon's Double Wins for Mackmen in 10th! ... Marchildon Wins With Bat!"

But the Second World War had started and it wasn't long before the word came: Phil Marchildon had been called up to serve Canada. It made an eight-column headline, even in New York.

"I was 29," said Phil, "and there were guys 25 and 26 at home who still hadn't been called up. I didn't think it was my turn yet. We were in Philadelphia, heading for a game in Washington when I got the telegram. I went to the Canadian embassy and they agreed to give me a deferment until the end of the season."

Only two pitchers won more games than

Marchildon that 1942 season, Bonham with New York and Hughson with Boston, both of whom won 20 with the top two teams in the league.

When the RCAF called him immediately after the season was over, the Babe went into training to become a tail gunner. In a story called "A Diamond from the Nickel Mines," J.G. Taylor Spink, publisher of The Sporting News, wrote:

"When Phil went into the service with the Royal Canadian Air Force in 1942, his fellow players said: 'Gosh, if he lives through that and his nerves aren't shot, it will really be something.' They were surprised that he picked the air force—so was he—but it was his way of making sure of going overseas. He is one of those gents who always wants to be in the thick of it, whether it is the ninth inning with three on base or a hot gin rummy game."

Now, in his living room in Etobicoke more than 20 years later, the Babe pulled a swivel chair to the middle of the room, sat in it and moved from side to side, aiming down an imaginary gun.

"We trained in dark rooms," he said. "You have to learn to rely on your night vision. You can see 200 yards at the most. They would flash dark silhouettes on a wall."

He was stationed at Skipton-On-Swale near York, in Squadron 433, the old "Porcupine Squadron," on a seven-man crew of a Halifax bomber named "P-For-Peter."

"I had been asked to go to London while on a three-day leave to pitch an exhibition game for an English team against a bunch of Americans," he said. "They didn't tell the Americans who I was—only that I had been a cricket bowler. I mowed them down. They didn't take their bats off their shoulders."

On his 28th mission, the crew dropped mines on Kiel Bay. When their work was completed, the plane suddenly lurched when hit by cannon fire and the order was given to bale out.

"I know what it was that got us," said the Babe. "It was an ME 110. I remember seeing the fire inside. In a situation like that, I was supposed to crawl back and bale out. I didn't have time.

"I opened the door of my gun turret and fell out. I remember hitting the wind. My shoes and hat blew off and I had the ring of my parachute in my hand.

"It was pitch black. I didn't know where we were. I remember saying, 'Parachute—you'd just better open.' I never did pull the ring, the wind just pulled it from my hand and the thing opened."

He floated down, watching the bomber fade into the distance, lit by flames, not knowing what his feet were going to touch. It was water—the cold, black water of the North Sea.

Of the seven men in the crew, only Babe and the plane's navigator, George Gill, survived. Gill, now with a breakfast cereal company in London, Ontario, always said that the Babe saved his life. He was yelling in the dark and the Babe told him to be quiet and conserve his strength.

More than three hours later, a Danish fishing boat found them. The Babe and the navigator couldn't converse with the Danes, and thought they were working for the Germans. In fact they were members of the Danish underground.

Cold, wet and exhausted, the two Canadians were helped from the boat when it reached shore.

But a German soldier stood there, machine gun pointed at them, and took them prisoner.

"Marchildon Missing in Action!" were the headlines in every baseball city.

The next word was a small news despatch:

"A letter from the German War Prison Stalag III, brings the information that Phil Marchildon straggled into that camp last September. The Penetang baseball pitcher, according to this information, was not in good health, but whether from illness or wounds, was not stated."

There was nothing to do but wait.

Stalag Luft III is where The Great Escape took place. That's where the Babe lined up with other prisoners of war to be deloused at the camp, near the town of Sagan, then in eastern Germany, now in Poland. Afterwards, he was issued prison clothing.

This was a new game. The Philadelphia Athletics and his incredible climb to baseball's major leagues were far behind him. Here, they didn't care that he had made it from Penetan-guishene to Philadelphia at age 28 to become Connie Mack's best pitcher.

"But they had heard of me," he says today. "See—look at what they wrote on my papers: 'Sportsmann.'"

One of the German guards had been raised in Brooklyn, New York. He knew about base-ball. The Babe told him that, when the war was over, he would be going back and that he'd beat the Yankees.

While he was in Stalag Luft III, F/O P.E. Marchildon, 528783, POW 7741, had written to Irene Patience, a girl he had met in Toronto, who worked at the Singer Sewing Machine office and was to become his wife.

The letters were in surprisingly fine hand-writing for a man with knotty hands like the Babe's, and they were sensitive and articulate.

"Looks like I'll be missing another baseball season again," he wrote on Dec. 11, 1944. "We can only hope for the best now. I, for one, am praying for the day it ends and hope it will be soon. We seem kind of useless here and feel it deeply. We feel the people at home do not realize our predicament as fully as they might. It makes us angry at times. . . ."

In another letter, he asked her to meet him at Union Station in Toronto upon his repatria-tion and to save him the first dance. "Presum-ably it will be a dreary Christmas for us," he wrote. "But we mustn't kick too much. I hope I know how to act when I get out of here. . . ."

And then the Russians began closing in and the camp had to be abandoned. The 2400 prisoners were ordered to march, and keep marching, from January to May. They were herded into a pen at nights, without food. . . .

"It started snowing," the Babe remembers. "We had a lot of food at the camp, but no way to carry it except in bags over our shoulders. I'm a Canadian—I knew what to do in the snow. I built a sleigh and made a rope from bed sheets. The Aussies didn't know anything about sleighs. I filled it up with food and, when they had to throw away food because their packs were too heavy, I'd pick it up and throw it on my sleigh."

But it stopped snowing three days later, and the Babe had to pull his sleigh in the mud. "We slept on the ground, wrapped in a blanket," says the Babe. "It was all we had, even in the rain."

One night, when a guy climbed the fence of the stockade to get firewood, they shot him.

When they were finally liberated, 10 months after his Halifax bomber had plunged into the waters off Denmark, the Babe had lost 20 pounds and his skin had taken on a yellowish tint.

Suddenly, he was home, his ship being one of the first to arrive back in Canada. He called Irene Patience from Montreal and she met him at Union Station in Toronto.

The Babe took a room at the Ford Hotel and gorged himself with food for two days, then he went home to Penetang.

Phil Marchildon was 32 when he got back from the war, a veteran by baseball standards, and he hadn't seen a baseball for three years—not since he had astounded the American League by winning 10 games in 1941 and 17 games in 1942 for the hapless, last-place Ath-letics. It was hard to win for Philadelphia. Twice he lost games in which he allowed only two hits. Once he lost a one-hitter.

Telegrams began arriving in Penetang from Connie Mack, the Grand Old Man of baseball who owned and managed the Athletics. "I ignored them" says Phil. "Hell, I hadn't been home two weeks at the time."

Mack finally reached him and talked him into rejoining the team at Chicago. The Babe was in terrible physical condition, his once-hard muscles turned to flab. He worked out slowly on the sidelines.

"We're having a day for you when we get back to Philadelphia," said Mack. "I want you to start."

"What!" said the astonished Babe.

Even his team-mates argued with Mack. Marchildon couldn't possibly pitch. He hadn't been in a game in three years and had spent the last 10 months as a prisoner of war.

Mack insisted and—only five weeks after he had been liberated—the Babe stood on the mound in Philadelphia. The A's, chronic last-place finishers, were drawing only about 3000 a game that season. Almost 35 000 turned out to greet Phil Marchildon.

He had caught their imagination before going off to war. He was the legendary busher who, somewhere up in Canada, had pitched in a place called Penetang and then in Northern Ontario, while working in the nickel mines.

They cheered as he warmed up to pitch. The papers kept referring to him as "A Canadian War Hero."

For two innings, things were fine. Then, when he tried to extend himself by throwing his twitching fastball, the Babe pulled a muscle in his leg. The tear was serious

enough to keep him on the bench the rest of that 1945 season.

"The Old Man gave me a war bond for $1000," he says today. "Imagine that? There were almost 35 000 fans there. He gave me $1000 and kept the rest."

His salary in the 1941 and 1942 seasons had been a paltry $4500; naturally, he expected a raise in 1946.

"I can't tell how you'll pitch," argued Mack, offering him the same $4500 contract. "You're older now and you've been away three years."

The Babe became a holdout, but finally joined the club at the $4500 figure when Mack promised to review his contract in June. The sportswriters were told about the deal.

Phil Marchildon, 33, won 13 games that season for the A's, making one of the greatest comebacks in baseball, surprising everyone but himself.

"But do you know," the Babe says, "when June came around, the Old Man never did say anything about my contract. The writers kept asking me and I told them to wait. Finally, they wrote it, that Mack hadn't lived up to his word. The next day, he called me into his office and gave me a new contract for $12 000."

In 1947, the Babe pitched the opening game for the A's and clipped the mighty Yankees in New York. He was 34, but he had developed a new fork ball to go with his mighty fastball and curve.

"I'll win 20 games this season," he told syndicated columnist Harry Grayson. "We'll get out of last place and maybe even into the first division."

It was the Babe's finest season. He won 19, lost only nine and lifted the A's to an amazing fourth-place finish. Baseball men still can't figure out why Allie Reynolds of the powerful Yankees, who also had a 19-9 record and a higher earned-run average, beat out Phil that season as the American League's top pitcher.

The highlight of the season was victory number 16, against the Indians in Cleveland's Municipal Stadium. The Indians had players such as Lou Boudreau, Bob Lemon, Larry Doby, Jim Hegan, Ken Keltner. . . .

It was Keltner who kept him from immortality. With a full count on Keltner with two out in the eighth inning, umpire Bill McKinley called ball four.

Keltner was the first man to reach base. There hadn't been a perfect game in the majors since 1922. It was a questionable call. The Babe blew up. He threw his glove at McKinley, catcher Buddy Rosar threatened to throttle the umpire. Pandemonium.

"What Bill McKinley apparently forgot last night," wrote a Cleveland columnist, "was that when there's a doubt and a perfect game at stake, the pitcher should be allowed to keep the change."

The Babe, slightly unnerved, allowed a hit in the ninth, then won the game himself with a double in the 12th inning.

Here's what writer Ed McAuley wrote the next day in Cleveland:

"But, ladies and gentlemen, there was only one story in last night's ball game and Marchildon, the slim and fiery Canadian who came back from a German prison camp to become the most effective pitcher in the American League, was easily its hero. . . .

"Where he really proved himself a fighting man was in the 12th, when Pete Suder singled with two out. Marchildon was angry—he was sick with disappointment—and many of the customers were booing. So Phil smashed a double to left center, and, for all practical purposes, the game was over. Suder streaked home with what proved to be the winning run."

The Babe was riding high. When he went to training camp the following season, 1948, he was shooting for 25 victories. Mack had sent him a blank contract and he had filled in his own figure—$17 500.

He won five of his first six starts. Start number seven, in Washington, was against the Senators.

"Froggy, you've sure got stuff today," said catcher Buddy Rosar, calling Marchildon by his nickname at that time.

"I feel great," said the Babe, throwing one final warmup pitch.

The game began, Marchildon wound up for his first pitch, and something went wrong.

("You can expect a reaction, perhaps in two years," army doctors had told him. "Come and see us if anything happens.")

Marchildon went into his delivery. The ball hit the ground before it reached the plate. He walked the first three men, all balls.

The Babe stalked off the mound, scared and confused.

"Something's wrong," he told Mack. "I have to go home."

That was the beginning of the end. He saw doctors in Philadelphia, rejoined the team, but couldn't get the ball over the plate. His strength was gone.

That winter he went into Sunnybrook Hospital in Toronto for tests. Nobody could explain anything to his satisfaction. His nerves had taken over.

The following season, 1949, he returned to the A's and seemed to have regained his old form. He was pitching in Philadelphia, against the Red Sox, and it was a scoreless game after nine innings. His nerves came back in the tenth. He walked three men, lost 1-0, and the crowd booed as he walked off the field.

When he was talking about the good years, the Babe was pumped up, strutting in his living room, puffing on a cigar, remembering the good things.

Now he was quiet. He did not want to remember the bad times. He sat quietly in his chair, lifted the bottle of beer to his lips and stared straight ahead, seemingly not hearing.

I was born too soon," he said quietly. "I was too late getting to the majors and I lost three years in the war. I had my best season when I was 34.

"As far as I'm concerned," he continued, "nobody could beat me. I could beat anybody. I'm a little hick town fella from Penetang and I beat the best in the whole world. Yankees . . . Red Sox . . . you name 'em."

The fact is, though, that he was finished after the game against the Red Sox. He couldn't believe the Philadelphia fans would ever boo Phil Marchildon—not after what he had done for them.

They had doctors test him arm. He said he couldn't raise it the day after they booed him. And he couldn't, for some mysterious reason. It was hell. Everybody started trying to analyze him. There were stories that he had nightmares, that he had been sleeping in his backyard after returning from the war.

He did have nightmares for a while. But he didn't sleep in his yard. He'd go outside for fresh air when he couldn't sleep. "Two bottles of beer is better than any sleeping pill," he said.

Then he was sent to the minors. It was the last day of spring training in 1950 and he was assigned to Buffalo.

"I heard it from one of the other player's wives," said Irene. "Where did you hear it, Phil?"

He sat quietly, staring ahead. No answer.

"Jodie and Sam Chapman were good friends of ours on the team," said Irene. "Jodie and Phil didn't get along very well, but she said to me that day, 'Irene—stick by him. He's really going to need you now.'"

He played a season with Buffalo, tried one game in relief for the Boston Red Sox, returned to the Toronto Maple Leafs and they finally let him go.

He kept hoping his arm would come back. The doctors said his arm was okay. It was his nerves. He kept pitching, kept throwing wild. He would pack his arm in ice between innings. Nothing helped. He was getting older. But there was no place to go. Nothing else he could do. He was a pitcher. He was Phil Marchildon from Penetang.

Nobody wanted him in pro ball anymore. He wound up in the Inter-county League, a semi-pro league in Ontario. He played with Guelph, played with Waterloo, won the batting championship with an average of .367.

In 1950, Irene was pregnant. She was worried about Phil. She got pneumonia. The baby died. Phil was out of work. He would just sit around and drink beer. He didn't know what to do. In baseball, he had stomped around on a mound, defying hitters like Joe Dimaggio and Ted Williams.

"Finally," said Irene, "I bought a house with what money we had left—thinking he might be forced to get a job. But Phil couldn't seem to face anything else. Friends would arrange interviews for him and he wouldn't show up. He seemed afraid. He had no confidence at all."

Finally, a friend brought an application to the house. For a job at Avro in Toronto. Phil went to work there and did a good job for almost nine years, until the day the plant shut down, due to the scrapping of the Avro Arrow fighter.

Phil moved to a company that made aluminum screen doors. It was sold and he moved to his current job, making hospital beds. The manager there is Bob Knight, who used to live next door to him in Penetang.

The fellows down at the plant know Phil used to be a major leaguer, but they're not all sure just how good he was.

"I took a ball to work the other day," said Phil. "I threw a few for them and they were catchin' it barehanded. Then I followed through on one—like this—and they didn't hold on to that one, I'll tell you.

"You ask me why I won't talk about the bad years," he said. "When you got a sore arm, boy—you just don't want to remember.

"Yeah . . . it still bothers me to think about it. It bothers me a lot. That really hurt, when they booed in Philadelphia. I didn't think I'd ever hear it."

And so, today, he rarely talks about baseball. That was another life—another world.

Instead, he comes home from the plant, uncaps a beer and relaxes. He and Irene have two fine children, Dawna, 14 and Carol, 22, a nice house, a new car, his salary, his baseball pension, and Irene's salary. She works as a switchboard operator and office clerk.

He doesn't look his age and friends still wonder how he can stay up late and still be at work on time every day. But the Babe is tougher than most people know. His hands are still like steel traps.

"I was throwing the ball against the wall of the house with the kid next door today," he said. "I didn't feel a thing. The kid? His name's Stephen Gully. He's about 10 or 11. You know, I was throwin' so hard the ball was going flat.

"It got me to wondering—I wonder . . . naw, I'm 55 and my legs wouldn't be any good. I wouldn't last. But I'd like to think I could still go in there and get them out myself. I watch some baseball today. It's not the same game.

"I was born too soon. I should have been born later."

You say goodbye to the Babe and start thinking again that professional sport can, indeed, be cruel. The athlete never forgets, but the people do.

There was the Babe—the best pitcher, perhaps, ever to come out of Canada—and he has been forgotten. Until Fergie Jenkins won 20 games for the Cubs in 1967, no Canadian had won as many games as Marchildon.

And maybe nobody ever will again with a team that was as bad as the Athletics. ●

Epilogue *Eleven years later, Phil Marchildon looks exactly the same, lives in the same house and has the same friends, none of whom really knows how great a baseball player he was.*

There have been two big changes, however. Phil Marchildon has been named to Canada's Sports Hall of Fame since I did the story about him and, he no longer makes hospital beds. He is retired, by golly, and lives a full life, satisfied to putter around his home. And, each winter, he tries to get down to Orlando, Florida, with his wife Irene.

Irene answered the phone when I called. Something in the back of my mind told me that they had not been ecstatic with my story. I couldn't remember what it was. Maybe it was too honest.

"Hi, there," Irene said warmly, putting me at ease. "We've been going to call you for so long now. How's everything?"

She said Phil was in the backyard, recuperating from a weekend of socializing at a couple of Hall of Fame functions where the newest members were admitted.

"Irene," I said cautiously, "was Phil angry with me over that story?"

"Naw," she said. "Only the pictures. He didn't like the pictures they took.

But, between you and me, he always takes bad pictures. Just a minute, I'll get him."

And there was Phil, friendly and warm. Something still bothered me.

"Say Phil," I said, "was Irene mad about something in that story?"

"She sure was," he said. "You called her a switchboard operator. Heck, she runs the show down there at Rexo-Therm. She's the office manager. She'll never forgive you." He laughed.

So that's what it was. And here I had been worrying for a couple of months about it, knowing we wanted to include his story in this book. What a relief.

"And I'm still working," Irene broke in. "I couldn't be retired like Phil or I'd go crazy. Now when we go out on Friday nights he wants to go home at 10 o'clock because he worries about the dogs being alone. He's just getting old."

"I feel pretty good," said Phil. "And, remember how I used to complain about my baseball pension? Well, it's all been fixed up. I got a letter just three weeks ago."

Phil always complained that baseball had forgotten players like him, the original guys who started the pension plan. He was getting only $190 a month and even that was cut off back in 1952.

"Well, they put us all in a new category and now we're going to get triple what we got, retroactive back to April," he said. "Now I've got two or three pensions. I'm not rich, but I can live as well as I want to."

It was really an uplifting call for me, one that I should have made years ago. Phil Marchildon is one of the toughest little guys I ever met, and you could know him for years and he wouldn't bother mentioning that he had been a prisoner of war or a ball player.

I have promised to go golfing with him one day soon.

In and out of focus

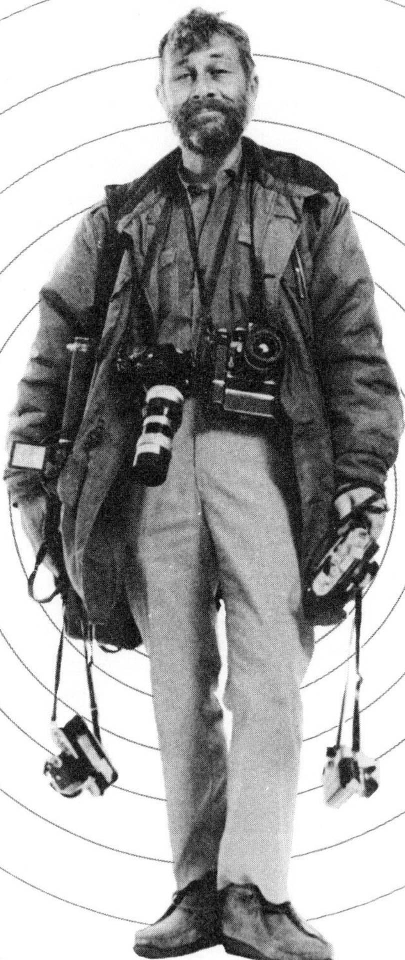

IF YOU EVER THINK you might like to become a newspaper or magazine photographer, the first thing you have to do is go out and find an army surplus store. That's where you buy your clothes. You know, used, old army fatigues, a couple of khaki shirts with those button-down flaps on the shoulders, and some heavy boots, preferably without laces. You can get by with a denim suit as long as it's rumpled and faded enough and in warm weather you wouldn't be out of place wearing leather sandals instead of the army boots. But you must make certain that somewhere in your wardrobe you have one outfit so worn and ragged that you can be sent on assignments to cover black-tie dinners or, perhaps, a Royal Visit.

I once described a photographer I knew as a person you felt like running through a car wash with the top down before taking him home to dinner.

Surely you have watched live television coverage of elections, political conventions, and major press conferences. The reporters sit back politely taking notes, wearing tweed jackets with leather patches on the elbows. Meanwhile, jostling for position in the front lines are photographers, dropping to their knees or standing on their heads if that's what it takes to get a good picture.

Photographers will climb trees or hang from barn rafters to get a good shot. And, no matter how important or busy the subject, a photographer will rearrange an entire seating plan if it looks better through his viewfinder. They look at life through that viewfinder and their only interest in current events is how the lighting happens to be on that particular day.

You'll also have to learn to make your way through crowds while wearing about four cameras and a light meter hanging around your neck. These cameras should have different-sized lenses, some loaded with color film, some with black and white and some, I suspect, not loaded at all.

Since 1971, I have worked with a guy named Norm Betts at *The Toronto Sun* who, I swear, sleeps with his cameras around his neck. It doesn't matter where you meet him, whether he is on assignment or not, Betts has those cameras hanging on him. At the company Christmas party he will get up on the dance floor wearing a camera. I'm willing to bet he wears one while shaving himself in the morning, just in case, perhaps, he cuts himself and wants to take a picture in the mirror. Betts and his wife visited me and The Missus (in the days when we were all married) when I was living in Mexico.

"I've just got to find out if Bettsy ever takes those cameras off," I whispered to The Missus.

So I organized a trip one afternoon to a mineral hot springs called El Cortijo about seven miles from town and rented the private pool for our own use. This was a totally private pool only four and a half feet deep with a small waterfall at one end, and with separate dressing rooms and showers. Finally I would find out just how attached Betts was to his cameras. He was the last to come out of the dressing room.

"I don't believe it!" I said to myself when he appeared.

There stood Betts, in the middle of nowhere, only the four of us there, in his little bathing suit, a camera and a light meter around his bare neck.

"Bettsy!" I said. "You're not going to swim with that thing are you?"

"I just want it close by," he said, taking a reading with his light meter.

He adjusted his camera and set it carefully on the edge of the pool. Do you know, we couldn't even get him to leave that side of the pool when he was in the water. I guess that's why he doesn't miss many pictures.

◀ The complete photographer: Ken Elliott.

When I was working at *The Canadian* on the stories in this book, I was fortunate to work with photographers who were sane—most of the time anyway. And they were all talented, despite their idiosyncrasies. Take Don Newlands, for instance, who travelled the world as the original and only staff photographer on *The Canadian* when it was launched.

Don Newlands absolutely hated to fly and, when it could be avoided, such as when the story was somewhere in North America, he would drive. His favorite form of transportation was his sparkling new Mercedes-Benz which he equipped with airplane landing lights.

"I only switch them on when it's late at night and I'm on a deserted and straight highway," he once explained to me. "I can see about a mile ahead and just sit back and open her up."

I will never forget the day he shot a story in Quebec City and drove back to Toronto—more than 500 miles—only to stomp out of the darkroom with the news that none of his pictures were any good. His camera had malfunctioned.

"Hell, don't worry about it, Don," said Editor Denny Harvey. "I'll just call a local photographer there to re-shoot it for us tonight and put the film on a plane."

Newlands wasn't listening. He kept packing his camera bag and then stormed out of the office straight to his car and a return drive to Quebec City. He must have used those airplane lights that night because, when Harvey got to work the next morning, there was Newlands with prints from Quebec City. He drove more than 1500 miles—Quebec-Toronto-Quebec-Toronto—shot a job twice, developed his negatives and made the prints, all without sleep. That's another quality the good photographer possesses—pride.

I remember one assignment, when I was in West Palm Beach, Florida, covering spring training the year the Montreal Expos became the first Canadian team to make it to baseball's major leagues. Newlands was in Hollywood, shooting pictures of a movie star on a Wednesday and drove, non-stop across the United States, to arrive the next day in West Palm Beach. I couldn't believe it. He felt better than I did. I had spent the night in a roadhouse bar playing pool.

And then there was Terry Hancey, my Monopoly partner and a friend since the days we both served our apprenticeship on *The Sudbury Star* in Northern Ontario.

I worked in the sports department and would fall asleep over my typewriter at about 4 a.m. only to be awakened by the police reporter who would arrive each morning at six. Hancey would live for days at a time in the darkroom, sleeping on a table where nobody could see him. Unfortunately, I was right out in the newsroom and everybody would know I had spent the night there from the marks on my forehead where it had rested on the typewriter carriage.

We were both hungry in those days and our work was an obsession because we wanted desperately to get to one of the newspapers in Toronto—the big time. Finally, our big chance for recognition arrived. Well, for Hancey anyway.

An older reporter who had left the paper had turned over one of his side jobs to me, as the stringer in Northern Ontario for *Time Magazine,* including *Life, Fortune,* and *Sports Illustrated.* If I thought something was happening that might interest one of their publications, I would send a wire to Chicago and they would reply immediately—send more information, go ahead and send everything, or forget it. They used three or four small stories I suggested in *Time* and then came the biggest assignment. I wired them that Branch Rickey, the legendary baseball manager and executive was vacationing on a nearby island along with thirty-eight grandchildren and great-grandchildren. *Sports Illustrated* was using a picture of the week at that time—a centerspread over two pages—and asked me to fly to Rickey's island with a photographer to shoot a photo for possible use the next week. Mike Dudowich, the head photographer at *The Star,* was the natural choice but, I knew it would mean more to Hancey, so I asked Terry and told him he would make $1500 if his picture was used.

We heard that Rickey, when he flew to Sudbury each summer, would stop and pick up baskets of fresh fruit to take to his island, so Hancey and I went to the fruit store and bought a twelve-quart basket of peaches, Rickey's favorite. We hired a small plane from Austin Airways and headed for the Rickey island out in Georgian Bay.

Old Branch, who died in 1965, wasn't actively connected with a baseball club in those days but was back in the news because he was trying to start a new circuit he would call the Continental League. And there he was, a living legend, awaiting us on his dock, looking like a bleacher bum. His old pants were rumpled, his sneakers worn, his T-shirt stained, and he had a two-week-old gray stubble on his chin.

I could practically hear Hancey's creative juices start to flow. The picture possibilities were endless. There were kids all over the place and Mr. Rickey really wanted to have the picture taken. We rounded them all up and they sat on a rock, surrounding their famous patriarch, who hadn't even bothered combing his hair. Instead, he reached into his pants and pulled out a pocketknife and placed the big basket of peaches at his feet. He would peel a peach with his old knife, then stuff a slice into his mouth. The juice ran down his whiskers, and then he would spit the stone out. After eating a peach, he would then trim a couple of his fingernails with the same knife, wipe it off on his pants and start on another peach . . . .

Hancey was ecstatic and my heart pounded, thinking of that picture in *Sports Illustrated* the following week. I watched as Hancey tried for one super shot. He would hide behind a tree and try to frame the picture through an opening in the leaves, lie on his stomach and shoot from behind the long grass.

"Pssst, Terry . . ." I whispered to him. "Why don't you take one safe shot. You know, just a regular shot of the entire group."

"Later," he said.

Later never came. Hancey was satisfied that he had the picture he wanted and the pilot started warming up the plane. Hancey worked all night in the darkroom back at *The Star* developing his works of art. Unfortunately, that creativity, which he possesses in abundance, was about two years ahead of his technical ability and none of the pictures turned out. Not one blankety-blank picture! I sent a telegram to *Sports Illustrated,* apologizing, and they never called me again.

We had to pay for the plane out of our own pockets—and the peaches. I suspect, however, that Hancey had borrowed the film from *The Star.* The only picture I ever saw was a print Hancey gave me, one of my prized possessions, of Mr. Rickey and me, arms around one another's shoulders, standing on the dock in front of the plane as we were about to leave.

Anyway, I left Sudbury first and Hancey left a year later. We went our separate ways, working in various cities until we both wound up at *The Canadian* about ten years later. By then Hancey was well on his way to being one of the top sports photographers in the country, having mastered his camera to the equal of his imagination. And, most recently, working as a freelancer, he has published two hardcover books of his sports photographs.

Despite his talent and our friendship, however, I have got to say that Terry Hancey is the most predictably unpredictable guy I have ever known. I don't think he will mind if I say that during our days together at *The Canadian* he was, well, rather irresponsible and totally undisciplined. He was the only guy I have ever met who could totally disappear; he would drop right out of sight for anywhere from a week to a month.

"Hey, Terry!" I'd say the next time we met. "Where have you been?"

"Oh around," he would shrug. "You know, here and there."

And that was the end of the conversation. However, I always suspected a girl was involved because Hancey had a way with women. Mind you, she never had to worry about exposure because he was also the most secretive guy I knew.

I remember when *The Canadian* sent him to Vancouver on a very rush job. His film was to be sent back to Toronto by plane the same day. Hancey wandered into the office three weeks later.

"Where the hell have you been!" demanded the editor.

"Oh around," he shrugged. "You know, here and there."

Later I learned he had met a girl and had completely forgotten his assignment.

ometimes, when we travelled together, Hancey would drive me absolutely crazy. We would agree to meet at the Toronto airport and he would show up at the last minute carrying his metal camera case.

"Where are your clothes?" I'd ask.

"Didn't get a chance to pack," he'd say. "By the way, can you buy my ticket?"

"Where's your ticket?" I'd demand.

"Didn't get a chance to pick it up at the office," he'd say.

"And I suppose you didn't pick up your advance and you have no money," I'd say.

"Right," Terry would answer. "But, that's okay because I'll have them wire it to me when we get there."

No two guys ever travelled together who were worse with money. We would spend double our expenses in bars and fancy restaurants and never file expense accounts. When Hancey's money would finally arrive, I would be flat broke after paying for both of us, including the cost of his plane ticket. We never held financial meetings. Hancey would just dole out tens and twenties when I needed them and, somehow, I always felt something wasn't right. The fact he had no toothbrush or change of clothes never bothered him. Hancey had this incredible ability to wear the same clothes for a week without ever looking rumpled.

Another way he got to me was during an interview, especially with a hockey player. I'd tell him to take some shots of the guy's expressions while I was talking to him, but Terry would be so interested in the interview, he would join us and start asking questions.

"Terry, the pictures," I would say coolly.

"Yeah, yeah," he'd say. "But I know what this guy is talking about."

Once we spent four days with a hockey player in Montreal and, when we headed back to Toronto, Hancey hadn't taken a single picture.

"That's okay," he'd assure me. "I'll go back next week."

I finally left *The Canadian* after four years of travelling. My marriage was showing danger signs and I had a young daughter I hadn't spent nearly enough time with. Actually, I was just fooling myself. After changing jobs, I spent too much time in bars and still not enough time at home.

Anyway, because we were travelling in different circles, I didn't see Hancey for about two years.

"Hey, Terry," I said. "where have you been?"

"Oh, around," he said. "You know, here and there."

Again we went a couple of years without seeing one another until we met in Ottawa in the lobby of the Four Seasons Hotel. We were working for different publications, both covering a hockey game that night between Canada and Russia. When we finished working, we got together in the hotel bar, closed that and went up to my room for a touch of scotch. We had several touches, actually, and about 4 a.m., suddenly got lonely. We took our drinks and went downstairs, just in case there were two lonely girls hanging around the lobby.

We were sitting there, in front of the elevators, talking about our broken marriages, and wondering why our respective wives had finally decided, individually, that we were both lousy husbands. Suddenly, two very classy ladies walked up and pushed the elevator button.

"Ahem," I said, clearing my throat, "would you ladies care to join us for a cocktail?"

"No thank you," one of the ladies smiled politely.

But the elevator arrived, the door opened and they ignored it, allowing the doors to close again. By golly, Hancey and I thought, they've changed their minds. So we stood up to join them. At that precise moment, two gentlemen came up the stairs and one towered about two feet over me.

"We were just waiting for our husbands," explained one lady with a smile.

Holy smokes! It was singer Harry Belafonte, who, I remembered, was in Ottawa with his show. I never realized just how big Belafonte is. He looked absolutely ominous that night and not too pleased.

"Oh, heh, heh," I said, trying to make a joke. "I was just trying to pick up your wife."

"It's a damned good thing you didn't!" he boomed as they all stepped on the elevator.

"Well, we haven't changed much," I said to Hancey as the elevator door closed. He was doubled over in laughter.

"You were trying to hustle Harry Belafonte's wife!" he said, tears running down his cheeks.

I got up hesitantly the next morning, very thirsty for some reason and started to make my way to the bar. I pushed the down button for the elevator, the door opened, and who do you think was standing inside? Yep, Harry Belafonte.

"About last night," I said. "I'd like to apologize. We, uh, had had a lot to drink."

"Yes," he said. "I noticed."

I went straight to the bar and joined some media guys for an eye-opener. About half an hour later, Belafonte strolled into the bar to meet someone and, for some reason, I had about four drinks in front of me.

"You never quit, huh?" he said, stopping at the table.

Belafonte, it turned out, was a hell of a guy. He even joked about my indiscretion the night before. I decided on the spot, however, that a man should never try to pick up another man's wife, especially when he is bigger than you and is following her in a hotel lobby.

As sports photographers, Terry Hancey and Don Newlands had one advantage over Ken Elliott—both were born in Canada and were familiar with the rules of North

American sports. Elliott, a bewhiskered little guy and a great travelling companion, was born in England. There were times when it showed.

will never forget the year we were in Lakeland, Florida, at spring training with the Detroit Tigers. We were doing a story on pitcher Denny McLain, the oddball who had a meteoric but short major league career. The late Mayo Smith was managing the Tigers and he approached me one day before an exhibition game, the first baseball game, I suspect, that Ken Elliott ever saw.

"Paul," Mayo said after calling me aside, "what is it with that photographer of yours?"

"Ken Elliott?" I said. "He's a great little guy and a very good photographer."

"Well," said Mayo, "he just asked me if he could stand behind the pitcher during the game."

"Well, uh," I said, rather embarrassed, "he's from England. Maybe they let them stand on the playing field in rounders or cricket. I'll certainly explain it to him."

"I already have," said Smith, turning away.

Poor Ken Elliott. But, what did he know about baseball, football, or hockey? They don't play those sports in England and, besides, he was a photographer, not a sports fan. Fortunately, his fresh approach gave us some of the best sports photos we ever had.

The biggest scare Elliott ever gave me was at Pimlico race track in Maryland at a race which included the top three-year-olds in North America, many of them prepping for the Triple Crown races.

I explained to Ken that the horses would start at the top of the stretch, pass the finish line once, circle the track, and wind up at the finish line a second and final time. This would give him two chances for an action picture as they went by him.

I went up to the second-level bar to watch the race and Elliott lumbered across the track with his tripod and the rest of his gear. As the horses were entering the gate, I peered over my glass and looked across the track to the finish line where Elliott had set up shop. He was on his knees, focusing his camera, his tripod firmly imbedded in the ground, but with one of its legs protruding onto the running surface. I almost choked and must have broken some kind of world speed record as I raced downstairs and through the crowd to the railing.

lot of people do not realize that when a horse is galloping it throws its hind legs out sideways. That is why the inside rail at every track is set on posts shaped like an upside-down L. A horse can lean against the rail, brush it, and throw its legs out under it without catching the supporting poles. Elliott had placed his tripod even with the rail which meant one leg was sticking out where the inside horse would trip over it.

"Ladies and gentlemen, the horses are in their starting position," said the track announcer.

"KEN!" I screamed across the track.

"They're at the post . . . ."

"ELLIOTT!"

"They're off!"

"KENNY! KENNY!" I yelled over the crowd. "ELLIOTT!"

The horses were charging down the stretch towards him. My hands were sweaty and my heart pounded. The first horse would catch a hind leg on that tripod, go down and the others would crash down behind it . . . . At that precise moment, Elliott looked up from his camera, located me on the other side of the track, and casually waved hello. I was making frantic pushing motions with my hands, trying to tell him to back up.

Elliott looked at me, looked at the oncoming horses—the most expensive horses in the world—looked at his camera, and then raised one hand to give me the okay sign. Slowly, ever so slowly . . . Elliot straightened up, placed his hands on his tripod and backed away, just as the horses thundered past him. My knees were so weak I had to hold onto the fence to keep from slumping to the ground in a rush of relief.

A picture is supposed to be worth a thousand words but, so are the photographers.

"Ain't nobody has as much fun as cowboys"

PROLOGUE *I thought I had seen almost everything professional sports had to offer, until I spent a week with the rodeo cowboys. One of the very best who ever lived was Canada's Marty Wood. Not only was I impressed with his ability but also with the cowboy's lifestyle, honesty, and genuine hospitality. I doubt that I ever had a better time.*

The rodeo cowboy works hard at his trade, risks injury every time he performs and, compared to other professional athletes, is paid a pitiful sum for his talent and effort.

I suspect it is pride in their skills, the comradery and the fact that they can have fun while working that keeps them on the circuit. Unlike other athletic performers, they have no general managers, coaches, or owners. They can, and do, live life the way they damned well please.

I'll always be grateful to Marty Wood and his sidekick Freddie Greer for introducing me to their unique world.

JULY 13, 1968—It was early on a Monday evening when the Arizona state trooper strolled into the tiny bar at the Western Village Motel in Phoenix.

He hesitated at the doorway, hands on hips, slightly taken aback by the scene before him.

And that's when they got him. One around the ankles, the other around the waist. Two big cowboys wrestled him to the floor, stole his hat and raced out into the street.

"Yip! Yip!" yelped the customers. "Eeeeee-hawwwwww!!!".

"My Gawd!" said the bartender to no one in particular.

The trooper, though, was grinning as he picked himself up and dusted off his trousers. Not even the police, it seems, bother the rodeo cowboys when they come to town.

And these were the pros who travel from city to city, town to town—bulldogging, roping calves and riding wild Brahma bulls, bareback and saddle broncs. They were in Phoenix for the Rodeo of Rodeos.

Somebody jammed a Stetson on the bareheaded trooper and everybody laughed. Suddenly, above the din, another commotion.

"What the . . ." yelled the bartender as thick, blueish smoke billowed up from behind his bar.

"Yip! Yip!" A smoke bomb. Now another one went off near the door to the men's washroom. And another in the lobby, as unsuspecting diners looked up in alarm. "Eeeeee-Hawwwwww!!!'"

"Craa-ck! Pop! Bang!" Firecrackers went off behind the bartender as he bent to smother the smoke bombs with a wet towel. "Yip! Yip!"

A bespectacled, middle-aged salesman from the East, wearing a conservative, grey business suit, watched, bug-eyed. He slid off his bar stool and left so hurriedly he forgot to pay his bill.

Three cowboys, wearing false handlebar moustaches, pressed into the open spot. They looked straight from one of those old posters: "Wanted—Dead or Alive."

"Say, bartender," one of them drawled, slapping the bar for attention, "whar's mah drank?"

"Ooooooo-eeeee . . . lookit that smoke," another one said. "Looks like them Indians is after us agin. Yip! Yip! Get 'em! Get 'em!"

Another smoke bomb, more firecrackers, laughing, hollering, and, above it all, the blaring of the jukebox—the country beat of the California Jug Band. A shapely cowgirl—a barrel racer from Arkansas—shifted on her stool.

"Ain't nobody has as much fun as cowboys," she said to the bartender.

"Hell's Angels, maybe," he grunted, adjusting his string tie.

"Bar-tender!" yelled one of the fellows with a moustache. "Ah needs a towel, pronto!"

The bartender shuffled toward him reluctantly, towels draped over his arm. They grabbed him, stole all of his towels and passed them around to be used as neckerchiefs. And, as the frustrated man stood protesting, one of the cowboys leaned over and gave him a playful slap on the back, so forcefully that the bartender almost lost his balance.

"Aww, hell, have a see-gar," one of the cowboys said in a consoling voice.

The bartender accepted the cigar hesitantly, another cowboy reached over and lit it, and, after a few puffs, the bartender started smiling again.

"BANG!" It exploded in his face.

He turned around, the ragged cigar stub still clenched between his teeth, held his head in his hands and moaned: "Why, oh why, didn't I take this week off? Ohhh, and this is just the first day. . . ."

Marty Wood had said on the telephone that the Western Village was the place to stay if you wanted to go to a rodeo in Phoenix. But he hadn't arrived yet.

"Gee, I don't know Marty Wood," the girl in the office had said. "But we shore have heard a lot about him. And everybody and his brother's lookin' for him, it seems."

Marty is from Calgary and they say he's the best saddle bronc rider of his time, the toughest and the most consistent. Now he lives with his wife and young son in Diamond, Missouri, where he runs a horse motel—a place where people are able to leave their horses when they're passing through.

"Do I know Marty Wood?" said the tall, young cowboy at the bar. "Hell, he's about the toughest damned bronc rider I ever seen. He should be comin' in tomorra with Freddie

Greer. Marty don't get wild like some of us, but he shore likes to drink."

With that, the cowboy walked over to the jukebox to play that record by the California Jug Band once again. And, as the lone waitress passed him, he grabbed her around the waist with a whoop and holler.

Later, you would learn that this was John Edwards, at six-foot-four one of the tallest, and one of the more talented, bareback bronc riders. He is a New York cowboy, a kid from Poughkeepsie who saw his first rodeo at Madison Square Garden and decided that this was what he wanted to do. He joined a dude ranch in New York State, learned to ride and now lives in a little log cabin he bought in Montana.

John, wavering slightly on his feet, was throwing the waitress around the room, his long legs going in all directions, but, surprisingly, in time to the music.

The crowd urged him on and, for the grand finale, he lifted the squealing waitress high over his head. He held that position for a few seconds, then started leaning to one side. They hit the floor with a resounding crash. But instead of being angry, as you might expect, the waitress jumped up, flushed, pushed him away with a laugh and returned to work.

John staggered away, the unofficial greeter for a group of young girls who had entered the bar. There were lots of girls now, office girls from Phoenix who had gone home to put on their cowgirl outfits.

"What's the Denver tomato's name?" one cowboy asked another, pointing to a girl in the corner.

She was one of a pack that follows the cowboys. The situation is similar in golf, hockey, football and baseball, but those athletes are beginners compared to the cowpokes. For some reason, a lot of women are crazy about cowboys. Perhaps it's their smooth line, like the one overheard at the bar.

"Yore shore purty and sweet," a young cowboy said to the girl sitting on the next stool. "Ya smell good, too."

"Silly," she giggled. "I'm a girl, I'm s'posed to."

John Edwards had turned his attention to a buddy sitting with company at one of the tables.

"Yip! Yip-eeeeee!!!" he yelped. He climbed up on the other man's chair, sitting partly on his shoulders, partly on the chair back, his arms around the fellow's neck. He was pretending he was on a bronc.

The chair kept tipping backwards until finally, CRASH! They hit the floor hard. The man laughed, everybody laughed, and John did it again. CRASH. It was beginning to look as if John Edwards wouldn't last long enough to make the rodeo.

The remarkable thing is that no one seemed to mind. Not even the bartender. And, after having been twice pulled to the floor backwards, the fellow in the chair was still laughing.

The cowboys never show anger. They hug one another a lot and their standard greeting is a slap across the shoulders that might hospitalize an out-of-condition office worker. They yip and holler and slap the bar with their palms when they laugh. And they never remove their hats.

They make more noise than anyone you ever heard, but they watch their language. They might throw their ladies from one side of a room to the other while dancing, but they have respect. Rarely do they use cusswords.

John Edwards passed out three times that night. They carried him to his room on each occasion, but he kept waking up and coming back.

Marty Wood and Freddie Greer didn't arrive until very late Tuesday night. They parked Freddie's half-ton pickup truck with the camper on the back and checked in at the Western Village. At 9:30 Wednesday morning, there was a knock at my door.

"Hey, you made it," said Marty Wood. He's not a big man, but he looks hard. And most of the time, even in the morning, a chaw of tobacco stuck under his bottom lip.

With him was a tall, rawboned young man in his early twenties. "Meet Freddie Greer," said Marty. "Freddie rides bulls."

"How do," said Freddie, a bachelor cowboy

from Dallas, Texas. "Shore is a purty day, ain't it."

They said to meet them for breakfast, but that turned out to be in the bar.

"Might as well start the day right," said Marty, surrounded by a group of cowboy friends.

A squat, square-jawed cowboy joined them for lunch. Ronnie Rossen from Montana, twice the world champion bull rider.

"We call him Punch because he's been throwed off so many bulls onto his head," said Marty.

There were drinks with lunch, too. Marty, obviously, was the leader. Freddie is a very quiet guy and Punch just seemed to agree all the time.

"Say, let's go to the track this afternoon," said Marty.

"Shore is a purty day for it," said Freddie, and Punch said it was okay with him, too.

First, though, they had to make a stop. Someone had given Marty a case of V.O. and he had to pick it up. They smacked their lips as they put it in the trunk of the car.

Rodeo cowboys don't have to pay to go to the races in Phoenix so they walked right in. People could tell they were important because of their belt buckles. Marty and Punch wore the huge, diamond-studded buckles that are given to winners of the National Finals. Freddie's, proclaiming him as champion of a specific rodeo, was somewhat smaller.

There was a bar at the track, and that's where they stood—two gulps and order another round ... two gulps ... "Think I'll go down and watch 'em walk to see if they're sure-footed or not," Punch would announce before each race.

"Shore is a purty day, ain't it," said Freddie.

Marty, it seems, knows most everybody. When he arrived in Phoenix, his room slot was jammed with messages, his conversations were continually interrupted by telephone calls. And people kept coming up to him at the track.

The rodeo was opening that night in the Phoenix arena, but none of the three had drawn rides. There are three go-rounds in each event, which means three rides on three different broncs or bulls spread over five nights.

They arrived back at the motel at 5:30 in the afternoon and, of course, went straight to the bar. Then, at 8 p.m., Marty announced that it was time to go to the rodeo. Punch, who was starting to sit lower on his stool, figured he had better go to bed.

Marty cracked open the case of whisky, wrapped three bottles in newspaper, put them in the camper behind the pick-up truck and drove off. Most of the rodeo performers live in trailers and campers, so the parking lot behind the arena looked somewhat like a gypsy camp. There were cowboys and cowgirls everywhere you looked, leading horses, riding horses, driving teams.

Marty took one of the bottles with him and asked the gate man for directions to the clowns' dressing room. The clowns are used to attract the attention of runaway broncs—and especially bulls—after a ride. They tease them, chase them, then leap to safety. It's amusing and it's also important.

"They're my buddies," explained Marty, who was starting to weave a little. "Gotta give them a bottle."

His goodwill mission accomplished, Marty led the way to the arena floor, which was covered with dirt. The house was about half full and cowboys lined both ends of the floor and sat on the rail fences of the temporary corrals.

"I wanted you to be down here so you can get the feel and smell of it," said Marty.

"Helloo Marty," cooed a cowgirl as he passed.

"Hi there, sweetheart," he answered without stopping. "Ain't she the prettiest barrel racer you ever saw?"

She smiled appreciatively.

One of the first things you learn is to watch for the tobacco juice. The brown streams fly all around you. Marty is an expert when it comes to spitting, neat and with a low trajectory.

"Been chewin' since I was 14," he explains. "Here—go ahead and try some. Lot better'n cigarettes. Look, you mosey around for a while. I'm gonna do some visitin'."

He wandered around the floor, his Stetson perched jauntily on the back of his head, exchanging greetings with other cowboys and people in the stands. Periodically, he and another cowboy would disappear, out to the pickup for a little taste.

"Y'all ready to go back?" Freddie asked as the evening wore to a close. His words were almost drowned out by a sudden roar from the crowd. One of the bulls had thrown a veteran rider named Joe Green and Green had been injured.

Marty Wood watches the rodeo action.

A knot of cowboys gathered as Joe was led, stumbling, holding his shoulder, off the floor and behind the corrals. They cleared a place for him, removed his shirt and put him on the cold concrete floor. Joe, his pale face almost the color of his greying hair, moaned as people tried to decide the next step.

Marty strode up through the cowboys and stood over Joe. He reached down, grabbed Joe's arm and yanked.

"Okay," Marty announced casually. "Let's go, clumsy Joe. You need a drink."

"Thanks," muttered Green, beads of perspiration on his forehead.

They've been on the road a long time. Marty knows about Joe's trick shoulder. It just needs that yank to put it back in place.

Marty led the way to the pickup, opened the camper door and produced a bottle. There were Marty, Freddie, Joe Green, and an Easterner and two more cowboys who had been invited. A little circle was formed, Marty uncorked the bottle and passed it to Joe first. He took a big swig and passed it along.

"Gawsh, I dunno," said Freddie. "I ain't use'ta drankin' it stray-it."

He took a small swig, passed the bottle off hurriedly, turned his back on the circle and was sick. It was one of the funniest things Marty had seen in a long time. He kidded Freddie about it until the bottle was emptied.

"Guess I just ain't use'ta it thata way," said Freddie, embarrassed. And he climbed shakily into the truck.

"Y'know, I don't want you to get the wrong idea about rodeos," Marty said on the way back to the motel. "We don't party like this alla time. But we always do in Phoenix. This is kind of a party place.

"Aw hell, I guess I party alla time," said Marty as an afterthought. "Course, I been doin' it all my life, no sense quittin' now. But I'm all business on a horse. You'll see tomorrow night.

"Y'know, that's the best thing there is for a hangover—a buckin' horse."

It was almost midnight when Freddie turned in the motel gate.

"Tell you what," said Marty. "Let's go brush our teeth and go to the bar. It's open until 3."

And they went to bed at 3, of course, because they had to ride the next day.

Despite the hot Arizona sun and the fact that they both had slight hangovers, Marty Wood and Freddie Greer looked pretty good when they stepped from their room.

"Shore is a purty day, ain't it," said Freddie.

"C'mon for breakfast," said Marty. "No drinks today. We gotta ride."

Freckles Brown met them in the lobby with the news that stew was on the menu.

"Mmmmmm-hmmmmm," said Freddie. "Ah shore do like stee-yew."

Freckles is a character, a legend. He's 48 and still an annual contender for the world championship in bull riding. Five years ago, Freckles broke his neck—for the second time in his career—but he'd piled up enough points to win the title anyway.

Marty is perhaps the best saddle bronc rider of his era—three times the world champion, and he hasn't been out of the top five since 1957.

Years ago in Bowness, a suburb of Calgary, his father operated a riding academy, and Marty rode show jumpers. The kid showed a lot of promise, too, winning ribbons at all of the local shows. But he was a tough little guy. Breaking the horses appealed to him more than riding them in shows.

He grew up on the legend of Pete Knight, a cowboy from Crossfield, Alta., who won the world's saddle bronc title four times before he was killed in 1937.

"A buckin' horse throwed him off," said Marty.

Saddle bronc riding is the showpiece of rodeo events. Riding bulls is more dangerous and riding bareback has been compared to "grabbing the handle of a suitcase and jumping out of an open window." Riding a saddle bronc, though, takes more skill.

nd now the young cowboys talk about Marty the way Marty talks about Pete Knight.

On the previous night, in the crowded bar, Marty had been talking to a youth named Jackie Phipps. Jackie is from a community named Cochrane, just west of Calgary. He'd had a few drinks and he called Marty over to him.

"Pssst," he said. "Put this in yore pocket and give it to me tomorrow."

He handed Marty a $100 bill. He was afraid he might have a few more drinks, break it and start spending more than he should. When Marty left to talk to someone else, Jackie said: "That Marty's the greatest. I really mean it. You're Canadian, you know hockey. I used to play junior in Western Canada. Well, Marty's the Bobby Hull of the bronc riders. Know what I mean?"

Marty averages about $20 000 a year in prize money and needs $10 000 to break even.

Shawn Davis of Whitehall, Mont. was last year's saddle bronc champ and earned $25 277 to second-place Marty's $19 907. Kenny Mc-Lean of Okanagan Falls, B.C., who was the world bronc riding champ in 1962, was eighth last year but earned $20 843 from his various events.

Actually, many Canadians have done extremely well in rodeo's toughest event. First there were the four world titles won by Pete Knight, three by Marty, and one each by McLean, Winston Bruce of Calgary and Carl Olsen, formerly of Fir Mountain, Sask., who now lives in Sweetgrass, Mont.

Also in the top ten last season were Bruce (6th—$12 596) and Mel Hyland of Port Kells, B.C. (7th—$12 563). And Malcolm Jones of Lethbridge, Alta. was seventh in bareback riding, which was good for $11 247. This year there were about 30 Canadians on the professional rodeo circuit.

"Well, I've got me a horse this afternoon who has his bad days," said Marty. "Let's go and see what we can do with him." He grabbed the bundle that included his handmade saddle, riding boots, rope rein, elastic tape, resin and sheepskin.

"The worst kind of a horse to draw is one you can't win no money on," he said. "That's what I may have today."

He explained the procedure. There are two judges, each about 15 feet from the chute. Each gives a possible 25 points for the way the horse bucks and another possible 25 for the way the cowboy rides. That makes a possible total of 100 points, but no one has ever been rated that high.

"So it's better to get a horse that will buck," said Marty. "Otherwise, you gotta make him buck."

The best bucking horses—many of them from stock contractors in Canada—are old horses that are set in their ways. Some are as old as 25.

Some assistance in making the horse buck, much to the chagrin of the Society For The Prevention Of Cruelty To Animals, is a jerk blank, a strap covered with sheepskin, placed around its flanks. As soon as the cowboy has been thrown, or removed from his mount by the pickup men, it is released.

"**T**hem people in the SPCA, they're talkin' about puttin' a stop to the business," scoffed Marty. "The jerk blank just tickles them, is all. If they stop that they'll ruin rodeoin'. And, see, the spurs are dull."

Marty is described in the program as "a rider with a slashing style." That means he can work his spurs the way the good bronc rider must.

Points for a ride are given according to how far up on a horse's neck the cowboy can work his spurs. He sits back, toes out, his spurs raking the horse from the neck back to just behind the saddle. And, for the entire 10-second ride, he is allowed to hang on to his rope rein with only one hand.

Marty slipped off his expensive dress boots and sat on the floor, his back against a pillar for support. He was wearing one blue sock and one white one. Carefully, he wrapped elastic bandage around his left foot and around a piece of protective sheepskin on the inside of the ankle.

Then he wrapped the bandage around his right leg, holding a piece of sheepskin in place along the inside of his calf. Then he slipped into a loose-fitting pair of riding boots (which could slip off in an emergency) and strapped on his leather chaps.

Now he took resin and rubbed it into his saddle. He also rubbed resin liberally along the inside of his legs, on his chaps.

Marty and the other cowboys grabbed their saddles and ropes and went to their respective chutes. His horse, Moon Face, was in number five. Marty and two handlers saddled the horse, attached the rope rein (all by reaching inside through the bars) and measured its length carefully. Then Marty climbed up the rungs to await his turn.

The announcer would introduce each rider, the jerk blank would be tightened, the cowboy would slip down on the horse and the gate would open. They come barreling out, one after the other. A 10-second ride, or shorter, and the horse, its jerk blank loosened, would be chased out of the arena.

Suddenly, there was a gasp from the crowd. The third rider, Pat Howey, formerly of British Columbia, had been thrown but his foot was caught in the stirrup. The horse kept bucking, dragging Howey by one leg. The crowd screamed, but finally Howey broke loose and jumped to his feet to show them he hadn't been injured. They cheered.

Marty's face was tense as he straddled Moon Face, his body over the saddle, but his weight still on the wooden rungs of the chute.

"That's where you can get crippled," he had said that afternoon. "The chute's the dangerous place. A horse can flop over on ya. It happened to me last year."

Another danger is catching your leg when you come out of the gate. Because the trick is to rake the horse's neck the first time it plants its front feet on the way out.

And Marty knows about injuries. He has broken both ankles three times, has been kicked in the head, has broken ribs and his collarbone and has two screws in one leg that once was broken in five places.

"Once I rode with a broken ankle," he said. "The doc gave me 27 shots of novocaine that week and I lost seven pounds. He gave me some pills, too, to take every four hours. But one day I took them every two hours. I was higher than a kite, but I won."

He also has a crooked back that bothers him from time to time, a reminder of the day when he was a kid in Calgary and broke three vertebrae when he fell from a hayrack.

"Marty Wood . . ." said the announcer, and Marty slipped into the saddle, the gate sprang open and his legs shot forward, toes out, to rake old Moon Face's neck.

He raked and he raked, rocking in the saddle at a furious pace. But, as he feared, old Moon Face was having a bad day. He scored 69, most of them for his ride, compared to the leading score of 74.

No matter how often they have ridden, there is a feeling of relief when a cowboy has finished a ride.

"Well, that's half a week's work," said Marty. "Ten seconds. Let's go get a drink. I don't ride again until Sunday. But I got a good horse, Drifter. Ain't never had a bad ride on him. Sometimes you can go along for months and not get a good draw, and you don't win nothing."

Freddie Greer was in the bar at the hotel and just grunted when asked how he had done on the bulls. A bad draw.

"Ah bin thankin' of goin' to San Bernadino," he said. "Maybe ah'll hop on over they-er with the pickup."

That's the tough part about rodeoing. Sometimes there are as many as three rodeos scheduled within 200-300 miles of one another. And the prize money is so scarce that a cowboy, when he hasn't done well at one, may skip to another if he can get back in time to ride his second go-round. So Freddie headed for San Bernadino, California, 300 miles away.

Because of his background, Marty is probably one of the best horsemen at the rodeo. "Some of these guys ride broncs, but they never learned to ride a horse," he said. He's never regretted his decision to leave show riding.

"Y'know, I don't like those people with the show horses," he said. "They're a lot different. Their noses are way up in the air. The cowboys are great people. I know if I'm broke that I can walk up to any one of them and ask for a loan of $100. They'd give it to me in a minute."

When Marty showed up to ride Drifter on Sunday afternoon, an old friend from Calgary, Dave Abrahams, was waiting for him. Abrahams is retired now from the feed business and was still recuperating from a heart attack.

Marty scored 74 for his ride on Drifter, highest mark of the day, and good enough to win him over $300.

"Most cowboys wind up broke," Abrahams said after the ride. "Marty, I was happy to hear about your place in Missouri."

Marty, 35, moved to Diamond, Mo., a while back and opened a horse motel, where horses can be left overnight. His wife Jean, who used to be a professional square dancer on the Red Foley television show, stays there with their five-year-old son, Chip.

"I'm tryin' to build for the future," said Marty. "Wish you could come and look over the place. Good location."

Freddie Greer was back at the motel when they returned. "Didn't win a danged thang at San Bernardino," he said "Nawthin' here neither."

The next day was a Monday; the rodeo was over. Freddie and Marty were having one last drink in the bar and a woman walked in.

"Say cowboy," she called to Marty.

"Yes'm."

"Do me a favor, willya? Be standing here talkin' to me when my boy-friend comes in–I wanta make him jealous."

"Ma'am," said Marty. "I'm a happily married man, thank you. I don't hardly need trouble like that. Sorry."

"Shucks," said Freddie. "She coulda asked me, ah'm a bachelor."

"That woman's nuts," said Marty with a grin. "C'mon Fred, get the pickup goin'. We got to get to Long Beach."

"Okay," said Freddie. "Shore is a purty day fur a drive, ain't it." ●

EPILOGUE   *Good times don't last forever, not even for world champions.*
Usually, when the riding is over, the money is gone. Only a few, those who made enough from endorsements and other outside activities retire with a bankroll. Marty Wood always refused to endorse products. He did his talking on a saddle bronc. When he rode his last bronc, in Edmonton in 1976, he was far from being financially secure for the rest of his life.

"He was awful generous when he had money," says his friend Al Sewall from Okotoks, Alberta. "Too generous. And Marty always travelled first class.

He flew first class on planes and you wouldn't see him sharin' a motel room with ten other cowboys."

The surprising thing is that Marty rode as recently as 1976. He was medically dead just a year earlier when a car fell on his chest while he was working under it while living in Denver.

Marty had two old Lincolns and, by taking parts from one to repair the other, had one on the road all the time. He was always good with his hands. On this particular day, Marty had one of the cars up on blocks or jacks and suddenly it slipped, crushing his upper body so that his lungs collapsed. A friend saw it happen, called the police, and they called the fire department. Help arrived in minutes but Marty had stopped breathing. An electric shock brought him back.

He was in intensive care for a couple of weeks and a guy could have made a lot of money if he had bet that Marty would be up on a horse again a year later. They were just worried about him living. Marty Wood, however, was as tough as any horse he ever rode.

And then, in 1978, tragedy struck during a family reunion near Calgary. Marty's father, who had taught him to ride, pulled onto a highway and was hit by another car travelling at 100 miles an hour. Mr. Wood was killed and Marty's mother spent four months in the hospital. Word also came from Texas that his old pal Freddie Greer had cancer. . . .

Marty still hasn't settled into anything permanent to take the place of rodeoing. It was his entire life. And, just to prove he hasn't forgotten, in 1979 he entered an Oldtimers' rodeo in Las Vegas and astounded everybody by scoring a remarkable 78 on his first go-round in the saddle bronc competition.

If rodeo cowboys received as much attention as other athletes, Marty Wood would certainly have been elected to the sports hall of fame long ago. Nobody ever knew a horse any better.

So Strong-so what?

The Story of Doug Hepburn

prologue *I have never been certain how to describe Doug Hepburn or where to start. It began one night in Toronto, while I was a hockey writer and weekly sports columnist for* The Globe and Mail *and suddenly wondered whatever had happened to Doug Hepburn, the guy from Vancouver who had become the strongest man in the world, lifting on one leg because of his club foot. It was midnight and, as I passed the telephone, I decided to take a very long shot and call him. There was one D. Hepburn in the Vancouver telephone directory, the operator said, and she placed the call, person-to-person to Doug Hepburn, the former weightlifter.*

"Hello," said the far-away voice. "Yes, it is I."

I was amazed. There he was, on the line in about thirty seconds. I was totally unprepared. No pen, no paper, no coffee, no cigarette.

"Let's see now," mused Hepburn after I had introduced myself. "You were sitting around and suddenly wondered, whatever happened to Doug Hepburn . . ."

"Uh, yes, that's exactly it," I stammered.

"Do you have a pen, some paper, a drink and a cigarette?" he asked.

"No, as a matter of fact," I said, startled.

"I'll wait until you get them," Hepburn said, "and then I'll tell you a little story."

Three hours later, I put down the receiver realizing that I had just heard one of the most amazing stories of my life. There was far too much for one sports column. I didn't know where to start.

I sat on the Doug Hepburn story for a year, until I joined the staff of The Canadian. *Actually, I think that unwritten story I heard that night was the reason I became a magazine writer. I had to have some place to do it at length. When I tried to relate it to Editor Denny Harvey, he didn't seem to believe it. Still, he told me to get out to Vancouver to talk to the guy in person. Fortunately, the story was still good. No one else had thought of Hepburn or bothered to find him.*

I spent eight days with Doug Hepburn, talking into a tape recorder until late into the nights and, as I flew back to Toronto, my head was whirring. I sat looking at those tapes at home, almost afraid to transcribe them. One of my idiosyncrasies in times like that was to drive to the old Victoria Hotel in downtown Toronto where I would rent a room on the top floor for five dollars a night. There was a phone and a washbasin. I shared a washroom with the bellydancers who worked downstairs in the bar. Then, with only my type-writer and a tape recorder, a dozen packs of cigarettes and a couple bottles of sherry, I punished myself for three days, transcribing those tapes, cutting up the typed pages and gluing the pieces together in chronological order.

I finally emerged with a three-day growth of whiskers, my head into Doug Hepburn again, fingers yellowed by nicotine, and in a state of near exhaustion. And I still had to write the story. It was the most difficult piece of work I have ever attempted. This, then, is Doug Hepburn.

O O O

MARCH 11, 1967—It all started in Vancouver—the day he was born. His eyes were crossed, and his right leg was withered and he had a club foot.

About the only good thing that happened was that the doctor on duty realized from the start that Doug Hepburn was going to need help. So he grabbed the little head with his forceps and gave a tug. Doug still has the scars from those forceps and he kids everybody about them: he offers them as proof that he didn't want to come into this world in the first place.

People who complain about the psychological effect of coming from a broken home should speak to Doug Hepburn for therapy. He could tell them what it is like to have crossed eyes and a club foot and come from a broken home. To put it mildly, he didn't have much going for him in those early years. Nothing, really, that you would want to build a foundation on.

Let's start with that leg—the one he had to favor when he was lifting world records. He can

remember being sent to a hospital in Winnipeg before he was old enough to speak. The doctors—who could have corrected it today—were still experimenting. They removed a bone, fused the ankle and wrapped it all up in a cast. Hepburn remembers crying all night because of the pain.

"I don't give a damn what the doctors say," his father yelled one morning. "That cast is coming off." So he took a jackknife and cut it away. "The cast had been pressing against the top of my foot," says Doug, "and gangrene had set in."

Shortly after that, the family split up. While his mother went off to Seattle to await a divorce, Doug moved to Edmonton to live with his grandmother, who spent night after night massaging that bad leg. Doug's mother subsequently returned to Vancouver, got a job as a comptometer operator and took back her son.

By this time, Doug was at school. Kids are cruel and you can imagine what a natural target this one was—with his cross-eyes and club foot. It didn't take long for them to spot him.

The school bully, a bigger kid who was four years ahead of him, tested him the first day. And he got a surprise: little Doug felled him and pinned him to the floor. He hated school. It was a prison. He wouldn't work and he wouldn't concentrate. But one day they gave the class IQ tests. The principal skipped him a grade, despite a C-minus average. The teachers started to give him strange looks, as if they couldn't believe it; he was smart after all.

He was also strong: he forced himself to swim farther, ride his bike farther and to throw and kick a ball farther than anyone else. "I wanted to do more than fit in," he says. "I wanted to be better." It didn't impress the girls. They liked the fellows without crossed eyes and with two good legs.

His eyes were fixed when he was 15 and he says that made a big change in him. Then one day he went down to a beach and saw all these guys with the great big physiques, local body-builders. "I said, 'Look at that fella—he's not the same. Look at the arms! Look at the legs! Boy, I'm gonna get me one of those.'"

So Doug Hepburn went out and bought his first set of weights.

He didn't know a thing about them, but he lugged them home to his basement. If lifting them would make him look like those guys on the beach—then he'd lift until he was blue in the face. It became an obsession. Every spare moment was spent grunting in that basement. It got so that his schooling was interfering—so he quit midway through Grade 11. And that's when the friction started at home.

His mother had remarried, but her new husband wasn't prepared for this. There was a monster in the basement and it ate too much food. "I didn't want to work," Doug admits today. "I just lay around the beach, ate a lot and lifted those weights."

"At first," he says, "I started lifting to get a physique so that people would notice me. But now there was a change. Now something inside of me was compelling me to be strong."

Late one night, when he came home from the gym, he found his suitcase packed. There was a short family meeting and it was unanimously agreed that he was a big, lazy bum. There was only one chance for him to make something of himself. He would have to get out on his own so that he'd be forced to work.

When he left home, he found a cheap room in the basement of a boarding house, and he got his first steady position—as bouncer in the beer parlor at the Devonshire Hotel. It paid $1.50 a night. In the summer he worked as a lifeguard at Sunset Beach. He spent most of his time there walking around on his hands, developing more shoulder strength. He was getting extremely big and very strong, but his withered right leg still bothered him. He always made sure, when he was in a bathing suit, that he kept the left one crossed over it so nobody would stare.

People started to notice him now, but Doug found that he was still in the shadow of another lifter, a friend named Mike Poppelle, who ran a boy's club. "This gave me more incentive," he says, "because Mike was getting all the attention."

That's when he started to really eat—even though he was making only $1.50 a day at the time. And did he eat!

"It seemed logical to me that if I wanted to get bigger, I would have to eat everything I could get my hands on," he says. "I ate three times a day and three times a day I had to fight to keep from throwing up. A couple of times I did. One day I gained seven pounds." He learned which foods built muscle—milk, eggs and bananas.

He bought a blender to turn food into liquids. His favorite drink was made of milk, a banana and three raw eggs and he would flavor it with chocolate. He always liked chocolate. Every time he passed a bake shop he would buy a 40-cent chocolate cake. He would eat the whole thing and wash it down with a quart of milk as an appetizer. Once he sat down and ate two large tins of spaghetti, a dozen eggs and a loaf of bread. He drank three or four quarts of milk a day.

When he started he weighed 145 pounds. Soon he was 255. He had to turn sideways to get off streetcars and buses because of his wide shoulders. "People were starting to laugh again," he says, "but now because I was so big."

Odd as it may seem, Doug Hepburn at this point didn't know anything about competitive weightlifting. All he was doing was trying to be bigger than Mike Poppelle. He didn't know the three lifts used in competition: he would just pick up a barbell and hoist it over his head—something weightlifters call a press.

One day he dropped into Mike's club and started fooling around with his shoulder strength. "I used to get these tremendous surges of power," he says, "and I was feeling stronger every day." There was a barbell on two raised platforms and he picked it up for fun and held it on his shoulders. "Something inside of me said, 'Go ahead—raise it over your shoulders.' So I did. It went up quite comfortably."

Everything stopped in that gymnasium. Mike Poppelle and the other lifters looked at him in amazement. There was that crazy Hepburn—the guy with the withered leg—standing there holding 320 pounds over his head. When he put it down, they explained to Doug that what he had just done was match the world record, that's all.

The best press in history was 320 pounds, done by John Davis, the world champion from the United States. They shook their heads and laughed. Hepburn's press hadn't been done in strict accordance with the rules. So what? Hepburn hadn't even been in competition. "What it did," he says, "was let me know that if that was the record, I could do it."

There are three Olympic lifts: the press, the clean and jerk, and the snatch. Points for all three are totalled to decide championships. Doug figured he had better learn the latter two. Finally he entered a competition and pressed 300 pounds. Officials in Vancouver sent it to weightlifting headquarters in Montreal for acceptance as the new Canadian record.

The forms came back with a note saying: "Impossible. This man could not possibly have lifted 300 pounds. Why, the best in the east does only 220. You have made a mistake." Three times they sent that form. Three times it was sent back. It never was accepted. Who the heck was Doug Hepburn, anyway? Nobody had ever heard of him.

They didn't hear about him until he went to Los Angeles for the U.S. national championships to face Davis for the first time. Davis won,

but this unknown from Canada pressed 345½ pounds to break his world record.

Now he was serious. Now it became a religion with him. He moved out of the basement room in the boarding house into an old, empty store on Commercial Drive, right next to a Chinese grocery store. He and some other weightlifters moved their equipment there and fixed up some bunks with gunny sacks. They ate there, too, when they had the money.

Hepburn had already discovered that the North American public looks down its nose at strongmen and weightlifters. After breaking the world press record, he had been invited out to a couple of places to put on exhibitions. One night he was trying to break his world record between innings of a sandlot baseball game sponsored by local businessmen. "C'mon, get it over with," blurted the man on the loudspeaker—in front of the crowd. "We've got to get on with the ball game." Doug was both hurt and embarrassed. "What kind of man was this?" he asks. "In Europe or Japan, this would have been an important event—this was a great thing about to take place."

Although he was a big man, a strong man, Hepburn always disliked violence. That's the reason he walked out in the middle of the evening one night and quit his job as bouncer at the Devonshire Hotel. The Shriners were in town—up to their usual hijinks—and Hepburn feared what he might do in the heat of the moment.

Hepburn kept grunting and lifting in that old store, sleeping on gunny sacks at night and eating the cheapest of foods. Not even the people of Vancouver realized what was going on behind that door on Commercial Drive. They still didn't know who Hepburn was. He had been mentioned in newspapers, but never in headlines and not often. If he could raise the money, he would go to a competition and win it with ease.

Weightlifting officials knew his potential, and a fellow named Harry Brown, who was always sympathetic toward Doug, tried raising money to send him to the 1953 world championships in Stockholm. Local sportsmen were apathetic. They didn't know Hepburn and they didn't know weightlifting. However, three weeks before the championships, enough money had been raised to send him—not with the trimmings, not even with a coach or companion—but he was going.

The stadium in Stockholm was packed. On a raised platform, representatives from 20 countries strained to gain attention. Al Murray, coach of the British team, noticed the big Canadian training by himself. He noticed the withered leg and saw that Doug Hepburn was limping. He had strained his weak ankle and now, with his biggest moment before him, it looked as though he would have to withdraw. "No," Hepburn told Murray, "I'll go through with it."

Weightlifting is big in Europe and the 5000 fans were aware of what was going on. Hepburn was an unbelievable underdog, but he was the choice of the people. After two lifts, Murray—who had adopted him—yelled: "You've won, Doug! You've won! Davis will never make it up on the third lift." The arena went wild and Hepburn—the kid who had been born with cross-eyes and a club foot, the misfit—was the heavyweight champion of the world. They tacked his photographs to telephone poles all over Sweden.

Back home, Vancouver was caught unprepared. The news had been flashed home but nobody knew much about this big guy Hepburn. They had never taken him very seriously. The headline in one newspaper read: "Hepburn's Mighty Heart Earns Plaudits of World."

The story began, "A 26-year-old Vancouver man, with a club foot and a partially withered leg, is the toast of Europe today. Doug Hepburn, who has worked at his chosen sport for eight long years, virtually unrecognized in his home town, has brought Vancouver its first world record and first world championship of any kind since Percy Williams won in the 1928 Olympics." The rest of the story was partly an introduction of Hepburn to the public and partly an apology to the world's strongest man. "All Vancouver can do," said the last paragraph, "is humbly welcome home a great champion and take pride in the fact this is his home."

The reporters found Mrs. Hepburn and asked her for some inside stuff on her son. "The only thing I can say is that I am very proud of him," she said. "But please, don't mention me or make him share his glory. I did everything in my power to discourage him."

Back in Stockholm, Doug Hepburn limped down the aisle in the plane and took his seat—or rather he took up two of them. Subconsciously, the world's strongest man crossed his left leg over his right one, then settled back and began to dream. He dreamed of all the good things that were going to happen now. He'd shown them—he'd done it. The world was his oyster.

He had no idea that he soon would have no appetite for oysters.

There weren't many people out to meet Doug Hepburn when he returned. But the Mayor of Vancouver was there, the press and a police escort. For a few wonderful days he basked in this new feeling—the one that heroes know.

Nothing much had changed, though. On his first night he had to go back to that dirty old gym on Commercial Drive to sleep in his bunk made of gunny sacks. And, as things turned out, he couldn't even use the bunk. A friend had celebrated his victory by drinking too much and had passed out on it. Doug went down Hastings Street, to the toughest section of Vancouver, and got a room for $3 in a flophouse.

"Can you imagine how I felt, that first night home?" he asks. "Here I was, the strongest man in the world, sleeping in a flophouse." He admits he didn't know much about the way things went. He had foolishly hoped that maybe the people of Vancouver would do something for him—like setting him up in a little gym to teach kids.

The only offer he got was from a wrestling promoter in San Francisco. Doug had gone to a sports show in Oakland, California, and in one afternoon had broken three world weightlifting records. When he took off his shirt, the wrestling promoter leaned forward in his chair and declared: "We have another Yukon Eric."

But Doug didn't really want to take up wrestling.

That night there was a telephone call from Vancouver asking him to come home—Mayor Hume wanted to see him—and he was in a receptive mood. "I knew what it was all about," he says. "Vancouver needed me. Suddenly, Doug Hepburn was back in the limelight. I figured they wouldn't ask me to come home if they didn't plan to do something for me in return."

He was ushered into the office of the late

George Hume by a male secretary. "Okay, okay," said Doug. "I'll do it. I'll stay in training and represent the city in the Empire Games. Now—what are you going to do for me?" He says the mayor asked him how much he needed—"$250, $300 a month?" Doug said $150 would do—"just enough to eat, pay rent and train."

Mayor Hume put Hepburn on the official city payroll, listing him as his personal body-guard, and his pay cheque was mailed to him each month. "Sure, I guess it would have affected my amateur standing," Doug says. "But there are so many ways around it. I'd say 80 per cent of the athletes in North America have taken money. They don't talk about it." Naturally, he didn't work a day as Hume's bodyguard.

Doug once put his feelings in a poem, written to Avery Brundage, president of the International Olympic Committee, the protector of amateurism:

Deary Avery it's slavery
To train and strain for naught.
I took some dough, now I'm a pro
—what darn fool tommyrot.

To be true-blue with the AAU
I must be Simon-pure.
If Simon knew what I've gone through,
He'd change his tune, I'm sure.

Dear Brundage sir, may I demur,
There's something I must say.
I can't compete with sport's elite
Unless I get some pay.

About this time a big change took place in Doug Hepburn's life. He was living in a flophouse on Hastings Street again, mingling with the bums and the drunks, when he received a call from John Gunn. Gunn was a well-educated, elderly chicken farmer, and Doug used to do odd jobs for him when he was a kid. Gunn wanted him to move in with him—no rent, no work, everything on the

house. "What he did was introduce me to books," says Doug. "He tried to guide me. Those were perhaps my happiest days." Doug threw himself into his reading. He started to grow apart from his old friends who hung around at the gym.

As a member of Canada's team for the 1954 Empire games, Doug was invited to a big dinner in its honor at a Vancouver hotel. He went, alone, with his bag of equipment. "I was always by myself," he says. "I wasn't even one of the athletes. I was somebody else—alone and aloof." But he was a world champion—the only one in the room. "Sure, I was proud of myself," he says, "and I knew where I stood. I didn't want these guys to fall all over me, but I wanted respect. I don't care if a man is president of the largest corporation in the country—if he doesn't respect me, I don't respect him. Not one bit. Here they all were, all these executives at the head table—and some of them were drunk.

"They shouldn't have been drunk. They should have been sober. They should have had more respect for these young athletes. They wouldn't get drunk at one of their board meetings. Then I saw something. They had the young girls—these fine and clean young athletes—doing the can-can or something for them. I was sick. I went into the back where one of the daughters of these men was with her boyfriend. She said, 'Why aren't you out there?' I said, 'I won't go out there under these circumstances. Never. I came here to lift weights. That's all I'm going to do—nothing more.'"

As Doug turned to walk away, he overheard the girl say to her boyfriend, "Big, fat pig."

Naturally, Doug won a gold medal in the Games. But something the public never knew was that he had injured his knee severely six months before. One wrong move, one slip and the muscle would have snapped and he'd have been finished. But, even in victory, he found himself in a controversy again.

He was sitting in the back row of Empire Stadium when his name was called to proceed to the victory podium on the infield. Alexander of Tunis was already there, waiting. "The stadium was packed and I was confused by all the doors and hallways and things. I tried to get

◄ Hepburn won a gold medal at the British Empire Games with this lift in 1954.

there as fast as I could, but it wasn't fast enough. Alexander was waiting, leaning on one of those high jump pits, looking bored. When he pinned the medal on me, he said 'You're quite a man.' I said, 'You're quite a fella yourself.'" Next day the newspapers called Doug, "The Man Who Kept Alexander Waiting." And the next night, at an exhibition in a curling rink in Victoria, people scolded him for it.

* * *

Somebody was always telling Doug Hepburn that there was only one way for him to make money: he had to be a wrestler. His father—who had popped up again in his life—told him. His aunt hold him. His friend John Gunn told him. The country hadn't thought enough of Doug Hepburn to bother sending him to Germany that summer to defend his world championship. And the cheques from the city stopped as soon as the Games were over.

He went to Montreal where a promoter figured he would be a good strongman act to bolster the wrestling shows on his circuit. Doug put on a show in Montreal and made $200. Then he went to North Bay and to Toronto. After his show at Maple Leaf Gardens, wrestling promoter Frank Tunney called him into his office. Tunney was in there with Whipper Billy Watson, his star attraction and partner. They wanted Doug to wrestle and he agreed. He took a room in a nearby hotel.

"It's funny, but something told me it was wrong from the very beginning," says Doug. "I was mad. Mad at Canada for making me do this. I know I could have lifted much more. I could have broken every world record there was." Whipper took Hepburn into a little gym in the basement of the Gardens twice a day for two months to teach him how to wrestle. They worked on the reverse bear hug—a hold where Doug would grab his opponent, lift him in the air like a barbell, turn him over and hug him into submission.

As he wasn't an accomplished wrestler, he was presented as the world's strongest man. But even that was wrong. A weightlifter develops his strength by pushing. A wrestler pulls. Some wrestlers were much stronger in this sense. In his first bout, a semi-final, Doug won—as expected—and soon moved up to main events because of his name. When wrestling in Toronto he earned from $500 to $900 a night, and in smaller towns as little as $35. He averaged three or four bouts a week. He says some of the other wrestlers resented him. They knew they had more skill but that he had moved to the better paying main events because of his name.

You could dismiss Hepburn's one-year wrestling career simply by saying he hated every minute of it. But there was more to it than that.

Things got progressively worse. He would be billed to wrestle and he wouldn't show up. He would be in his hotel room trying to figure things out, unable to get up and go to the arena. The crowd would be waiting, but no Hepburn. "I would be overcome by remorse," he says. "I felt like I was fleeing. The other fellows were down there doing their jobs and I was running away. Yet I had to run away."

Tunney sent him back to Vancouver for a match. As soon as it was over, Doug took off and went out of town, to a little place called Preston Beach. "I wanted to think things out," he says. "I was mixed up really bad. I was throwing this thing away, this fine gift of strength."

That night at Preston Beach, he went into a beer parlor and started to drink heavily. Soon a group of loggers recognized him and joined him. "They were really nice fellas," he says, "and when the beer parlor closed, one of them invited me to his home. I was drunk. We drank more. I went out to the kitchen where his wife was and he introduced me to her. He went out and woke up the kids so they could meet me. They were being so nice to me I just blew up. I broke down and I ran out in the back yard and cried. I really cried.

"This man was so happy. He had his wife and his home and his family. Yet here I was, with all of those muscles, wandering about the world with no place to go. I was trying to be something I wasn't in a world I wanted no part of. Whatever it was I was looking for, it wasn't in wrestling."

The first thing he did when he got back to Toronto was go to the biggest new-car showroom he could find. "I said to myself, 'You're here, you've got money—you need something to make you keep on wrestling. Something to show you it's all been worthwhile. You've always wanted a Cadillac Eldorado, buy it—maybe that'll do it.'" He took a silver one with gold wheels, price $9300, and slapped $4500 down. "It was a symbol," he says. "The world hadn't respected you as a weightlifter, but you showed yourself what you could do with what you had."

One night, driving home from a bout in Buffalo, N.Y., Doug turned to Pat Frayley, another wrestler who was his buddy and his roommate on the road. "I'm quitting," he said. Tunney and Watson tried to talk him out of it, but, as Whipper said: "We pushed him too hard. He got there too fast."

The day Doug walked into Frank Tunney's office and quit, he was in bad shape. "I was drinking to the point where it was no longer in control," he says. "And a psychological situation existed in me similar to battle fatigue."

Tunney and Whipper Billy Watson had $800 coming to them as their share of Doug's earnings, but they handed it to him. "Keep it, Doug," said Tunney. "You're going to need it."

So Hepburn—black moustache, 305 pounds, withered right leg, $800 in his pocket—got into his big silver Cadillac with the gold wheels and pointed it west—to Vancouver.

Had he known, had he only known—he probably would have stayed right where he was.

* * *

Doug Hepburn is 39 now, weighs only 189, and he writes poetry. For only $40 a month he's the tenant at 4650 Hastings Street. People should have kept track of him after his gymnasiums closed. He could have used some help.

"I've known only poverty since I left wrestling," he was saying recently. "Theoretically, I own only the clothes on my back, and the spoon I eat with. They have to leave you that much or you can't live."

He lives alone with a cat named Wizard and an old Husky dog named Boris. He had his usual breakfast that morning—one small slice of Roman Meal bread he makes himself, with cheese, two pieces with honey and a cup of weak tea. He planned to have a small tin of salmon later that night and another piece of Roman Meal bread with honey. That's all. It's about all he has eaten each day for the past two years, which explains how he lost 116 pounds.

Last summer, a man from the income tax department paid him a visit. He looked at the surroundings, knew that Hepburn still owed $2400 in back taxes from his wrestling days and said: "You're a big, strong fella. Why don't you go out and get a job?"

"I must be free," says Hepburn today. "I can't work for anybody else. I have to be the boss. I have to prove to myself that this new Doug Hepburn can make it in the world of business the same way the old Doug Hepburn made it in the world of weightlifting."

Wrestling promoters figured he threw away a million dollars when he left the ring. But he quit, because he hates violence. He says other wrestlers probably considered him a coward. He admits he does not want to hurt other people nor does he want them to hurt him. When he finally did quit wrestling, he says he was sick mentally.

When he pulled into Vancouver in that big, flashy car, his aim was to open a little gymnasium on Commercial Drive. He did. But everyone told him he should have a nicer place. He said, "Why not?" and opened another gym in neighboring New Westminster. Then he opened another one in downtown Vancouver, which was designed for the businessman, and he turned the Commercial Drive establishment into a gym for women. You can dispose of this phase of his life—although it covered two years—by saying simply that he was a lousy businessman, he drank too much and he lost everything.

Finally the gyms closed down, the creditors moved in, and he had already sold his Cadillac for $2500. The only thing he could think of was wrestling. A Vancouver promoter lined him up a bout. "I got excited in that bout," he says. "I got kind of rough. I know now that if I had continued in wrestling I would have gone berserk. If they wanted a man with guts they would have had a madman." His opponent that night told the promoter never to match him with Hepburn again.

Four years before he had been the toast of Europe, the world's strongest man. It was rock bottom now.

His only income was from a mail-order course he sold in bodybuilding. Cheques would arrive from young subscribers and he would pick them up at the post office. "The first day I went in there (the post office) I was wearing a suit," he smiles. "Now I was down to old gum boots and jeans."

He rented an old house on the King George Highway, running south to the U.S. border from Vancouver, and became a regular drinker at the Clover Inn in suburban Cloverdale. "That's where I lost my soul," he says now. Still a well-known figure, he would sit in the beverage room from opening until closing, telling stories about his career while somebody else picked up the tab.

"It got so they asked the same questions over and over," he says. "I used to drink just to get numb so I wouldn't have to think about it." And he could put it away—as much as 50 bottles of beer a day.

Hepburn has always loved Huskies and he tried breeding them out at the old house. But finally he couldn't afford to feed himself, let alone all the dogs—"I guess I must have had about 30 of them"—and they started to die.

An old man walked up to Doug one day in the Clover Inn, introduced himself as Clark Peden and had a drink with him. He was in his sixties, but they felt their philosophies were somewhat similar, so they became close friends.

Peden was a hermit. He lived in an old shack on the Serpentine River, not far from Cloverdale, but away from people. Every once in a while, when he had a few dollars, he would come into town to buy some grub and have a few drinks. Sometimes he would stay overnight with Doug at his old house, sleeping on the floor. Finally, when all the dogs were gone and he couldn't raise the money for rent, Doug packed up his stuff and went to live with Peden.

"He lived there alone in this old shack," he says. "The windows were all boarded up, he had a newspaper for a tablecloth and he read by candlelight. There was an old stove that was falling apart, an outhouse and a rain barrel outside where we got our water. He lived on porridge. When I got there, I got a kerosene lamp, put some window panes in and cooked up some wheat cakes. Not many men could live the way Peden lived. He's tough. They don't make them like that any more."

Looking back on this period, Hepburn says it wasn't so bad. "It gave me something I never would have had—something you have to go through to acquire an understanding of other people. An ability to understand a man who is drunk and sick, a man other people would condemn." He was drunk and sick himself many times out there, sometimes taking two or three days to get over a hangover after a trip to town.

When Hepburn had lived in his old house on the King George Highway, an English couple, Roger Williams and his wife, had lived with him for a while. Now they came to get him and took him to their house. He stayed in the basement, writing a little poetry, trying to sort out his troubled life.

"Finally," he says, "I admitted it. I was walking around in their living room one day and I suddenly realized—you have a problem you don't understand and you need help. I went to the Hollywood Hospital and admitted myself."

Vancouver's Hollywood Hospital is for drunks. It is a place that has had considerable success in alcoholism cases with LSD treatment. They told Doug they wanted him to take it.

He remembers a man named John Holloway who spoke to him the night before. "Doug," he said, "tomorrow you're going to have to do something that will be harder than winning 10 world championships. Because you're going to have to overcome the will that made you a world champion—it has been misdirected and now it is working against you.

A slimmed-down Hepburn with one of his trophies ▶

Tomorrow, under LSD, you are going to have to die. The situation will be presented symbolically."

The next day, an intern handed him a tray with a glass of amber-colored fluid—the LSD—and Doug drank it, saying it tasted like varnish remover. He says the LSD accelerates the mind and all sensual mediums about four times their usual power. "I remember, I could hear something that sounded like a plumber clanking and banging on a pipe. It was the scratching of the needle on a stereo set. That's how it affected my hearing." Then he slipped into another world—the world of LSD.

"You can only *try* to describe it in words," he says. "It's not like a nightmare, it doesn't happen all at once. I was going through a dark valley. I was floating. Coasting down . . . and down . . . and there were caverns. On each side were these caverns and rocks and skulls and bones. You were still floating, going somewhere and you felt as if someone else was talking to you.

"I reached the bottom of this pit, or whatever it was, and I was strapped to the ground, naked, lying on my back. And from the forest or jungle or something, they kept coming—these demons. And they had pitchforks and it was all in technicolor.

"They were staring at me, brandishing their weapons and you knew they were going to cut you to a million pieces. And you're fighting them. You're fighting, and you're fighting. And then, if you have the courage—and I understand only 30 per cent of the people do—you let them do what they came to do. They are standing over you with their swords and pitchforks raised and you let them plunge them into you.

"But they don't. When you give in to them, they turn and run away. The minute you give in, they are afraid of you. I saw the fear transferred to their faces. They came back and tried to scare me again but I just lay there and laughed at them." Doctors explained later that the demons represented the many fears he had built up. By facing them, giving in to them, he had overcome them.

Whatever it was that happened, it worked.

That was in 1963 and Doug hasn't had a bottle of beer since.

After taking LSD, Doug stayed at the Hollywood Hospital for a year, working as a strong-arm orderly. If a drunk was admitted and had an attack of the DTs, it was Doug's job to wrestle him down and hold him while the nurse gave him a shot to calm him down. Doug then would take the patient to a back room they call East Berlin, where all disturbed patients are taken to cool off. This powerful man, once a headliner who was paid as much as $900 a match, had returned to wrestling in a sense—for $50 a month and room and board.

He also started lifting weights again, just for self-satisfaction, and met an old friend, Bill Copeland, a former bodybuilder who once was Mr. British Columbia. Copeland, married with three children, is now a fireman in Burnaby. He wants to help Doug make something of himself and has gone into partnership with him in a barbell and food supplement business.

Hepburn does a lot of singing these days, and his voice, a powerful tenor, would surprise many people. It's still a hobby, but he spends much of his time at Vancouver's Espresso coffee house. They allow people from the audience to go up and sing and Doug goes up as often as they'll let him. It isn't the crowd for his type of singing, though, they want folk songs and he sings such tunes as Oklahoma!

He was asked about his many trophies and medals. "Oh, some of them are up there," he said, pointing to a dusty old shelf. "But that's the one that counts." He gestured toward a cheap, tin cup, about six inches high—worth less than a dollar—that sat on a shelf beside his bed.

"I won it for singing one night in an amateur show in a place down on Hastings Street," he said, taking it down and shining it up. The engraving said: "Shamateur Night Winner."

"Hey, is that what it says, shamateur?" he said. "Geez, I never noticed that before. What an insult."

Upon the shelf, covered with dust and cobwebs, was the Lou Marsh Trophy, presented annually to Canada's best athlete—amateur or professional, male or female. Any man in the country would be proud to own it. Doug, who shrugged and said he wasn't sure what that one was for, won it in 1954.

He figures he still owes about $8000, including back taxes. If he ever gets clear of debt, his dream is a home, paid for, that will allow him to be away from the world while still part of it, with freedom to think. One room he visualizes would be a bedroom-sitting room-library-solarium.

There would be a glass roof so he could go to sleep at night watching the stars. It would be beside the sea, so he could watch the waves roll in. And in the winter he could lie in the sun. "It would be as if the world was in a glass bottle and I was just sitting there looking at it," he says.

And what about a woman to share it with? "Naturally, every man wants a woman," he says. "But for me she would have to be a very unusual woman. People have no conception of how a man can live as I live, alone, and exist with only the freedom of his mind. To me, the freedom of my mind, the freedom to be what I want to be and do what I want to do—that means more to me than any woman. Women, generally, do not want my kind of man. They want the man to become involved. Thinking is the greatest pleasure. Thinking is beyond sex."

He doubts if he ever again will go into a gymnasium. If someone walked in tomorrow and offered to buy him one outright, no strings, he would turn it down.

"I know it might sound strange—living as I have lived, looking as I look—but I really believe I can make it in business. I'm convinced that somewhere, somehow, I'm going to do something else. I don't know what it is, but I have to nurture it, I have to let it bud."

His plan, if he ever makes big money, is to make a presentation to the City of Vancouver. "I always thought maybe I'd have a monument made—a bronze statue of myself, life-size, holding the world record over my head. But hell," he smiled, "they wouldn't get a chance to use it. You see, I'm contemplating immortality. I feel too good—I don't think I'll ever die." ●

epilogue It was thirteen years later and now the long distance operator said she had no listing for a Douglas or D. Hepburn in Vancouver.

"However," she said, "there is a number for Douglas Hepburn's Village International Health Products Limited."

"That," I told her, "has got to be him."

It was late at night but, if he was the Doug Hepburn I knew, he would be living and sleeping on a cot in his place of business.

"Hello," said the familiar voice.

"That's a fancy title you've given your business," I said.

"Yeah, I started getting tongue-tied trying to say it every time I answered the phone," he said, "Now I just say: 'Hepburn's!'"

He sounded great—relaxed and happy—and there was the sound of machinery in the background.

"I've got my own machine shop now," he said. "A lathe, power drills, and even a machinist. Yeah, I sleep right here. I never was one for big, fancy houses."

After all these years, he is still trying to invent the perfect exercise machine, this time with the entire mechanism encased in a tube, and his machinist is assisting him.

"Maybe nothing will come of it," he laughed, remembering failed business ventures of the past, "but, I'm enjoying myself trying."

He briefed me on his last thirteen years, how he returned to the gym, started lifting again at age 50, built his body back up from 189 to 278 pounds and, at 51, broke yet another world record.

"I looked it up," he said. "The world record for the bench press for senior Olympians was 335 pounds and I lifted 445. And I did 175 pounds with the one-arm military press. The media here still doesn't know anything about lifting. One guy wrote that it was like breaking the world record for the 98-yard dash."

Instead of the old frustrations, Doug seems able to laugh at his foibles now. He has since returned to 189 pounds, has quit smoking, drinking coffee, and has been living on fruit and vegetables.

"What about this new-found wealth and the health products.?" I asked.

"I have them made to my specifications and they're sold in health food stores across the country," he said.

It was Mike Poppelle, the bodybuilder he had first tried to emulate years ago who gave him a loan to get started.

"I've had a couple of setbacks since I saw you," Doug said. "You know, similar to when I was a hermit living in that cabin in the woods. I just felt I had tried everything I could to be successful and had failed and then Mike told me: 'Doug, you know, everything going through your head is flyshit. It can't solve anything. You'll have to solve them externally. Work from the outside to the inside.'" Whatever that means. . . .

Doug started his machine shop and says he now has about $70 000 worth of equipment. He also drives a Lincoln.

"For the first time in my life," he says, "I have enough money to explore the various facets of myself. Now I can weld and I build entire gymnasiums. And I'm still the same guy you met who was living in that dump on Hastings St.—still looking for some kind of a pot at the end of the rainbow."

Hepburn says he's still a rebel, still cut from another mold and that he continues to experiment with his body.

"I still won't accept the possibility of aging," he says, "or even dying at a specific age or time. Do you know why we die? Because the body doesn't know how to do anything else."

And, just before I got the impression that Doug Hepburn, the most unusual man I have ever met, had changed completely, he said, "Excuse me for a minute, okay. My machinist is just leaving."

Then I heard him say quietly in the background: "Say Harry, can I pay ya tomorrow or the next time I see you?"

Doug Hepburn's rather unusual story, I suspect, is not over yet.

An Odyssey: Rimstead on the Loose

I WAS A DISASTER on the road.

I drove editors, business managers, and comptrollers crazy. The mere mention of my name in a business office would make grown men weep. Others threw their hands up in the air. Some snapped pencils in two . . . .

There was a constant battle over expense accounts. It wasn't that I spent too much, although that did happen regularly, but that I would sometimes wait a year before filing my expenses. And then, at best, it would be a sketchy account without receipts. But, expense accounts were not nearly as troublesome as the actual travelling.

My problem was that I never learned how to travel. If a story was to take three days, it took me five. One-week assignments lasted ten days, two-week jobs could last a month. I missed planes, trains and buses, forgot what hotel I was supposed to be staying in and, once, wound up in the wrong city.

In those days, I carried Diner's Club, Carte Blanche, and American Express credit cards. One month, my three bills totalled more than $10 000 but I could only charge the magazine $3500. As I fell further behind each month, there was a race among my creditors to see who could garnishee my wages first. Needless to say, I am not allowed to have any of those cards today.

The main problem, I guess, was that I would sometimes forget what I was supposed to be doing on an assignment and get involved in other things. These, uh, other things usually began late at night, one foot up on the brass rail of a bar when, suddenly, I would turn and say: "Why not!" I would have saved myself a lot of grief had I gone to bed earlier. But, hell, I wouldn't have had nearly as much fun.

Once I spent three days with Gump Worsley in Montreal, fourteen hours at one stretch, and then still had to call him, when I got back home, to do the interview. But it wasn't all my fault. I flew into Montreal on a Friday night to watch Worsley play goal in a Montreal Canadiens' exhibition game, and to set up an interview for the following day.

This was during training camp and on the Saturday morning, after the Canadiens' workout, I approached the irascible Gumper.

"Not today, okay?" he said. "How about tomorrow afternoon?"

"Sure," I said, as we walked down the street together, away from The Forum.

"Feel like a cold beer?" Gump asked. "C'mon into my favorite little bar here, but no talking about business, okay?"

Actually, neither of us drank beer. A few years before, when Coach Phil Watson called Gump "a beerbelly" while they were both with the New York Rangers, the rotund Gumper retorted: "Watson doesn't know what he's talking about. Hell, I don't drink beer. I drink whisky!"

We sat at that little bar from noon until about 3 a.m., laughing, talking, drinking whisky and playing darts. The next day, both of us were too tired to do the interview. Gump slept in the afternoon after practice and then shut out the Detroit Red Wings that night. I had to go back to Toronto Monday morning and, as I flew home, I realized I didn't have a solitary quote from Gump that was fit to print. I had to call him a week later and interview him over the phone. It was not one of my deeper stories.

Sometimes I almost got in trouble, like the night in 1969 in West Palm Beach, Florida, at the Montreal Expos' first training camp. I went out to play pool with Maury Wills after we had spent the day talking. The great shortstop and legendary base-stealer had really levelled with me. Those were especially racially-tense days, the time of ghetto burnings, and Maury, who is a very light-skinned black, told me about his own situation—how he wasn't accepted by whites and, because of his color, not really accepted by blacks either. Anyway, the talk got around to pool.

"You would be no challenge for me," I boasted.

"You wouldn't stand a chance," he replied.

Our interview was over. We hopped into a cab and decided to settle the issue on a pool table in a bar. We started our game, ordered a couple of drinks and, while Maury was shooting, the owner called me aside.

"I can serve you," he said quietly. "But I can't serve your friend."

I was so dumb I didn't know what he was talking about until Maury, after I told him, placed his cue back in the rack and said, "Let's go."

I was livid after he had explained the facts of life to me in the parking lot. He had been turned down because he was black!

"Don't worry about it," he smiled. "It's something we've got to live with. What could we do if we went back in there?"

He didn't like it, but, no matter how hard he complained, he knew he couldn't change the attitude of a redneck. We found a second joint, and there was no pool table but, a large, U-shaped bar. We sat on two stools, ordered drinks from the gum-chewing barmaid and she delivered them without question. I noticed the manager call her aside. She returned, stood in front of us and, looking directly at me, said: "Uh, yore friend is Puerto Rican, ain't he?"

"No, he isn't," I said coldly.

"Oh, I'm sorry," she said, right in front of Wills. "I was shure he was a Puerto Rican."

She took his drink away. I was dumbfounded. It was my first actual confrontation with blatant discrimination, and I was really only a bystander. Wills displayed remarkable composure, even though he is, by nature, a rather volatile guy on and off a baseball diamond. He shrugged. The people weren't worth getting all worked up over.

"I'll pick the bar this time," he smiled.

We took a cab into the heart of West Palm Beach's black community, and went into a bar that was jammed. I was the only white, another experience that helped me realize how a single black must sometimes feel. I sat there like a lighted bulb. But, not one person looked at me sideways. I was treated with so much more respect than Wills had been by my people. We closed the place and, when we returned to the hotel, told a few other writers what had happened.

The next day, the story was carried by Associated Press and appeared on every sports page in North America. It described how Maury Wills, one of the biggest names in baseball, had been refused service twice on the same night in West Palm Beach, Florida. When the story broke, the management of the Expos and the Atlanta Braves, who shared the West Palm Beach training facilities, demanded an official apology, threatening a change of site the next season.

I really got to know and like Maury Wills and, because I was travelling with the team on that first road trip of the season, we spent a couple other evenings together. One night in Chicago, we went to a banjo bar and Wills joined the entertainers on stage. He is one helluva banjo player.

Naturally, after our encounter in Florida, we often discussed the race problem and the quota in sports, which allowed only so many blacks per team. Maury laughed, recalling one night in Pittsburgh, when he played for the Pirates. The manager, making up the lineup for that night's game, made major league history by mistake. When the players ran out to their starting positions, chuckling to themselves, it was suddenly apparent that, for the first time ever, all nine starters were black.

"We couldn't have lost that night," smiled Wills. "And, as far as I know, it never happened again."

The Expos finally headed for Montreal and their home opener after the road trip and, because it was a significant event—the first major league game ever played in Canada—my boss Denny Harvey was in Montreal to go to the game.

We had dinner the night before, went out for a few drinks and, at about 1 a.m., Denny decided to call it a night. I hated sleep in those days. I was always afraid that if I slept, I'd miss something. Instead, I made my way to Slim's, a notorious after-hours hangout for the night people. It wasn't listed in the yellow pages. In some cities, they call them booze cans. The Montreal term is a blind pig.

Slim's was an ordinary apartment in a building with walk-up steps from the street that was operated, obviously, by a guy named Slim. You had to be known by the management to be allowed inside seeing as how it was not really a licensed place. Slim didn't open until the regular bars closed and his clientele included guys and girls who worked in the bars, a few criminals, and a handful of neighborhood hookers.

A German barmaid took me there the first time, vouching for me at the door, in appreciation for getting an autographed hockey stick for her young son. I cultivated my relationship with Slim, a tall, jolly kind of guy, so that I would be able to go there by myself when I was thirsty. I seemed to be thirsty every time I was in Montreal.

Slim ran a respectable place and kept things in order with a heavy crowbar which hung on a spike next to the door. Actually, it was just a tobacco-stained, drink-spilled bootleg joint. There were plain chairs, little tables, an old sofa, and a stuffed chair in the living room-dining room area. The select circle sat on a couch in the kitchen, which also served as the bar. This meant you could sit there and joke with Slim, who was a great storyteller. I remember meeting Preacher Red in there, a character who, one night in the infamous Chez Paris, performed a mock wedding for one of the strippers and her slow-witted boyfriend who was in the audience. They went off on their honeymoon, certain they were married and have not been seen since. The appreciative groom paid Preacher twenty bucks and The Preacher, his collar still turned around, used it to buy the next round of drinks after the honeymooners had left.

I was always alone, so Slim would invite me into the kitchen and we would talk and drink until sunrise, although you never knew when that was. Slim's establishment reminded me of Las Vegas, where there are no windows, no clocks, and you never know what time it is. On this particular night, I was in a rather jovial mood, went straight into the kitchen at Slim's and was soon joined by a sad-faced woman, her head covered with a bandana, who introduced herself as Shirley.

"Goddammit, what a lousy night," she said, throwing her coat over the back of a chair to reveal a rumpled sweater covered with matted little wool balls. From her excessive makeup and general disposition, I pegged her for a stripper, hooker, or both.

"Hey Shirley," Slim grinned. "How goes it?"

"Shitty, Slim," she said, throwing back a cognac.

And then Shirley told us this very sad story. She was, indeed, a hooker and had had a very special appointment at a downtown hotel at 1:30 a.m. with a generous, out-of-town businessman. Shirley, it seems, had returned to her apartment after her evening engagements to put on a special dress and to freshen up a little.

"I sat there, watchin' the goddamned TV," she said. "And damned if I didn't fall asleep and miss my best trick of the week."

"Did you call him?" Slim asked.

"The bastard got somebody else," said Shirley.

We allowed as how this was a very sad story indeed and, to try and cheer her up, I started calling her Shirley the Sleepy-Headed Hooker. She had a great sense of humor that kept getting sharper with every cognac and we were having a great time in the kitchen when there was a loud knock on the front door.

Slim, one hand free in case he needed the crowbar, opened it cautiously because it was so late and I watched from the kitchen as a rather hard-looking guy grunted hello, entered and walked towards the kitchen. I could tell by the look on Slim's face that this was a rather special customer. Another guy, wearing a cast on his foot, had wandered in from the living room area and plunked himself down in the kitchen. The new arrival, Slim following him, looked at the guy coldly and said: "Get the hell out of here!"

The guy with the cast left hurriedly and Slim looked nervous. The new guy looked squarely at me, and Slim blurted: "He's okay, Billy. He's a friend of mine from Toronto. A sportswriter."

"Hi Billy," said Shirley.

"Hello Shirl," he said, not looking at me as he took the place of honor at the end of the kitchen.

"I am Shirley the Sleepy-Headed Hooker, if you please," Shirley smiled, one hand to her head, as if posing for a photographer. "This is my buddy here from Toronto and that's what he calls me."

We told Billy her sad story, he grinned, and sipped quietly on his drink.

"Who d'ya write for?" he suddenly demanded of me.

I told him and, suddenly, the tension eased, we all relaxed and had another round of drinks. It wasn't until hours later, after he left, that I learned that Billy was one of Montreal's best-known strongarm guys who had done several stretches for armed robbery and whose name was known to every rounder in town. I had even heard of him back in Toronto.

I have never cared how a guy made his living as long as he didn't bother me and that night at Slim's was one of the most enjoyable I ever spent. Shirley the Sleepy-Headed Hooker, Slim, and Billy were super company. We liked one another and just talked and laughed the night away. When I finally emerged from Slim's, I had to shade my eyes from the sun and, still blinking, hailed a cab to find that it was 11:30 in the morning, less than two hours from the opening ceremonies at little Jarry Park.

Denny Harvey and our art director, Ken Rodmell, had already left for the ballpark when I got back to the hotel. I quickly showered, changed clothes, and left for the game in heavy noon traffic. I had no idea what seats they had and didn't see them anywhere at the park. I went down to the dressing rooms after the game and then caught a cab back to the hotel, yawning and rather fatigued after my long night. I fell asleep in the front passenger seat and was rudely awakened when, to avoid an accident, the cabbie had to jam on his brakes. Still asleep, I was flung forward and woke up when my head hit the open door of the glove compartment.

"Sorry," he said.

"No problem," I muttered, rubbing a lump on my scalp.

Harvey and Rodmell were having a drink in their room when I walked in. They both looked at me with what may have been mild disgust. I must have been quite a sight. My clothes were rumpled, I smelled like a brewery and, unknown to me, blood was trickling down my forehead and temples. My head had been cut and I still have a scar today.

In a situation like that how do you explain that you just had a wonderful time and you weren't really a hopeless drunk? Fortunately, Harvey just shrugged and told me to join them for dinner if I wished. I have always liked the guy. He didn't care how you did your job as long as you produced. He knew he would get his story. I must admit, however, that I was slightly embarrassed, especially when I had invited both of them to come to the Expos' game and hadn't been much of a host. I should explain that both of them could match me drink for drink when the occasion arose. However, they had more common sense.

A few months later, a well-known professional athlete with connections in Montreal called me aside.

"Rimmer," he said, "do you have any idea who you're hanging out with in Montreal? I've heard a few stories. You'd better be careful, buddy."

Frankly, I have never worried about the places I sometimes wound up at late at nights. I can list the after-hours clubs from coast-to-coast, starting with The Penthouse in Vancouver and finishing at The Coliseum in Boston. If you mind your own business, people are people, no matter what their suspected professions. I've known bookmakers, gamblers, hookers, drug pushers, and even a professional hit-man. We didn't talk about their jobs. I always felt that there, but for the grace of God . . . .

The hit-man's specialty was exploding cars but, when business was slow, he wasn't above breaking a few arms or legs just to keep food on the table. His friends were respectable people who felt he was some sort of salesman because all his business was conducted out of town. We only discussed his particular talents once, when a guy was harassing me about something I had written and the hit-man, out of friendship, offered his services free of charge. I hastily declined, of course, but, I didn't throw away his phone number.

Another guy who was my house guest in Toronto for three months was a painter I had met in Mexico, an Italian fellow I called Torpedo Sam. One night, when we were both reflective and in our cups, he admitted that he had been connected with the mob in New York, and imported pot from Mexico, but only because a relative was involved. He said he was straight now and, for self protection, had filed everything he knew with the CIA to be opened in the event of his breathing suddenly being stopped. A copy was sent to the other side. He said he had been left alone since then, but he wasn't ever sure for how much longer.

Even though he was a quiet and sincere guy, I didn't really believe his story—not until I took him to Woodbine Racetrack in Toronto one afternoon and two guys I recognized from the Buffalo family recognized him, followed him to the men's washroom, and offered him employment if he wished to stay in the area. Torpedo Sam politely turned down the offer and promptly left town the next morning in his big Lincoln Continental. I have not seen him since but he did send me a postcard one day.

My social directors, while travelling, were the cabbies, the guys who know their city even better than the mayor. If you wanted to know about after-hours places, the cab driver could take you to them. A well-placed tip will get you the best seat at a theater or, in my case, another drink after the bars have closed. I often wondered how much money is spent in a year by guys looking for hookers. The cabbie takes a fat tip, makes the connection, and then also takes a cut from the girl.

It was through a cabbie I first found The Coliseum in Boston, an upstairs joint that, although illegal, was quite fancy inside and catered to politicians and other influential people.

"This is the place," the cabbie said that night, "but, I don't think you'll get in without knowing somebody. They call the guy who runs it Canada Joe."

"Wait for me while I try," I said.

A rough-looking guy answered the door and asked me what I wanted.

"Is Canada Joe in?" I asked.

Canada Joe appeared and I took out my press card, told him I was a travelling sportswriter with a thirst, and had been told about his place by a well-known hockey coach who had said to say hello. Canada Joe squinted at me and, not wanting to admit that he had never met the coach I mentioned, motioned me in with a nod of his head.

I went out to pay my cabbie and, as I opened the door, he said "No luck, huh?"

"No problem at all," I smiled. "I'm in."

"Geez, you must have a good line," he said.

"I am an expert," I told him, "in two areas: Getting into debt and getting another drink."

I kept mentioning the hockey coach's name every time I went to The Coliseum and it always worked, despite the fact the coach had never heard of the place and Canada Joe had never met the coach. He knew I was lying, of course, but liked to have his doorman think that he was a bigshot. And, he always remembered me.

One morning, about 4 a.m., I was sitting there at a tiny table, almost shoulder-to-shoulder with a lady wearing a big hat at the table next to me. She was sitting with a man much younger than herself and seemed to be rather tipsy, slurring her words when she spoke.

"You're all alone," she said to me. "Why don't you join us for a drink?"

"Thanks," I said. "But, actually, I was just about to leave."

It was Judy Garland, less than a year before her tragic death.

Considering the problems I had travelling in North America, I was quite surprised when *The Canadian* agreed to send me to Europe for the first time. One of the stories was to be about the Canadian four-man bobsled team, which, under Vic Emery, had won an Olympic gold medal in 1964. This was one year prior to the 1968 Olympics at the world bobsled championships which were to take place at Alpe d'Huez, the proposed Olympic site about forty-five kilometres from Grenoble, France.

I stopped in Paris, full of myself and Hemingway, gawked at the Eiffel Tower, the Arc de Triomphe and sat sipping cognac in a sidewalk cafe on the Champs-Elysée. Frankly, I did not even like cognac, but that's what Hemingway drank. Fortunately, I fumbled with French well enough to find an all-night bar. It was a sleazy joint that was crawling with B-girls and the clattering of their false eyelashes sounded like applause. I perched on a bar stool to watch the show and ordered a small drink, pleasantly turning down the offers of female companionship. The B-girl works for the house, orders a bottle of expensive champagne, gets a commission on her sales and, when her duties are over in the bar, is allowed to negotiate for other attentions for the rest of the night.

A young man sitting next to me did not share my reservations. He had five girls and five bottles of champagne on the go at one time and seemed to be really enjoying himself. He was in his early twenties, spoke English, and kept asking me to join him. He was, he said, from Iceland and in Paris on his honeymoon. His new bride had fallen asleep at the hotel and he had slipped out for a cocktail. When I left, he was drunk and arguing over his bar bill of $851. I wondered how long his new marriage was going to last.

I flew to Lyons the next day and took the picturesque train ride north to Grenoble. I had a reservation at the Hotel Park, the best hotel in town and, after I checked in, I bought a magnum of champagne, took it up to my room on the fifth floor, opened the window, and placed it carefully on the outside ledge to keep it cold. Then I went out to discover the town. There was a message for me saying that a French policeman would pick me up in a lorry at 2 a.m. the next day to take me to Alpe d'Huez. Apparently, the sun was so warm up there that they were holding the bobsled races at 5 a.m., while the ice was still hard.

I hailed a cab and the driver took me to a little place about twenty minutes away. I spent about seven hours there, drinking champagne and trying to talk to my French drinking companions. It was a nice place with a continuous strip show, a lot more racy than I had seen before, but still a strip show. I have never liked strip acts and am of the old school that thinks a woman is far more sexy with her clothes on. Frankly, I have never liked champagne either because it makes me burp. But, while in France . . . .

I finally reeled out of the place at about 3:30 a.m. and there wasn't a soul on the streets. Also, there was absolutely no sign of a taxi. What to do? The bar had locked its doors, there were no phones, and I couldn't speak French. My feet were the only available form of transportation and so I started walking, rather unsteadily and not even knowing which direction to go. I headed down narrow streets with high walls along the sides and I couldn't see anything resembling a downtown area. I walked, and walked, and walked . . . .

After about an hour, I realized I had to do something smart or I would freeze to death before finding my hotel. I know—I'll borrow one of those bicycles outside of that apartment building, write down the name of this corner, find my hotel, phone a cab, and then return the bicycle to its rightful place. I would get the hotel night clerk to write a note and I would leave it with the bicycle along with a few francs. I approached the bicycles in the parking lot, selected one and wheeled it unsteadily to the street. Let's see, you put one foot on a pedal, push down, and then throw your other leg over the seat . . . .

It had been years since I had ridden a bike. Also, the champagne was still with me. I gave it the big push . . . BANG, CRASH, CLATTER! The noise was thunderous in the quiet night as the bike and I hit the cobblestone street. Lights started clicking on in the apartments. Shutters started opening. I started running. All I could think of was the headlines back home: "Canadian Journalist Arrested for Stealing Bicycle in France!" There would never be time to explain, especially in French.

I have never moved so quickly. I ran down the street, my heart pumping wildly, turned the corner and—Eureka!—there was my Hotel Park!

I stumbled breathlessly into the lobby and asked for my room key. When I said the room number, the room clerk started muttering at me in French, waving his arms and, obviously, very upset with me about something. Later I learned that I had almost killed some people that afternoon at a bus stop right underneath my window. The maid had gone into my room to prepare it for the night which included closing the wooden window shutters. The shutter knocked my magnum of champagne off the window ledge and it had dropped like a bomb, exploding on the sidewalk below, just missing the people.

I promised not to put champagne on my window ledge again and went out the next day to buy some warm boots, gloves, long underwear, and a hat for that night's trip to Alpe d'Huez. The policeman showed up at 2:30 a.m. and I climbed into the lorry's back seat beside a fat guy who only grunted something and then turned to stare out of the window. I guessed he was a television cameraman from Germany because of his accent and equipment. We rode along in the dark, not speaking. The French driver, the German, and I spoke only our native languages.

When we started up the treacherous mountain road to the ski resort, it scared the hell right out of me. At the bottom of the mountain was a junk yard, filled with the rusted skeletons of cars that had fallen off the mountain. This was before they had improved the road for the Olympics. There were no guard rails. We finally got to the top and I swore I would not make that trip up and down every day for the rest of the week. I would sleep on a bench up there, if necessary, until the championships were over.

When we finally reached the top, everything was in darkness. Nobody was there. The driver motioned us to get out and, when we did, he pulled away, back to Grenoble. The German cameraman had a large camera over his shoulder and was not dressed at all for the weather. It was bitterly cold and windy. The German had on an overcoat, shirt and tie, a pair of street shoes without toe rubbers, and no hat or gloves.

We stood stupidly in the dark, motioning to one another, shrugging our shoulders, and tried the locked doors of the little building that was there. Finally, we both decided we were obviously in the wrong place or the races had been cancelled. The bobsled run, icy and shining in the moonlight, stretched down ahead of us like a large snake. We could see no lights below, no sign, even, of the town. I motioned towards the run and the German grunted. We started walking through the deep powdery snow on opposite sides of the run. I kept thinking about those little shoes the fat guy was wearing and how cold his feet must be. His hands were red from carrying the cold, steel camera. We slogged along, downward in the dark. Suddenly I yeard a yell and then muffled cries that sounded like German profanities. I looked over and the poor guy had disappeared. He had stepped into a hole beside the course that snow had drifted over. It was one of the vantage points built to protect officials and the media so they could look over the edge, onto the course.

I carefully climbed down onto the icy runway and, when I couldn't climb up the other side to get to him, had to walk all the way back to the top and down the other side.

When I finally reached him, I was certain that the German's utterances were profane. The poor guy was up to his neck in snow, holding his camera high above him. I took the camera and then, puffing and slipping, finally pulled him out. He had snow in his ears, down his shirt, up his sleeves and pant legs and looked as if he wanted to quit his job on the spot. Mind you, we still didn't know where that spot was. Our only hope of getting back to town was to follow that bobsled run down.

I pointed to the icy run, suggesting we try it so that he wouldn't fall into any more holes. The German slid over the side carefully, his leather soles treacherous on the ice. I was lucky. The apres-ski boots I had bought in Grenoble had heavy crepe soles and they gripped the ice solidly.

We started down in the dark, me far ahead, my friend slipping and sliding behind me. Suddenly I heard another noise, a scraping sound and turned to see his television camera rounding the bend, high on the wall, speeding past me and down the course. Next, I saw him coming in the dark, spinning like a pinwheel as he slid down the ice on his back. I tried to get a piece of him as he sailed past but couldn't hold him.

I ran around the next turn, into the sudden blare of lights, just in time to see my German friend crash into two Austrian bobsledders who were getting ready to push their sled into a start from the grid. He bowled them over as a startled crowd blinked in disbelief.

What we hadn't known was that the top of the bobsled run was so treacherous the races had to start from the three-quarter point, which is where we were now. We hadn't been able to see the bobsledders, not even their lights, because of the high walls of the run which acted like a topless tunnel.

The television camera, apparently, missed everything and continued its way merrily down the bobsled run, the only fatality of that year's championships. My friend had skinned his hands and forehead on the ragged ice and had torn the knees from his pant-legs. He was helped, grumbling, off to the sidelines and into a car back to town. I never saw him again. I have often wondered how he told the story when he got home to Germany. Meanwhile, I eagerly gulped the cup of hot chocolate someone gave me and tried to explain what had happened. Eventually, order was restored and the races resumed.

For the rest of the bobsled competition I stayed in a little hotel right in Alpe d'Huez. When I got back to Grenoble, I quickly checked out of the Hotel Park, where I had slept only once in ten days, and caught the train back to Lyons. My plan was to fly from Lyons to Nice that evening, spend the night in Nice and then fly to Rome, where I would start working on my next story.

I had been up since 5 a.m. and when I got to the Lyons airport I was starting to doze off in the taxi. Then I discovered there were no flights to Nice until the next day.

Dammit—who wanted to waste a night in Lyons? I had hoped to include Nice and the Riviera in my sightseeing and now I'd have to fly directly to Rome the next day, seeing only the Nice airport.

I grumbled to the taxi driver that I wanted to go to the best hotel in town and he pulled up in front of an old place called the Hotel Royale. "Your best room," I said to the desk clerk. A little, old man, bent and shuffling along ahead of me with my bags, led me to an old elevator and then along a spacious hall upstairs to my quarters.

Well sir, I still have never seen another hotel suite like it—huge, ornate, and the walls were a rich mahogany. The large bathroom had a sunken tub in the floor that was the size of a tiny swimming pool. I was flabbergasted. There was even an expensive stereo unit built into the wall and there was a stack of records, from classical to jazz. I just shook my head in disbelief and then realized there was no bed.

"Aah, m'sseur," said the little man, pointing to the wall and pushing a button. Suddenly a bed folded down, completely made up. There were six of them in the room, three down one side and three down the other.

I felt more awake after freshening up and then left the hotel that evening to look for a restaurant to have dinner. I was growing tired of French menus, not knowing what I was ordering and dreaming of something simple like a good, old hamburger. Suddenly, as I walked up the street, I saw a little sign that said: Pizza. Well, I knew what pizza was and that was fine with me.

It wasn't a very large restaurant, more like a cafeteria back home with tables and chairs placed close together on an open floor. I slipped onto a chair at a table next to a round, little guy, ordered a pizza and a bottle of wine, and was almost dozing off when the waiter spoke to me.

"Excuse me sir, but where are you from?" he asked in English.

"Canada," I told him.

"Ah, this gentleman was right," he said, pointing to my neighbor. "He is the owner of the restaurant and would like to buy you a drink."

For the next half hour or so, the owner and I tried conversing, using the waiter as an interpreter. This was the year of Expo in Montreal and the man said he was going to make his first trip to Canada to see it. He must have thought Toronto was very close to Montreal because he insisted on getting my address and telephone number so that we could meet for lunch.

"He likes you very much," the waiter said as the owner got up to go, "and he thanks you for your information about Canada. He asks if you would like to join him, please, for an after-dinner drink downstairs."

"Downstairs? What is downstairs?" I asked.

"His nightclub," said the waiter.

I followed the little owner down the stairs into a cave-like club in the cellar, complete with a band, a long bar, and filled with drinkers and dancers. He moved to the bar, motioned to the bartender, and suddenly a bottle of very expensive Napoleon brandy appeared. But, we had lost our interpreter and all I could say was "merci."

The owner called to an attractive woman with long blonde hair, she joined us and then, in English, she said to me: "He would like me to join you for a drink to overcome the language difficulty."

That was okay with me. I think we finished that expensive bottle of brandy and had started on another when the little owner shook my hand vigorously and said goodnight. The bar was about to close. The bartender, meanwhile, was wrapping three magnums of champagne in newspaper and placed them on the bar in front of me. Oh, oh—the crunch. My bill would be about $300.

"No thanks, I didn't order that," I said quickly.

"Oh, but there is no charge," the girl said. "It is for us, for you and me. The owner would like us to have it."

"But . . . " I protested.

"You are staying at the Hotel Royale, non?"

It was all very confusing. Why me? But, hell, I had that fantastic suite and, at this stage wouldn't have time to sleep before my early flight anyway.

"But," I said, "the bartender should come with us."

She pouted. He smiled.

The three of us staggered up the street, each with a magnum of champagne under an arm, heading for the Hotel Royale, and singing some French tune I didn't know. They absolutely loved my suite. Heck, there were even champagne glasses on the bar. The first magnum popped and the girl started to giggle. The bartender had been drinking all evening, too.

I stood, rather stupidly, and wondered what I had gotten myself into this time. The girl went into the bathroom and, when she returned, started unbuttoning her blouse. The bartender started taking off his shirt. I cleared my throat. The next thing I knew, she stood there in her bra and panties and he was in his undershorts.

"Ooo, it ees warm . . . " she said.

"Wait!" I cried. "I'll turn down the heat!"

I heard water running and went into the bathroom. My sunken bathtub was overflowing. I had no idea how to turn the water off. I had never seen that kind of a tap before.

"We will sweem," cooed the lady, who now, along with the bartender, was stark naked. "Please, Canadian, take off your clothes."

"No, no, no!" I said. "I am not warm. I can't swim. How in the hell do we shut this water off?"

My two guests walked down into the tub and stood there, giggling, up to their thighs in the huge tub, champagne glasses in their hands. The water was running all over the place. It had now run out of the bathroom and was soaking the carpet in the suite.

"Please!" I yelped. "The water!"

They fumbled with the tap, fell into the tub, broke both champagne glasses on the tile floor and, finally, the water sputtered to a stop. They climbed from the tub, laughing uproariously and the bartender slapped her bare behind. They went into the suite, dripping wet, while I tried mopping up the lake of water with bath towels. I heard another magnum pop inside and then heard a thumping noise and squealing.

The sight that greeted my eyes! They had all six beds down from the wall and were bouncing from one to the other, as if on a trampoline, and she was chasing him, shaking up the magnum of champagne and squirting it at his behind. There were streaks of wet champagne all over those carved, mahogany walls, champagne all over the desk, the stereo set, the beds . . . .

She saw me, squealed again, and let me have it, champagne all over my face, jacket, shirt, trousers. They had both gone bonkers! I was dripping with sweet, sticky champagne and I had left my bags in a locker at the airport. I had no other clothes and would have to catch my flight in about ninety minutes. She squirted me on my back, gave an oil painting a shot for good measure, and the bartender tripped, fell off the bed, and hit his head against the wall.

What to do? What to do? Get the hell out, that's what! Fortunately, I didn't have to pack. I grabbed my one small bag, threw my razor and toothbrush into it and tried to wipe my face off with one of the wet towels on the floor. I tried to comb my hair, stiff with champagne, and looked like a 1950s greaser. Thank God I had a dry overcoat . . . .

"Au revoir!" I shouted as I left. They seemed very surprised. I have no idea how long they stayed or what happened next. The magnificent suite was a complete shambles. I put on dark glasses, told the room clerk I was in a terrible hurry, paid my bill, and jumped into a cab.

My wet clothes were practically frozen to me as I walked from the cab to the Lyons airport and you can imagine how I smelled in the plane. Nothing can compare with the smell of old champagne. My God, but I was a mess when I arrived in Nice for a two-hour wait between flights. I sat at the bar and, after several attempts in both English and French, finally convinced the bartender that what I wanted was a cold beer, an empty glass, and a glass of tomato juice on the side. The French, it seems, had never seen a red-eye before. They nudged one another as I mixed the beer and tomato juice and drank it. Maybe it wasn't that at all. Maybe they were pointing out the guy who smelled so bad.

The next plane got me to Rome. My clothes had dried and were sticking to me, my pant legs were like two wrinkled stovepipes. My hair was something to behold, practically cemented in place. I had to go through customs and immigration that way, shuffling along in long lineups. Then I had to go to the currency exchange and buy lira with my dollars and francs. I just couldn't understand how to convert it.

I was like a dead man when my cab arrived at the downtown Bernini Bristol Hotel. The only bright note was the friendly taxi driver who couldn't seem to do enough for me. He carried my bags to the registration desk (where they looked at me with alarm) and even offered to carry them to my room. When I got upstairs, I realized why he had been so willing. By mistake I had tipped him $50 instead of $5. It was about noon. I climbed into a hot tub, and, finally, crawled into bed.

I felt absolutely terrible the next morning. My stomach was grumbling, I had severe cramps, and an advanced case of what Mexicans call Montezuma's Revenge. This, however, was a terribly explosive strain of diarrhea the likes of which I had never experienced before. Obviously a reminder of my social evening in Lyons. I was in the bathroom for four hours.

When it had finally passed, I dressed slowly and prepared to see Rome for the first time. I especially wanted to go to The Vatican and St. Peter's Square. It was even more magnificent than I had imagined. I was still hung over from Lyons, weakened by my condition, but I tried to see it all.

And then it happened, one of the most embarrassing situtions of my life. I was standing smack dab in the middle of St. Peter's Square when the cramp hit me. I froze. I couldn't move. Remember, I said it was an explosive strain. I don't suppose I have to spell it out for you. That's right. It happened, right there at The Vatican. My first urge was to jump into one of the fountains. Nobody ever took longer to get out of the square and back to where the taxis were. I took baby steps all the way, wondering if anything was visible. Gee whiz! It was the first time that had happened to me since I was two years old and right there, with God watching . . . .

When I returned to Canada and submitted my expense account, they must have thought I had covered the entire Second World War. I felt and looked as if I had lost it.

Needless to say, *The Canadian* never sent me to Europe again. ●

The Comeback of a Jockey

prologue *I had watched Chris Rogers ride, heard stories of his destructive lifestyle, and had been told about the respect his enormous talent had earned him in racing circles.*

But, I had never met him. When I called him in Maryland to ask if he would consider letting me write a magazine story about him, he had no idea who I was or if I was out to condemn or praise him. Still, he was friendly, polite, and said that if I was willing to take the time, he could certainly make the time to see me.

When you read his story, you will realize how difficult it must have been for him to tell it and to talk so openly about incidents that might better have been left in the past. His warmth, honesty, and courage made me an immediate Chris Rogers fan. Some of his racetrack pals felt the story was damaging to him and, perhaps, embarrassing. Chris Rogers read it, shrugged, and said, "What the hell. That's the way it was."

I respected him for that.

○ ○ ○

JUNE 22, 1968—He was a runt of a kid and the first time he went to the racetrack it was with his father, who ran a crane at a steel mill in Hamilton.

It was the spring of 1934 and Chris Rogers was nine. His father had always liked the horses, knew everybody in the backstretch and it got so they were at the track every Saturday and Sunday morning.

Illness was one of the reasons the kid was a runt. Pneumonia set in after a routine operation for appendicitis and he almost died. Illness also had put him behind the others in school, and Chris began hanging around the horse barns more and more, despite the fact that horses scared the hell out of him.

"Say, kid, it's time you rode a horse," one of the older men said one day. He was leading one of the ponies used to accompany the spirited thoroughbreds to the gate. "But you can't ride 'til you get some shoes with high heels."

Chris bolted for home, rummaged through a closet and found a pair of his mother's pumps.

"Them heels ain't high enough," said the man when he returned, fighting to suppress a smile.

So the kid ran home again and, when nobody was looking, borrowed his mother's spike-heeled dancing shoes she had bought only the day before.

"Those are just fine," grinned the man. "You're ready to be a rider."

Lead ponies are supposed to be sedate, but this one wasn't. It took off with the kid, galloping through the barn area until three older men blocked its path. It stopped abruptly, sending the kid and his mother's high heels through the air. But they couldn't have handled it better in the movies. He landed, ker-plunk, right in the arms of a groom called Nick the Greek.

He spent the rest of that summer working around the barns for Medway Stables and, when he returned to school, the principal told him he would be better off at the racetrack.

A trainer named Fred Schelke took Chris to his farm in Gormley, Ont., for the winter and two things were to stand out in his mind forever. The first was having to break the ice in the basin to wash his face each morning, and having to ride horses without gloves or a hat in freezing temperatures.

"Gee, Mister Schelke," he said one day, "I sure need gloves and a hat."

"Nonsense," said Schelke, bundled up warmly as he watched. "Only infants wear gloves."

Chris Rogers was 13 at the time and there was nothing to suggest that he would earn $2 000 000 as one of the world's great jockeys. He had no intention of becoming a jockey. He was content to be working around the barns, 25 cents for walking a horse or for washing a bucket of dirty bandages.

The Ontario racing circuit in those days included Hamilton, Fort Erie, Stanford Park at Niagara Falls and the Toronto tracks, including Long Branch, where, at 14, Chris Rogers was introduced to his first bottle of beer.

It was the beginning of a relationship that would last more than 25 years, until the day two and a half years ago that Chris, finally realizing it had ruined his life, made a fresh, dry start. He joined Alcoholics Anonymous, for the second time, and went back to the track to try to make himself a leading, respected jockey again. But during those 25 years, he had established himself as one of the top drinkers, pound for pound, in the world of sport.

In those days, help around the track worked for room and board—no money—and Chris was employed by a stable owned by a trainer named A. J. Halliwell. He was ranked fifth among the exercise boys and jockeys which meant he would probably never ride in a race.

On the eve of the 1941 Buffalo Handicap at Fort Erie, however, Chris was the only boy left to ride a horse named Bon Marche. It was given little chance, but Chris won the race, and a few more before the week ended. Now he was a bug boy—an apprentice jockey.

The thing they all noticed from the start was that here was a kid with horse sense, one who could pick his way through a field and win. It's something every top jockey needs, but it can't be taught. There was no stopping Chris Rogers then—winning or drinking.

For Rogers became a notorious drunk. When he took a wife in 1946, he was a 22-year-old, five-foot-two jockey with money in his pocket and a bright future, and already he was known as the softest touch on the track. Life became one long, expensive party.

But despite his drinking, he kept trying to perfect his trade. One day, riding in the Appas Tappas Stakes at Hamilton, Rogers was head and head coming down the stretch with a horse ridden by Hedley Woodhouse, a Vancouver rider.

Rogers had learned a few tricks. He moved his horse in on Woodhouse, leaning on him so that Woodhouse wouldn't be able to use the whip in his right hand. But then Woodhouse did something Rogers had never seen before—he switched his whip, hit his horse with his left hand and beat Chris by a nose.

"Dammit, I'll learn to do that," Rogers vowed.

He eventually did, but instead of switching it from hand to hand in midair, Rogers would put the stick between his teeth with one hand and reach up and grab it with the other.

It was unheard of, but Rogers perfected it and today it is standard practice throughout North America.

His reputation grew and in 1949 he was given a mount in the Queen's Plate—a horse named Epic. It was just a ride. Epic won Canada's championship race for three-year-olds in a breeze. Naturally the drinks were on Rogers.

The drinks were always on Rogers and the parties continued and grew in size. Suddenly he was one of the most popular guys on the track.

In 1950, he came back and won the Queen's Plate again, this time on a horse named McGill. He shouldn't have won that one. He was beaten in the stretch but the less experienced rider on the other horse got excited and turned his mount's head loose. Rogers, cool now and experienced, breezed in for the win.

Later, in 1954, aboard a Hamilton-owned horse named Collisteo, Rogers was to win the Plate a third time—a distinction shared going into this year's Plate with only three others this century, the last being Avelino Gomez.

Veteran horsemen still contend that it was the greatest ride they have ever seen—the day that Rogers nipped E.P. Taylor's Queen's Own at the wire to win. Queen's Own was unbeatable—in a class by itself—and the way Collisteo won has been argued ever since.

Collisteo had no chance, and was a 17-1 shot. Chris had been riding in New York at the time and was sent for by another owner—whose horse broke down the day before the Plate.

So, as a last-minute rider, he took the mount on Collisteo. Nobody could ever figure out how he nipped Queen's Own at the wire to win it. It looked impossible, yet the photo showed him lurching ahead at the finish.

"A lot of people have asked me about that," Rogers smiled as he replayed the race for me. "They had me in looking at movies for hours. But I could never tell the real story. I stole that Plate.

"It is a story of a jockey's greed," he said slowly. "I've never told anyone about it. But what the hell. I didn't want the ride on Collisteo much, he didn't have a chance. Queen's Own was the class of the race.

"But I was sharing the same valet as the young rider on Queen's Own and riding that horse had gone straight to his head. I also heard the other riders talking. When a jock wins a stake race, he usually splits with the others around the horse, such as the groom, the exercise boys and, especially, riders on other horses owned by the same man.

"Windfields Farm had two or three entries in the Plate that year and this kid had already told them he had no intention of splitting his purse. They were pretty mad about it.

"Anyway, this kid had a bunch of stars pasted on his box in the jocks' room. I went into the corner and I ripped the stars off. I said to him, 'When in the hell did you get to be a star?' Then I turned to the other riders and said: 'Well, if I win, at least you know the party will be on me.'

"He was outside, leading down the stretch, and I was running second, on the rail. He looked back and saw me. He could have galloped in for the win—I had no chance. But he decided he wanted to zop me, just nip me at the wire so he could say he outrode me. He came over to the rail and slowed up a little. They never did see what happened in the movies.

"I reached down and gave his saddle cloth a tug to slow him up, and gave Collisteo the stick. He was caught. Boy, my old buddy Pat Remillard [a veteran jockey] didn't help me much. He was up in the stands and when he saw it yelled: 'Hah! Chris got him—he got ahold of him.' Somebody overheard him and they started checking. The kid doesn't even know what happened—but old Pat does."

But there's more to the story. Grabbing the

saddle cloth is for amateurs. There's a picture somewhere of that finish that shows how tricky Rogers really was. When he crossed the finish line, his crop was in his right hand—and so was Queen's Own's rein.

"You don't do things like that any more because the coverage of a race is better today," said Chris as he readied himself for his next mount. "There's no sense teaching young kids today about those things because the first time they try it, they'll be sent down. Some of us oldtimers will still use a few tricks when we have to, but only in the dark spots."

But a lot happened between the 1950 and 1954 Plate victories. Rogers had become firmly established in the U.S. as well. His pockets were full of money—until his friends encouraged him to drink so they could make a touch.

After his Plate win in 1950, Rogers was riding a horse at Gulfstream in Florida named Arise, a hot contender for the upcoming Widener handicap. Three weeks before the race, trainer Jim Bentley called Rogers in and told him he was being taken off the horse.

"The owner wants a name jockey for the Widener," he said. "So we've given the mount to Ted Atkinson."

Rogers stalked from the room and slammed the door. On his way across the barn area, he met an unshaven man leading a horse.

"Say, sonny," said the man. "Can you work this horse three-quarters of a mile for me in a minute and 12 seconds?"

A good rider needs a clock in his head and Rogers was a good rider. He worked the horse in an exact 1:12. The man was extremely impressed.

"How'd you like to ride my horse in the Widener?" he asked.

The horse, it turned out, was Royal Governor and the man was training for the affluent Mrs. Weir DuPont of New York. The reason for his appearance was that he had just arrived from New York and hadn't had time to shave.

Aboard Royal Governor in the big race, Rogers found himself five lengths behind Arise, the surprise leader, heading into the stretch.

Atkinson, riding Arise, looked over nervously as Rogers pounded after him and went

to his whip. Rogers slipped through on the inside and nipped him at the wire.

That was 1950, when Rogers was 26—a name rider now—and he kept drinking, riding, drinking and spending his money. His wife enjoyed a drink too, as did their friends, and the parties sometimes lasted for days.

About two years later, Rogers decided he was tired of it all. He wanted to stop having parties. So he bought a house in the east end of Toronto—away from the downtown gang.

But the gang followed him. The parties moved to the east end. Finally Rogers kicked them all out. Then the parties moved to his mother-in-law's house, downtown, and his wife moved with them.

"I'm a loser both ways," said Rogers.

So he joined them again, and partied.

It all came to an end at Long Branch late in 1952. Chris was coming out of the gate and his knee caught, forcing the cartilage to pop. A friend, a chiropractor, asked if he could look at the injury. He said the trouble was in his back, three vertebrae that were weakening his leg. After a month of back treatments, the knee popped back into place and it looked as if things were going to be okay—until arthritis set in.

It was between Christmas and New Year's when trainer Frank Gilpen dropped by at the Rogers' home to find him drunk, under the Christmas tree and unable to get up.

"I'm going south," said Gilpen. "Are you going to stay with these drunks or are you coming with me?"

Rogers couldn't answer. Gilpen flew around the house in a rage, packing Rogers' belongings.

They went to Arkansas, and Rogers decided to visit the famed hot springs to see if it would help his arthritic knee. The results were remarkable. In time he could bend his leg again and he started working horses for Gilpen.

Now he was ready to ride and, in his first three days, rode seven winners. He hadn't been drinking since he left home. He was starting fresh.

Rogers called his wife in Toronto to tell her

to join them and bring their two kids, Butch and Christine.

"I'm not coming," she said.

Rogers, bewildered, told Gilpen.

"There's something I wanted to tell you before," said Gilpen, "but I thought you'd start drinking again."

The divorce came through and Rogers gave the house and his money to his wife. And he resumed drinking, ruining a season in which people felt he would be the leading rider in North America. It wasn't so much that he couldn't ride, but that he couldn't get the good mounts.

Still, every horseman knew his reputation. If you could get a sober Chris Rogers, you had one of the best in the business. That's why he was up on Collisteo in the 1954 Plate. When he won three races that day—and there's only one way to celebrate a day like that—he crossed the street from the old Woodbine track (Greenwood) in Toronto and rented a bunch of rooms in the Orchard Park Hotel. The party lasted three days.

Meanwhile, the 18 to 20 bottles of beer he consumed each day were starting to take their toll and he developed a severe case of gout. The excessive drinking also meant he had to spend hours each morning in the sweat box to make 112 pounds.

But Rogers straightened up again, long enough to remarry, and in 1958 he and a horse named Lincoln Road got to know one another. Lincoln Road was a good horse but nobody could handle him—he would swerve every time he reached the quarter pole. Rogers quickly discovered the reason.

The big horse was afraid of the shadow thrown across the track by the quarter pole. Whenever he approached it, he would stop and swerve. Rogers worked him one morning and just before the quarter pole, rapped him on the read end with his stick and yelled. Lincoln Road burst through the shadow for the first time.

Rogers rode Lincoln Road in the Kentucky Derby, only to be beaten by half a length by a great runner named Tim Tam. Still, it was one of the highest payoffs ever recorded at the Derby for a place ticket.

Rogers was riding high again. He took Lincoln Road to the Preakness, the second leg of the triple crown, and again he was second to Tim Tam. Tim Tam, it appeared, was unbeatable. So, when Tim Tam went to Belmont, Lincoln Road was entered in the Jersey Derby instead. He was an easy winner.

Chris began riding again in Canada and, when things started getting good, he sent for his second wife and their two children, who were in Florida. His brother, Alf, was acting as his Canadian agent and sending Chris's money to Florida to meet payments on his new house and on his U.S. income tax which was supposed to be paid quarterly.

A bookmaker called Chris and told him he owed him $1500.

"I never bet with you," said Chris angrily.

"Not you, man, your wife," said the bookie.

Chris discovered that his mortgage payments were six months behind, there was a large charge account at a department store and his income tax hadn't been paid.

It shook him up badly and, in addition to having to make the other payments, he was ordered to pay $350 a month in alimony when the divorce, his second, came through in 1961. There was only one thing to do . . . .

In Rhode Island, Chris came down with yellow jaundice—an ailment that can be caused by excessive drinking. After more than a month, he was released from hospital to ride again. The U.S. government started confiscating his pay, leaving him nothing to meet all of his payments, including the alimony.

"The hell with it all," said Chris, and he returned to Hamilton. His father and brother, Alf, persuaded him to attend some meetings of Alcoholics Anonymous, but he only went to a couple.

Things came to a head four years ago, when Chris was thrown from a horse three times one morning on the training track. The supervisor of racing called him to the office and suggested, for his own good, that Chris move on—perhaps out to Western Canada—to get away from his drinking pals.

Chris drank a toast to that and headed for Assiniboia Downs in Winnipeg. "You know," he told a friend, "I really don't care if I live or die."

His weight went up to 136 and he quit riding. He didn't have a cent, no job and he didn't particularly care.

Finally, three years ago, he wandered on to a track at Detroit, a pathetic shell of a man. He had given up riding and was looking for work exercising horses in the mornings.

A few weeks ago, at Pimlico, near Baltimore, he recalled the bad days. "I've got four horses to ride this afternoon. Why don't you drop out to Laurel in the morning. I'd like you to meet the wife."

One of the trainers out at Laurel was a tall, blonde girl—Carol Rogers. It was 6 a.m. and she was saddling one of the two three-year-olds she trains, so that her husband Chris could work it out before going to Pimlico.

Chris was coming down shedrow, a plastic-tipped cigar jutting from his mouth, carrying a large load of fresh straw on a pitchfork. He flashed his easy smile, made introductions and quipped: "The thing you forget when you marry a trainer is that she has all these horses you gotta ride."

Another man appeared and Chris introduced him as his brother Alf, also a former jockey, who once had handled his bookings. Alf quit as his brother's agent, though, when Chris kept missing mounts because of his drinking.

"I'm back now," said Alf. "Chris has straightened up and we're trying to make a fresh start."

Alf had been working at Stelco in Hamilton in addition to running his farm, but had been hospitalized just a few weeks before with ulcers.

"I came down here to recuperate," he said. "Then I started booking some mounts for Chris and now we're trying to make it go again. He looks good, doesn't he? Hasn't touched a drop for more than two years."

"C'mon jock," said Carol with her Kentucky accent. "The horse is ready."

She's taller than Chris, pretty, but doesn't smile much when she's around her horses. She'd rather talk horses than anything else and you can tell that she considers herself the equal of any man.

She gave Chris a leg up and, while he galloped the horse on the training track, she leaned on the rail, watching closely. Carol, 28, is 15 years younger than Chris, and, people keep telling you, she's the reason that he finally straightened up.

They first met years ago, at Rockingham Park in New Hampshire, where Chris was riding and Carol training her horses. They lived side by side in rented cottages, Chris with his second wife and Carol with two girl-friends.

The extent of their relationship was an occasional game of horseshoes with friends, and he rode several horses for her. Carol knew enough to keep her liquor hidden when Chris was around.

Then, three years ago when he wandered into Detroit, his career ended, his life a shambles, Carol was there. She was one of the first trainers to give him work exercising horses in the mornings.

"That was the spring of 1965," she said. "Chris had been drinking all winter. He was heavy—about 130-135—20 pounds over his riding weight. He was having a lotta trouble. I had come up from New Orleans with five or six horses and I'd run a couple of them. Chris had won races for me at Rockingham and Lincoln Downs—I wanted the best I could get and I thought he was the best.

"You don't have to give him a lot of instructions. Most jockeys don't have that sixth or seventh sense that Chris has. So, I didn't care how heavy he was. I told him to drop around to the barn if he wanted to ride my two horses. I didn't know how heavy he was, though. And he took off for Canada without saying anything one afternoon and didn't come back for three weeks."

Chris talked about it after he had worked her horses, while Carol rubbed them down and walked them.

"I had quit," he said. "Hell, it was all over. She asked me to ride but it was impossible. I was working a lot of horses for a trainer from the Midwest named Buck McClelland and I

Chris Rogers and his wife Carol at an early-morning workout ▶

wasn't drinking as much. Anyway, one day I was with her and Buck was running three horses.

"I heard what they told the jocks and I watched the races. The way those riders handled those horses made me mad. I said, 'Dammit, Buck, I'll ride them for you next time.' And I was really surprised when I weighed myself. Riding all those horses in the morning had helped. I was 114. I rode them the next time out and they all won. But I still wasn't going to ride again."

"Chris was staying with his cousin in Detroit," Carol said, "and I used to visit them a lot. Finally, the meeting there was over and I planned to come here, to Maryland, with my horses. I asked Chris what he planned to do. He didn't have any plans so he decided to come along, too.

"I gave him as much encouragement as I could to stop drinking, but I really didn't know anything about the problem. I inquired about various ways people stop drinking. He kept getting sicker. Finally I told him I was going to a meeting of Alcoholics Anonymous here. He balked, but he came along.

"I don't think you'd be writing this story if he hadn't. He'd be dead now, or a vegetable somewhere in a hospital. You have to give AA credit. If there is an answer, they've got it."

Chris is still a superb rider, despite his age, but his past has hurt him with the owners. On this particular afternoon, he rode three horses—two 35-1 shots and another that was 70-1.

"I'm not getting any stock," he said. "When I was at the top, I didn't have to ride these kind of horses. With a bad horse all you can do is ride, push and shove, and hope your luck's with you. A good horse is different. You ride with your head."

Chris has always been an experimental rider and never hesitates to pass on information. Every young jockey knows he can ask Chris anything.

For instance, most riders in the starting gate grasp the horse's mane, the reins and the stick with both hands. They hold the mane so they won't be thrown back at the start.

"I'm the only one I know who holds the mane and stick with one hand and the reins with the other," says Chris. "That way I can slip my hand off the mane and use the stick right at the start. I've tried to show a couple of young apprentices down here."

He also was the first man ever to change hands on the stick by first placing it between his teeth.

Alf was in the jocks' room now and pointed to a gap in his mouth where two teeth at the front are missing.

"That's what happened to me," he said. "You get the horse's sweat on the stick and, if it gets into your gums, it rots your teeth. I lost these when I was riding right here at Pimlico."

The bottom front teeth in Chris's mouth are worn on a slant. "That's from the stick," he laughed. "These are false. I lost mine the same way a long time ago. Now I have the false ones made from a special rubberized plastic. An ordinary plate will crack if you bite hard."

Suddenly he started laughing, slapping his knee.

"Remember that time at Gulfstream," he said to Alf. "Hell, I pulled the stick out one day and my plate came out with it and went flying through the air. Well, that night we had everybody at the track out there lookin' for my teeth . Didn't find them for a week."

Chris, Carol and Alf live together in an apartment in Laurel, until Alf is able to bring his wife, Betty, and four children down from Canada. They go to bed at nine each night, get up at 4:30 each morning and head for the track.

Carol busies herself around her horses and Alf, notebooks and condition books bulging from his pockets, hangs around trainers and owners, trying to get Chris mounts.

"I don't know them all yet," he said. "But I've got to get him at least four horses a day to make it work."

The previous night, over dinner, the three of them had been talking about the job ahead of them and the difficulties in making a comeback.

"Look, order a drink if you want one," Chris had said. "It doesn't bother us a bit. In fact, it makes me mad when people won't drink around me. When we go to a party, I always ask if I can be the bartender. Now I watch them getting drunk and I laugh when I think how sick they're all going to be in the morning."

They talked about how many people might still be suspicious of Chris because of his past, and how it affected his chances of getting mounts.

"One of Chris's problems," Carol said, "is that he's so good he can tell an owner or trainer exactly what's wrong with the horse after riding it once. And he does. Now, that's wrong. They don't want to hear that their horse is sore. But, Chris—yes sir, he always tells 'em."

Chris had been riding at Aqueduct in New York this season and doing reasonably well. He moved to Pimlico because of one horse, and because he knows what cut-throat racing is.

The horse is Sir Beau, a three-year-old purchased by trainer Judy Johnson for only $4500 as a yearling. But this year in the Gold Cup, Sir Beau came second to the controversial Dancer's Image. Sir Beau hadn't been eligible for the Derby, but he did run in the Preakness last month at Pimlico, finishing sixth.

"I'm the only one who ever won on Sir Beau," said Chris. "So I thought I'd better move here, where the horse is, before somebody started cuttin' me out."

He was also scheduled to ride Sir Beau three days later in the Woodward Stakes at Pimlico, a mile race on the turf. But he was worried that Sir Beau might not be ready for the mile distance. His suspicions were correct: Sir Beau finished third behind Hand In Hand and Go Marching, the $200 000 horse trained by Horatio Luro.

"You'll meet Judy in the morning," said Chris. "She's quite a character. She used to ride steeplechase horses at Bluebonnets in Montreal. Won a lot of races, too. She's the only woman who ever had a licence to ride."

Judy Johnson didn't get to the track as early as most trainers that morning, not until 8:30. She was waiting when Chris arrived to work out Sir Beau. A good showing by Sir Beau would mean money and prestige for Judy Johnson. It would mean new respect and more mounts for Chris Rogers, and assurance for Alf that he could make a living again as his brother's agent.

"I asked Chris to ride Beau because I think he knows as much as any rider who ever lived," Judy said, "I knew him in the old days. Certainly, there's been pressure on me to change riders. They wonder why I'm not riding a younger man. But I tell them that Chris is one rider who can tell me something about a horse and I won't question him."

Later that afternoon, at the track, Chris mentioned that Luro had arrived in town with Go Marching and had asked him to work it a mile on the turf.

"I'm riding against him Monday," he said, "but heck, you can never tell when a favor will be repaid."

"He's what!" yelped Carol and Alf when the news was relayed to them down at the paddock area.

"Luro has used Chris for years," she fumed. "He wants him because he knows he can ask Chris about the horse and Chris can tell him. But will he get paid a cent for working it? No! What's the matter with Chris. Won't he ever learn? Will Luro ever give him any mounts? No!"

Chris has always been a soft touch. He and Alf had been trying to figure out the night before how much money Chris had given away in his drinking days, when anybody could make a loan.

"Yeah," Chris had said, "I did used to circulate my money a bit. They used to wait for me outside of the tracks."

"Circulate! Hell," said Alf, "he gave more than $50 000 away to total strangers."

How do the other jockeys react to the old man making a comeback?

"They're all for me," said Chris. "They were standin' up cheerin' at the TV set in the jocks' room at Aqueduct when I rode. I know them all, taught most of them something."

Will Chris ever return to Canada to ride?

"I'd really like to make things up to some of the people I hurt," he said. "But I don't think I'd get much of a chance there either. They're just as cold as the people down here."

"We hurt a lot of people," said Alf. "Chris would be scheduled to ride and he wouldn't show up. We'd like to some way make it up to those people now that things are straightened away."

"You know, that's what bothers me most about the past," a reflective Chris had said earlier in the week. "When you drink you hurt the people around you. You may help some, but never the right ones. I hurt a lot of good people."

That's all far behind the new Chris Rogers and he didn't bat an eye when asked: "What could be the best thing to happen to Chris Rogers now?"

"The best thing," he said, "is that Chris Rogers stays sober."

And Chris, who may be a grandfather soon, now that his eldest son, Butch, 21, is married, fully intends to do that.

"Pssst!" said Alf as the week came to an end. "There's something else. Don't tell them where you found out, but Chris and Carol are expecting a baby. Great, huh?"

And when you leave Chris Rogers, you think back to what Eddie Arcaro once said.

"He's one of the finest riders who was ever on a horse. But we'll never know how great he might have been."

You also suspect that you'll hear of Chris Rogers again. ●

ᗺᑭᎥᒪᝪᑫᑌᗺ *Eight years after I had interviewed him in Maryland, on September 30, 1976, Chris Rogers, now 53, stood in the paddock at Toronto's Woodbine Racetrack.*

He was waiting to mount a horse named Double Revival for a routine allowance race over the turf course. Chris had returned to Canada in 1973 and had arrived alone, having separated from his third wife, Carol, who had been with him in Maryland. He had met a new lady at Woodbine, an exercise girl named Lynn and they were happy together as Chris continued his straight, new life. It had been more than ten years since he had had a drink and he would never take another one.

During his three years back in Canada, Chris hadn't exactly set the Ontario racing circuit on fire, but, he won his share. Now he was on Double Revival at the starting gate and another race was on. They rounded the bend and headed for the spot where the dirt track crosses the turf course at the head of the long stretch. Only one other major track in North America has a similar crossing of tracks, Santa Anita near Los Angeles.

When the horses leave the bright, green grass of the turf course, they must cross over 106 feet of brown dirt, something that was of concern to the owners of the great Secretariat when he made the final appearance of his brilliant career at Woodbine, winning the 1973 Canadian International Championship. Horses will sometimes be startled by the sudden change in color and footing and, when this happens, it can be dangerous. Secretariat, however, handled the situation easily in a workout and his owners decided to let him run.

Chris Rogers knew all about horses that are frightened by color changes or shadows. After all, wasn't he the guy who had discovered why a horse named Lincoln Road kept running out at the quarter pole? He was afraid of the shadow and Chris had corrected him by using the whip and yelling when they approached the shadow so that he would jump over it. Lincoln Road had been written off and Chris rode him to thrilling second-place finishes in the Kentucky Derby and Preakness.

He was not expecting it on this day, however, when Double Revival jumped as he left the grass to cross the dirt track and stumbled. The horse went down, throwing Chris free but, as Rogers rolled, it was in the path of Hugo Dittfach who had been behind him on Swiss Mocha. Dittfach's horse kicked Rogers, shattering his right leg.

"The shinbone was sticking out of his leg at a right-angle," remembers publicity director Bruce Walker, who was waiting at the infirmary when they brought Rogers in. "His dad and his brother were there, too. And Chris just joked about it, telling them not to worry about a broken leg."

They had to remove his silks to take him to the hospital and that is when they first saw the burn marks on his chest. Burn marks left by radium treatments. Only a few people had known and they had been sworn to secrecy. Several months before, during the spring meeting, Chris had complained to the trainer in the jockeys' room that he seemed to be losing strength. Trainer Eddie Dalton, who looked after most of the jockeys' aches and pains, took Rogers to the track doctor and he suggested extensive tests. The results came back. Chris Rogers had lung cancer.

Assured that it would be kept a secret, Chris began radium treatments and took chemotherapy all summer long, booking his hospital visits so that he could continue riding. Now, as they prepared to take him to nearby Etobicoke General Hospital, they knew why his leg had snapped so easily. He was still cracking jokes as he left the track for the last time.

Chris Rogers never got out of the hospital. He died of cancer one month later. The thousands of people who had taken advantage of him during his drinking days, when he was riding high, didn't show up at the funeral.

There were no free drinks.

"My bulls–
I love them all"

When the bulls refuse to fight in the classic way,
there is only so much a matador can do,
even if he is very brave.

PROLOGUE *I was worried about turning in this story of bullfighting to my boss Denis Harvey.*

He had, after all, sent me to Mexico to cover the 1968 Olympics. Instead, I went to the Games on only three occasions and spent the rest of the time with my friend Enrique Lutteroth and the matadors. I did one story from the Olympics, on Canada's gold medal equestrian team, but did my interviews by telephone when I finally got back to Toronto a month later. So much for responsibility and self-discipline. But, hell, I know I had a better time than any other member of the Olympic media.

I had met Enrique the year before in Nanaimo, British Columbia at the annual Great Canadian Bathtub Race. This is an event that requires you to be drunk for five days, to dance all night in the streets and then try to pilot a little bathtub thirty-eight rough miles across the Strait of Georgia to the finish line in Vancouver. Actually, they were not bathtubs at all, but tiny fibreglass boats molded from a real bathtub and powered by a ten-horsepower outboard motor.

More than 100 of the 300 tubs either sank or disintegrated during the first ten miles where the waves were over eight feet high. Poor Enrique, the lone Mexican entrant, who had taken time off from managing his family's onyx mine in Baja, was one of them. The last we saw of Enrique was when he went high in the air and nosedived into the water, his huge sombrero floating on top to mark the spot. They never saw the boat or motor again, but Enrique surfaced and, as he swam to his escort boat, held up his hand for a drink.

There were more than 3000 craft on the water and it was the most fun I ever had on an assignment. The only time I did not smile was when I went high in the air off a wave and, when I landed, kerplunk, tore off the toenail from the second toe on my right foot. I had always wondered how something like that would feel and would like to report that it does not feel very good.

We partied for three days at the fashionable Bayshore Inn in Vancouver, eating kippers and drinking champagne on our balconies. When we parted, I had Enrique's telephone number in Mexico City and when I told him I might be going to the Olympics he offered to find an apartment for me.

When I arrived in Mexico City, in October 1968, Enrique picked me up after I had registered at the media center. He had a gallon jug of tequila from which we drank in the car, slinging the jug up onto our shoulders to take a slug. That night we wound up at an open food stand at the market with some of Enrique's Mexican pals, not a tourista in sight. Enrique had taken to calling me "El Presidente" because of my Mexican-like capacity for tequila and, as they laughed and jabbered away in Spanish, I knew he was telling them about the bathtub race.

"Here, have a torta," Enrique said, handing me my first mouthful of Mexican food.

I will never forget biting into my first, raw jalapino chili—Arghhh! My mouth was on fire, perspiration streamed down my face. I wanted to claw at the monster on my tongue. They laughed, slapping their knees as the tears rolled down my cheeks.

"Here, a cold cervesa," laughed Enrique. I grabbed the bottle of beer and began gulping. Geez! It seemed worse. They began laughing again. It was my first lesson. Beer makes it worse, reactivating the chili.

Enrique invited me to his father's home the next afternoon for comida, the late-afternoon dinner, their biggest meal of the day. Wow! I hadn't realized how wealthy Enrique's family was. Senor Lutteroth was clearly the patriarch and his three sons ran his various businesses under his guidance. In addition to the onyx mine, which was Enrique's responsibility, they controlled all professional wrestling in the country, and owned fourteen arenas, including the one in Mexico City where the Olympic boxing was taking place. They had three magnificent homes, not visible from the street, connected by large, flagstone paths behind a huge wall. The homes were sparkling and bright with glistening marble floors. The entire family had gathered for dinner at the home of Senor Lutteroth.

Each morning, at precisely 10 o'clock, the sons would dress in business suits and attend a formal business meeting in their father's study. After that meeting, Enrique would replace his suit with more casual clothes and we would head out for another day and night of gaiety and tequila in Mexico City.

Enrique would drive me to the Olympic media centre every couple of days to check for possible messages from home and I would regale my Canadian colleagues in the press bar with tales of my latest adventures. Those poor working stiffs had daily deadlines and here I was, free as a bird. My deadline was six weeks away and all I would have to do is grab an interview with one or two Canadian athletes before I left. Hell, I didn't even do that.

Our most memorable night occurred when four of us went to Garibaldi Plaza in Mexico City in Enrique's little compact car with a gallon of tequila—the special brand that Mexican wrestlers would pick up in a small town in the mountains when they were booked in that area. Garibaldi Plaza is little more than a square block of grass encircled by bars and nightclubs. But it is the home of the mariachis. More than thirty mariachi bands are there seven nights a week, until the wee hours, playing requests for a few pesos and trying to outdo one another for customers. It is strictly Mexican with very few tourists and we drove the car right into the park, got out and started passing around the jug of tequila.

Suddenly we were surrounded by a crowd of cheering Mexicans and about six bands, all playing different tunes at the same time, fighting for the fistful of pesos Enrique was passing out. The tequila was passed around to the musicians and the appreciative crowd. When the jug came around to me, I would throw it over my shoulder and guzzle, trying to live up to my El Presidente nickname. I was no El Presidente that night. One of the last things I remember is the sea of sweating, yelling faces and the way the crowd pressed in and started to rock Enrique's little car. We took off, with me lying on the floor in the back seat—absolutely drunk.

Enrique had to fill me in on the rest of the night. He had, for some unexplained reason, rented me an apartment in the city of Puebla, about eighty-five miles away, where army tanks had rolled out a week earlier to quell a student uprising.

"I had to stop every five miles," he said, "because you were sick."

Unfortunately, he provided proof of my embarrassing condition about a week later. When we arrived at the address in Puebla, Enrique pulled my lifeless body out onto the sidewalk and left me lying there while he carried my bags upstairs. When he returned, a common, yellow cur was sniffing at me *and, suddenly, lifted his leg and let me have it. Enrique, thinking it was a great joke, took a picture of Canada's canine relief station in action . . . .*

They never called me El Presidente again. I had the worst hangover of my life and stayed in bed for two full days.

As the days rolled by, somewhere in the back of my mind I realized something else was happening. Oh yeah, the Olympics. I shoved them to the back of my mind again. After my first day at the Plaza Mexico bullring, I never gave them another thought.

We sat in the midst of this mass of humanity in the world's largest bullring, eating cheese and washing our food down with red wine. I was feeling such strong emotions that it was almost scary. I knew instinctively that I had to write about this even though I would be risking ridicule by my friends at home who knew that Hemingway was my hero.

Enrique, with his family's connections in sports, spoke with a promoter to arrange an interview for me a few days later with Eloy Cavazos, one of the young matadors. I was hooked. I had no idea how Canada was doing at the Olympic Games and, what's more, I don't think I really cared.

P.S. My toenail grew back quite normally, thank you.

○ ○ ○

FEBRUARY 15, 1969—The enraged bull charged through the gate, snorting and tossing its massive head, and an audible gasp, punctuated by screams of alarm, went up from the 50 000-person capacity crowd in the Plaza Mexico.

"Espontaneo!"

A boy, perhaps 15, had leapt over the barrier and was trying to attract the bull's attention with a homemade cape he had smuggled into the arena.

Policemen made futile grasps at the boy, but stayed behind the safety of the barrier. Finally, while the bull's attention was diverted elsewhere, the peons (the matador's assistants) wrestled the boy down and took away his cape, but he broke loose and raced empty-handed to the center of the ring.

Absolute and total pandemonium!

The boy stood and faced the bull, a lonely figure in the center of the ring, his arms raised in defiance. The huge animal, bred to kill, pawed the dirt and began its charge.

The boy stood his ground, poised, and seemingly without fear. He would try to avoid the bull without a cape. He would try at the last possible moment to leap sideways, to prove to the world that he was brave enough to become a novillero, or novice bullfighter.

The bull caught him with his right horn, throwing it the way a boxer throws a right. The boy's body flew into the air and landed face down in the dirt. The boy lay motionless and the bull circled him, then charged again, lowering its powerful head and scooping him up with its horns. The boy landed on his back this time and the bull trampled him. Finally the toreros lured the bull away with their capes and the boy's limp body was carried out of the ring to the infirmary.

I looked at my companion, 19-year-old Fabian Ruiz, who had sat through the ordeal with an ashen-grey face, refusing to watch.

"How badly do you think he is injured?"

"Excuse me," said Fabian. "But I cannot talk now. That boy was me down there."

Becoming a matador is to the Mexican or Spanish boy what becoming a heavyweight boxer is to the black youth from the ghetto. It is instant financial and social success.

The reason that Fabian had not been able to watch the mauling of the young espontaneo is that he had been an espontaneo once himself. Going into the ring in this manner is the way that a would-be bullfighter proves his bravery and attracts the interests of the promoters. When the promoters decide the espontaneo should be given a chance to fight professionally, he becomes a novillero. It is also the promoters who decide when a novillero is good enough to be elevated to matador.

I had met Fabian a week earlier, at the home of Raphael Baez, a leading manager of matadors in Latin America. When they are in Mexico City, the bullfighters Baez manages stay at his apartment. I had gone there to talk to Eloy Cavazos, who, although he is only 18, is one of Mexico's leading matadors. Because Eloy does not speak English, Baez's wife, a blonde from Los Angeles who is now more Spanish than American, was interpreting. (When Baez's matadors are fighting, Mrs. Baez does not go to the bullring. She cannot bear to watch.)

I asked if Eloy was afraid when he went into the ring and why it was that he decided to fight bulls. Mrs. Baez translated and he answered her in Spanish, apparently with some candor as his reply upset the others in the room. Finally, because Mrs. Baez was not translating his reply, a young man who had been sitting there quietly spoke up. It was Fabian.

"He says that he is afraid of the bulls," said Fabian. "He says that he fights bulls only as a necessity, to earn money. They do not want him to say that because it is not good."

I was surprised to hear him speak English. He smiled and explained.

"I learned to speak English in two weeks, while I was in a clinic in Los Angeles," he said.

Fabian accepted an invitation to dinner the next night and suggested a little restaurant, a favorite eating place of the matadors.

"I do not come to downtown Mexico often," he said. "I am afraid of the crowds of people and the way they drive. More afraid than I am of the bulls. I am not afraid of the bulls."

Eloy's remarks had upset Fabian and he was trying his best to explain that he did not feel the same way. He fought bulls because it was his place in life to fight bulls—the complete fulfillment for the young man in Mexico.

"Eloy should not have said that," he said. "The people might not understand."

And the people are very important to a matador. It is the crowd who decides whether he should be awarded an ear, two ears, or two ears and a tail for his fight. A judge watches the flutter of handkerchiefs in the stands and makes his decision on the basis of the crowd's enthusiasm. After he has made his decision, the peons cut off the prize or prizes and give them to the matador and he makes a tour of the ring holding it or them aloft. Once, in Spain, a bullfighter fought so well that he was awarded two ears, a tail, four hooves and the testicles—the greatest tribute ever paid a matador. Fabian, in a small city, once was awarded two ears, a tail and a hoof.

The people can also end a matador's career, simply by expressing displeasure by whistling and throwing programs and seat cushions. If the people place him in disgrace, the promoters will not give him fights.

In 53 fights as a novillero, Fabian cut 87 ears and seven tails and also won the Silver Sword at the Plaza Mexico, where he fought seven times. Three months before I met him, he had been elevated to full matador at a ceremony in the ring at Tijuana. It was fitting that the ceremony took place there. Three years and three months before, he had been an espontaneo at this same ring.

"The bull threw me high in the air," Fabian remembered. "I landed on my head and fractured my skull. I was unconscious for five days. Some friends from Los Angeles took me to a hospital there."

His friends decided he would receive better medical treatment in Los Angeles. They stuffed him, unconscious, into the trunk of their car to smuggle him across the border. And, during his two weeks in the hospital, Fabian learned to speak English remarkably well.

He is still very close to that family in Los Angeles. While he was in the hospital, he asked the three young daughters in the family for locks of their blonde hair. Instead of considering another future, Fabian lay in his hospital bed and, from the locks, he made himself a coleta—the artificial pigtail the matador wears as part of his traditional dress. He still wears it today—a flash of yellow against the blackness of his own hair.

In the two weeks I spent with him, I could never think of Fabian as a matador. He was just a kid, a blithe young spirit who, when walking down the sidewalk, delighted in leaping over fire hydrants. And when we spent other afternoons together after that first interview over dinner, I noticed that he dressed in much the same manner as the teenagers at home: loafers, slacks or jeans, a golf sweater and a light windbreaker.

He was not at all like the fictional matador—the tall, dark Latin, surrounded by lovely ladies, lavished by the touristas, a connoisseur of fine food and drink. Fabian will not even have a glass of wine with his meal. He has no girlfriends.

"The bull," he said, "does not drink or have women. So I cannot drink or have women."

During the first week, Fabian told me about his younger days in Aguscalientes, a town in the central part of Mexico where his father, a carpenter, lives with his mother, three brothers and two sisters.

"I was a carpenter also when I was 10 years old," he said. "And then one day a man took us to a bullfight in Acatecas, near my home. When I saw the parade of matadors as they entered the ring, I said to myself that I would be a matador."

The Latin people will tell you that a man is born to be a true matador. Fabian cannot explain why he felt it so strongly. It was as if, at 10 years of age, he knew what he must do.

"I went to an old man in my town who had been a matador," he said. "I told him that I, too, wanted to become a matador. He laughed at me. He said I wanted to become a matador because I wanted to have a lot of money, women and cars. He said I didn't want to work. I was very angry. I told him that none of it was true and that if he would not teach me, I would find someone who would.

"He called me back and said that perhaps I did want to be a matador. He would help me."

Few people other than the Latins realize how much there is to fighting a bull. Casual observers look at it as a mere battle of survival. But it is complex—more complex than any sport (if it can be called that) with which I have been associated. Fabian spent two weeks talking about his profession without ever repeating himself. He also tried, without success, to teach me some of the basic passes with a large towel in my hotel room. His movements were artistic, impossible for someone with no training to do.

"I would go to the slaughterhouses early in the morning, before the caretakers arrived," he said. "And there I would fight cows in the corrals, not killing them of course."

When he felt he was ready, Fabian leaped over the barrier one day at Acatecas as an espontaneo. His near fatal experience at Tijuana was his second appearance as an espontaneo and there was one more, at Aguascalientes. Now, he was ready to become a novillero. He purchased a Suit of Lights for 7 pesos, made his own muleta and was given a cape and sword by a friend.

One day, Fabian and I decided to go to the Cortijo La Morena, a combination restaurant-bullring in Texcoco, a one-hour drive from Mexico City.

It is owned by Luis Barroso, owner of the Ganaderia Ranch which produces the excellent Mimiahuapan bulls, and customers may try to fight their own bull, young Brave bulls (the breed's official name) from the Mimiahuapan strain. These range from six-month-old calves to yearlings. I was to try my hand at it with Fabian acting as my coach.

During the drive he told me about the dangers of his sport. He had raised his shirt to show me the ugly scars on his lower abdomen, reminders of the six serious gorings he has suffered in his short career. His friend Eloy had been gored five times, twice on the right thigh, once under the left armpit and on each cheek of his rump. Eloy had also suffered fractures of two fingers, his left ankle and a vertebra.

"My worst was when the horn went in here," Fabian said, touching the right side of his lower stomach, "and came out here." He touched the left side.

Years ago, before penicillin, bullfighters often died from the infection passed from the horn. Now, penicillin is the matador's best friend. You need to see one of these bulls lift a horse off the ground to realize how powerful they are in the neck. A man has no chance when the bull finds its target.

"I'm not sure how you say it in English," Fabian said. "But the worst part is the trajectory, we call it. They need to open your stomach to find out where the horn went inside. There may be only one hole where it entered, but, when the bull shakes his head, the curved horn goes in different directions inside. I had five wounds inside once."

There are the usual facial scars, similar to those suffered by hockey players, but they don't bother mentioning them.

"It is good that you are to try to fight a little bull today," he said. "It will help you to understand. The people in the plazas, they do not always understand.

"I want only to think about bulls," he explained. "The only thing that is clean and pure in the sport is when you are in the ring with the bull."

The sport, for shadiness in dealings, is a close rival to professional boxing. The matadors, for instance, must pay the sportswriters who cover bullfighting if they hope to receive publicity. If you don't pay a writer, he will write bad things about you. If you do pay him, he may even overlook a bad fight. The going rate is 2000 pesos ($160) for a fight at the Plaza Mexico. Managers and promoters are not always to be trusted.

"I want only to have enough money to have a big car," said Fabian. "The car will come after I have built a big home for my parents. I send my money now to my mother. I only ask God that I will be ready to fight well. I know that the bull will be strong. So I must eat and sleep to be strong, too."

The genial manager of the Cortijo La Morena, Manolo Arjona, greeted us, told Fabian how happy he was to have him drop by, and took us on a tour of the corrals. The calves were in pens, snorting and pawing at the ground when anyone looked in. There was a machine into which a calf is led so that its horns

Fabian Ruiz, the young matador, in his Suit of Lights.

136

can be trimmed at the points to make them less dangerous.

It is an impressive place on acres of landscaped grounds, a building in the middle with tables instead of seats in the spectator area. People dine and drink while someone tries his hand at fighting a bull below him. Musicians stroll from table to table.

"Are you ready, matador?" he asked.

I nodded. More ready now, after the tequila.

There is a resident matador to teach people the basics of the sport but Fabian had looked after that with the hotel towel. They strap leather chaps on you to protect your legs and place a black Spanish hat on your head. A man runs at you with a pair of horns to warm you up.

"The old story about a bull charging anything that is red is not true," Fabian had explained. "He charges the movement of the cape. You must keep it a few inches ahead of his horns so that you can direct him. Do not let him touch it."

Suddenly, over the public address system, your name is announced. The quadrilla forms a line and marches into the ring to the traditional music, then the matador salutes the crowd.

In a moment of bravado—over the tequila— I had asked for the largest, most ferocious calf in the house. They believed me. It wasn't large at all by other standards, but large enough at 200 pounds to turn my feet to lead as it charged toward me from the gate. You hear the pounding of the hoofs and watch as the lowered horns bear in on you. Now, what was it that Fabian had said to do? Your only thought is to get the hell out of the way.

Someone yelled a light-hearted "Ole" as he swished through the cape, which was as far from my body as my arms would permit. The idea, of course, is to keep your feet together, bringing the bull past as near to you as possible without touching. This calf would have needed a 10-foot horn spread to touch me.

After surviving the first stage of the fight, Fabian handed me the muleta, the smaller red cape that is used for the really artistic passes just before the kill.

He missed me the first time, but, on his second rush, the calf knocked the muleta from my hands. Okay, I thought, we'll have to call time here while I retrieve it. That was a mistake. The calf had no intention of waiting for me. I looked up as I wandered over to pick up my muleta and he was on top of me. Whomp! I went down and the first reaction I had was to grab its horns and hold on. I lay, struggling in the dirt and heard Fabian shout: "Okay, I'll take him."

He took the calf away with his cape and I retired permanently, without so much as a single handkerchief waved on my behalf. No ears, no tail, no hoof. No more, either.

And, when I looked back into the ring, Fabian was putting on another show, facing the charging calf without a cape and, at the last second leaping high in the air so that the calf charged through his outspread legs. It was the same leap he did over fire hydrants.

"I was surprised when I saw that calf come in," he said later. "Its horns weren't clipped. It could have gored you."

"What you did was good," he said on the way back, "because now you know how it feels. I wish that everyone who goes to the Plaza Mexico would do the same thing. Just so they know."

Just thinking about it, how it would be if that animal had been five times as big, five times as ferocious, five times as strong, was enough to prevent me from getting a sound sleep, even though I was physically tired. I woke up with a nightmare during the night. It was one of several I was to have about bullfighting. The telephone awoke me the next morning. It was Fabian, excited.

"I have a fight!" he blurted. "The most important fight of my career. Next Sunday at Acapulco, mano-a-mano against Manola Martinez!"

Mano-a-mano is a program involving only two matadors, each with two bulls. Usual cards involve three matadors, each with two bulls. But, mano-a-mano pits one matador against the other. Comparisons are easy to make. And Manolo Martinez is the best matador in Mexico.

My thoughts went back to that Sunday at the Plaza Mexico, when we had seen the young espontaneo trampled and mauled. Later that afternoon, when the matador Finito was fighting his first bull, he had had a great deal of trouble with his kill.

The fans had whistled and jeered, expecting too much of him with a bad bull. And then, when he struck bone time after time while attempting to sink his sword, the entire plaza expressed displeasure. Seat cushions were thrown and Finito, in extreme distress, could not finish the job.

Finito heard two avisos (time signals) with that first bull, then finally killed it with his tenth thrust.

I watched Fabian while the crowd was whistling and jeering. He was pressing his ears closed so tightly that his fingers were white—perspiration appeared in beads on his forehead and the veins bulged in his neck. There was a look of hatred on his face, extreme contempt for those who were whistling. He was praying for Finito to finish well.

He would not discuss it until we had left the Plaza. Then he tried to explain to a Canadian how a matador feels when the whistling begins. It is total disgrace, the worst thing possible, worse almost, than being injured. And the reason Fabian had been so upset was because the people had been wrong. The bull was a terrible bull and, when they jeered Finito's attempts to make it fight, it had unsettled him accounting, perhaps, for the terrible kill.

"But it was his first bull," said Fabian. "I knew he had another bull left and would probably do well. Then they would forget the bad one."

Finito, indeed, had triumphed with his second bull, cutting an ear.

There was no question about it. I had to go to Acapulco with Fabian. But thoughts went through my mind: the mauling of the espontaneo, the scars on Fabian's abdomen, the jeering directed at Finito, the hours spent with Fabian while he explained how important it was for him to be a success. . . .

What if something went wrong?

Suddenly, things had become very serious. Outwardly, I am not a particularly religious man but, curiously, I found myself in the religious section of a jewelry store, asking the saleslady if she had a medal of the patron saint of the matador.

Later, I dropped in to see Fabian and told him I would be going to Acapulco. He seemed genuinely pleased, and asked me to meet him at the ring early Sunday morning. We would select his bulls together, he said, and I could stay with him during his dressing ceremony. He would get me a good seat, on the shady side in the barrera, I would see him fight and then we would have dinner.

I gave him the case containing the religious medal. He lifted it out slowly and his reaction indicated to me that, without knowing, I had done the right thing.

"Thank you," he said quietly. "I hope that I will fight well."

For the most important fight of his career, Fabian boarded a bus and took an overnight ride to Acapulco. With a whooshing of air-brakes, its motor whining, the bus wound through the mountains, picking its way down to sea level. Fabian relaxed. He put his head back in the dark and closed his eyes.

On Sunday, his 14th fight as a full-fledged matador, he had a chance to prove that he belonged with the best.

A triumph would ensure solid bookings for the season, especially at the Plaza Mexico, the world's largest bullring, where a matador can earn from $8000 to $10000 in one afternoon. A humiliation would mean starting all over again. But Fabian thinks positively. He intends to one day be the leading matador in the world. He slipped off into a restful sleep.

Three elaborately tooled leather cases were unloaded at Acapulco, each with the name "Fabian" emblazoned on the cover. Fabian loaded them into a taxi for the trip to the villa of Raphael Baez, his manager.

The largest of the three cases held his suit of lights, slippers, coleta and undergarments. It also contained his religious medals, rosaries, holy candle and holy pictures with which he would make a shrine.

Another case was a hatbox containing his montera, the traditional black hat of the matador.

The third case, long and narrow with a handle, was his scabbard. It contained two swords, hard steel, razor sharp on both edges and with a bend in the blades. The blades are flat, the bend slight, so that when the matador plunges it between a bull's shoulder blades, the bend carries it in a downward direction where it can sever the aorta artery.

The opening is three inches in diameter between the bull's shoulders and the matador must hit it while the animal's front feet are together. Otherwise, the opening will close and he will strike bone, his sword flung high in the air.

Hitting the artery is important. A half-sword can kill and a full sword fail. When a full sword has not killed, the peons—assistants to the matador—can assist by making the bull move from side to side so the sword will move inside, until it finds the artery. In the perfect kill, the bull's legs stiffen, a gush of blood shoots from its mouth and death is instantaneous.

Raphael Baez was waiting with his wife in the villa, situated high on a cliff overlooking the blue Pacific water. All rooms opened to a large patio and Fabian would share his room with his brother José, 18, who had come from Aguascalientes to act as his sword handler. Fabian greeted them, then settled down for a day of rest before his big fight.

Sunday was a sweltering day in Acapulco. Fabian had asked me to meet him at the bullring at noon, where I would accompany him as he selected his bulls.

From the taxi, I noticed the posters throughout town: "For the First Time, the Maximum Bullfighter—MANOLO MARTINEZ—Competing for the Honors with Fabian Ruiz of Aguascalientes." Manolo, of course, had received top billing.

The Caletilla bullring—with a capacity of only 8000—is small compared to the Plaza Mexico. Fabian was in the office of the promoter, a fat, elderly gentleman, casually passing the time of day. There was lots of time; the corrida, or performance, did not begin until 5:30.

"Come," said Fabian. "We will look at my beautiful bulls."

These were bulls from the ranch Guayabe, two for Fabian, two for Martinez. They stood in pairs in corrals separated by a narrow runway, from which people could peer at them through the fence.

I looked around for Fabian. While the others wore worried looks, he was at the far end of the alleyway, trying to see how many times he could chin himself on a two-by-four. The kid had no nerves at all.

"Okay, Paul," he grinned. "How do you see my bulls?"

"Big," I answered. "How do you see them?"

"Beautiful—I love them all."

He laughed and went to join the men as they made the draw. Each bull has a number branded on it. The numbers of the pair of bulls in one corral are written on a flimsy cigarette paper, the numbers of the other two on another paper. Both papers are rolled into tight balls and dropped into a hat. Each manager selects one of the papers, determining which bulls his matador will face.

"I will rest now for an hour," said Fabian. "Join me at my room."

Fabian's brother José, Raphael Baez and two doctor friends were in Fabian's room for the traditional dressing ceremony. One of the doctors was Gabriel Espinosa, head surgeon at the Mexico City Hospital. Dr. Espinoza, handsome and in his 40s, is the nephew of Fermin Espinosa, who fought under the name of "Armillita" and was Mexico's greatest matador for 25 years.

Fabian was stripped to the waist, prominent scars on his stomach, four religious medals hanging around his neck. A shrine was set up beside his bed—his rosaries, crucifixes, more medals, and holy pictures in plastic holders. A red glass with a candle was in the center.

His suit of lights was on a chair, covered with a white sheet. He sat on the bed and began. The mood changed. Things had become serious.

He pulled on a pair of red stockings, up to his thighs, then a pair of pink embroidered ones over them, spitting on his hands so that he could pull them tight. These were held up by an elastic band high on each leg and another under each knee. Next he slipped into his pants, white with gold embroidery on the sides, which came up to his armpits.

He walked over and lifted the medals from the shrine, kissed each and hung them around his neck. He now wore 11 medals. The pants, short like breeches, had gold tassels at the bottoms and these were now tied tightly around his calves, so tightly that a piece of paper was wrapped around each leg first so the laces would not cut off circulation.

A stiffly starched white shirt came next, with ties at the bottom that went around his waist and tied to his suspenders. Next was a green ribbon tie and a green sash or cummerbund around his waist. He kept leaning back, arching his back, to see if he could move freely.

As Fabian was tying his blond coleta in place, the telephone rang. Senor Baez was speaking in Spanish and when he turned back to the others in the room, his face was dark. One of Fabian's bulls had killed the other in the corral. He would fight a substituto. The problem was, this was a small ring. Would a substitute bull be any good?

Fabian continued dressing, sewing his tie to the front of the shirt so that it wouldn't flap in the wind, adjusting his hat, combing his hair for the third time. He was ready for his suit of lights. The magnificent jacket, stiff and ornately decorated with brilliant red, gold and green sequins, was slipped over a bright red and gold vest.

He went into the bathroom, returned with a towel and spread it carefully on the floor in front of his shrine.

"A match," he said. He struck it and lit the candle, knelt before it, bowed his head and prayed. He rose, touched each of his holy pictures with his fingers, kissed the rosaries and crucifixes then headed for the door.

The ceremony had taken more than an hour. There wasn't a wrinkle anywhere that a bull's horn might catch. There also was not a single piece of protective equipment, not even an athletic support.

In Mexico they say the only thing that ever starts on time is a bullfight. At 5:30 sharp, the cuadrilla appeared in the ring to the traditional music and the two matadors saluted the crowd.

"MAN-O-LO ... MAN-O-LO ..." they chanted for Martinez. Martinez smiled, turned and acknowledged a redfaced and grinning Fabian.

Manolo fought first, a bull named Chocolate. But it was a bad bull and he could do nothing with it. It was not a particularly important fight for him so he wasted little time with it, making an excellent kill with his first sword.

Fabian was next. His bull was the substituto, named Tapa Bocas. The gate swung open and the crowd groaned. Fabian's biggest fear was realized. They had not got a good substitute. This was a small bull, not fully grown and the crowd began whistling its displeasure—not with Fabian, but with the promoter.

They did not know it was a substitute, though. They thought it was a little bull for a little matador. Fabian's face was red with disappointment and rage. The veins bulged in his neck. He looked up to where the judge was sitting, his face saying: "You don't really expect me to fight this, do you?" They waved for him to continue. He made a few passes, trying desperately to save the situation. But, in addition to being small, the bull was useless.

The stage of the fight arrived where the picador, a man seated on a padded, blindfolded horse, sinks his steel pic, attached to a long pole, into the bull's tossing muscle, the morillo. It is between the shoulders and, when picked, is supposed to slow the animal down and make it lower its head.

The whistling reached a crescendo. This little bull didn't need a pic. Fabian's face became redder and redder. He seemed flustered, embarrassed. They whistled again when he went for the kill. He looked up at the judge again, as if asking if he really should kill it. Things became even worse. He couldn't sink his sword. He could not even kill it with the descabello, or dagger, which is plunged into the bull's brain, just behind the head, as a last resort. Finally, it died. Now the whistles were turned on Fabian. Never have I seen a face a more brilliant color of red.

Manolo's second bull, Bien Vendo, was the best of the day and, while he performed adequately, he did no more than he had to, then

Action at the Plaza Mexico ▶

took four swords to make the kill—the first time I had seen him use more than one.

It was Fabian's turn again, the last bull of the afternoon. A lot of his friends, aware of the importance of the fight, prayed that his bull would be a good one.

During Manolo's fight, Fabian had stood, motionless, staring, waiting. Now he strode into the ring, a scowl of defiance on his face. The gate swung open, a full-sized bull charged into the ring, butted the fence, and started looking for another target.

Fabian waved away his peons. He would do it alone. Usually, the peons make the first few passes so the matador can read the bull, watching it to see how it takes the cape, whether it goes left or right or charges true.

It was a lousy bull. An artistic fight would be impossible. Still, Fabian had to try to make a fight out of it. He made a few passes then turned, saluted the crowd, removed his hat, turned his back to the people and flung the hat over his head, into the stands. The bull would be dedicated to whoever caught the hat. He had thrown it to me.

The pic was sunk, the blood shining on the bull's shoulder. Time for the banderilleros to place the banderillas. Fabian waved them away. He would place them himself. A banderilla is a steel barb attached to a stick 26 inches long and gaily wrapped in colored paper. There are three banderilleros, (men who place the barbs) each of whom has two banderillas to place between the bull's shoulder blades, where they hook into the skin and remain flopping throughout the fight. They add to the color, and to the irritation of the bull.

Fabian raised a pair of banderillas high in the air. The bull charged and Fabian ran in a path through the charge, leaping high in the air, placing them perfectly and hurling himself aside. He placed the second two.

Now, he took his third pair and snapped them over his knee, breaking them, so they were only six inches long. The crowd cheered in appreciation. It isn't often that a matador will do this. It is too dangerous. Fabian was giving them the works. And, if there was perfection in his fight, it was the placing of the shortened banderillas—a direct hit, square between the shoulder blades. The crowd's cheer was deafening.

Fabian grabbed his cape and began a series of passes. The band struck up the "Diana," the tune that is played in appreciation during a good fight. They didn't play long, however, the band leader realizing that the bull was not charging in a true line, preventing Fabian from preforming artistically. Still, the crowd gave him a series of "Ole!"s for his cape work.

Now I was seeing the real Fabian. He was like a man possessed. When there is no bull, there is no fight. But he was charging around the ring, trying to force something to happen. He kicked dirt in the bull's face, made menacing gestures at it. If there was no artistry, there was bravery. He took chances, moving in closer and closer to the dangerous horns.

The bull caught him, throwing him high in the air. There was a gasp from the crowd. The peons attracted the bull's attention to take him away from Fabian, others rushed to his aid. He stood, his pants ripped open at the crotch, where he had been gored twice before, and waved them away.

But you never know how serious a cornada, or gore wound might be. The matador will continue if at all possible. Fabian once was gored with the horn entering the right side of his stomach and coming out the left side. He stayed around to kill the bull before going to the infirmary.

He took his muleta, the small red cape used in the last stage of the fight, and made several passes, falling to his knees. The bull caught him again. This time, his pants were ripped on the other side of the crotch.

The bull caught Fabian once more and, when he stood, blood streamed down his face. Still, he kept going—charging, pressing, fighting to overcome that earlier humiliation.

His first sword hit bone and flipped into the air. The second went in but missed the artery. The bull took several minutes before falling.

It had not been a triumph in the sense that he was awarded a trophy such as an ear, two ears or a tail. But the people had liked the excitement and admired his bravery. Youngsters rushed into the ring, lifted Fabian to their shoulders and gave him a tour of the ring. People threw garlands of roses which were gathered up and placed in his arms. He raised his free arm and grinned wanly, the blood still streaming down his face. Then they took him to the infirmary.

Miraculously, he had not been gored. There were red marks where the horns had scraped his thighs. But his nose was cut, scraped—perhaps broken—and his upper lip was swollen to three times it size. He lay on a table in the infirmary while a doctor taped his face. He was very quiet.

Fabian had little to say on the way back to the villa and, when he got there, he went into his room, threw himself on the bed and cried. It had been a frustrating day and he was unhappy with the way he had fought.

The others hadn't returned yet. I stood out on the patio, talking with Mrs. Baez.

"He's so different from the others," she said of Fabian. "It seems to be more important to him. He wants so badly to do well."

Later, Fabian, his brother José and Dr. Espinosa joined me for dinner at my hotel. Fabian was sullen, had trouble chewing and didn't talk much.

Suddenly he looked at me and asked: "What are you going to write about my fight?"

"That you were very brave."

He looked away. He was returning to Mexico City on an early-morning bus and I was staying in Acapulco, so we shook hands and said our good-byes that night. I told him I hoped he would, some day, be the world's leading matador.

I dined with Dr. Espinosa again the next night and he tried to explain to me why a young man wants to become a bullfighter, how the matador is the epitome of masculinity to the Latin.

"Fabian is perhaps the most knowledgeable matador his age in the world," he said. "He could be the best in the world one day—if he lasts. He is in too much of a hurry. He becomes very excited."

I had not realized that Fabian was so highly regarded as a technician. And, as I left Mexico, I wondered if perhaps I had gotten to know a young man that one day would be as well-known as Mexico's Armillita, or Spain's El Cordobes. Or, the incomparable Manolete, the greatest of all time, who died on a bull's horn on August 28, 1947.

Dr. Espinosa did not have to spell it out. "If he lasts. . . ." ●

EPILOGUE *There was one incident in Acapulco that I did not mention because* The Canadian *was a family magazine.*

The scene was Fabian's room at the villa as he prepared to pray before his little altar. It was a sombre occasion and an uneasy silence hung in the air.

"Please Paul," Fabian said, reaching his arm out behind him, "a match to light my Holy candle."

Fear of the upcoming fight possessed me and I fumbled nervously in my pocket, finally finding a book of matches. I took them out, looked at them, and suddenly, jammed them back in my pocket. The others looked at me, puzzled, until someone else handed Fabian a match. My face must have been flushed with embarrassment. The matches were from La Huerta, Acapulco's most notorious whorehouse.

I had been there the night before and I just couldn't give those matches to the matador to light his Holy candles. Maybe they wouldn't work or they might offend Someone Upstairs so that it would mean bad luck. Perhaps I should explain that La Huerta is a legalized house of ill repute, the largest and least expensive one in town which, under its huge, straw-thatched roof, employed more than 200 girls.

It is a famous hangout for tourists and visiting sailors and you are quite welcome to go in and order drinks without partaking of the house specialty, which is served in motel-like units that encircled the mammoth bar. The girls paraded down the aisles and between the tables wearing outrageous costumes to attract the customers. They wore everything from babydoll pyjamas and high heels to gowns made from an American flag.

The girls smiled invitingly at the male patrons but would not speak to them unless invited to sit at their table. No selling or dickering was necessary. The price was a standard one hundred pesos, eight dollars in those days, and, if you had the urge, you took your girl to one of the various checkout counters, similar to those in supermarkets, and paid your money. In return, they gave you a key to one of the units that had been freshly made up and you were given thirty minutes with your medically-inspected companion.

I was staying at the famous, old El Mirador Hotel, a huge, pink structure where you could sit in the dining room and bar and watch the divers holding lighted torches leap from the cliffs each night. About twenty Canadian newsmen, who had been covering the Olympics, were also staying there and now were spending a couple of relaxing days in the pool before going home.

I told them all about this quaint place I had discovered and invited them to join me there that night along with a young Mexican doctor I had met with Fabian.

"We have no interest in prostitutes," they scoffed.

"But," I said, "it is a regular bar. We can just have a few drinks, watch the girls as they parade around, and leave."

Eleven of them, came along and, within twenty minutes, had all checked through the cashier with a new friend.

"Tomorrow morning," I said to my doctor friend as we sat at the bar, "I would like you to help me play a trick on them."

It was their last day in Mexico and they were all in the pool the next morning when I walked up with the doctor and called them aside.

"Guys," I said quietly, "the doc would like to speak with you."

"Gentlemen," said the young doctor in perfect English, "the girls you were with last night are supposed to be clean. But, just in case, I suggest you take these penicillin tablets. We have a strain of venereal disease here in Mexico that takes five days to clear up. I would recommend that you take one pill each day and avoid being with another woman during that time."

The doctor carried it off perfectly. We left quietly as they looked at one another in the pool, terror-stricken. They had been away for a month and were going home that night. I am not certain if any of them were married, but, I often wished I could have eavesdropped for the next week as they made excuses....

Meanwhile, I had problems of my own. I didn't have enough money to pay my hotel bill. I placed an emergency call to my bank manager at home and he said he would wire me $500. But, by the time it got there four days later, my bill had increased so much I was still short. I had a terrible argument with the management because they didn't want to accept my personal cheque for the balance when I checked out.

It was a direct flight back to Toronto and, as it happened, Canada's skiing heroine, Olympic champion Nancy Greene was on the same plane. She had been at the Mexican Olympics as an amateur sports advisor to the Canadian government. We sat together and Nancy was a most pleasant travelling companion, despite the fact she was still miffed at me because of a magazine story I had written after her triumphant return from the 1968 Winter Games. I wrote of my relief to find that this oh-so-perfect Mary Poppins figure actually enjoyed guzzling beer.

She was a captive audience and I bored her for the entire flight, talking about bullfighting and the new friendships I had formed. Actually, in the back of my mind, I was somewhat worried. I did not have one story from the Olympics and I had spent three times more than my allowed travelling budget.

Fortunately, editor Denny Harvey accepted my bullfight stories and a hurry-up piece on Canada's equestrians without complaining. But, as time went by, they started demanding that I file my expense account. Oh, what to do? I had all of these receipts but they were made out in pesos. Suddenly, I got it! I filed my entire expense account in pesos, pages and pages of pesos. The company comptroller, to whom I had always meant disaster, threw his hands up in disgust and frustration.

It worked. He didn't have time to go through every item and convert the pesos to dollars so he made out a cheque for the end amount. By golly, I had slipped through again.

●

I tried for the next four years to get some news about Fabian Ruiz but, always without success. And then, on January 1, 1972, I returned, with my family, to Mexico, crossing the border at Laredo, Texas, to Nueva Laredo in a dilapidated Volkswagen camper which had my worldly belongings strapped to the roof. The first thing I did when we arrived in San Miguel de Allende was to ask again about Fabian Ruiz and to telephone Senor Lutteroth's home in Mexico City to see if I could reach Enrique to tell him I was now living in his country. Nobody had heard of Fabian Ruiz (Favian Ruiz in Spanish) which gave me a chilly feeling. They would certainly know him if he had become a famous matador. Did he quit? Was he dead? I couldn't find out, but, Enrique would know.

A maid kept answering the phone at the Lutteroth residence in Spanish and I couldn't understand a word. "Enrique?" I kept repeating. She kept hanging up. Maybe she was telling me that Enrique was at his home in Baja, looking after the onyx mine—I couldn't tell.

I lived in Mexico for six months and never did reach Enrique or Fabian. It was as if they had just disappeared, as if my Olympic trip had been a figment of my imagination . . . .

There was a quaint, little bullring in San Miguel which looked to be centuries old. We would sit on the concrete seats each Sunday afternoon while third-rate matadors wrestled with skinny bulls and the band—half of them drunk—sprawled together in one corner trying desperately to play in tune. "Let the bull live!" a guy yelled one afternoon. "And kill the trumpet player!"

I remember one reluctant bull that leaped the barrier eleven times one afternoon, hoping for safety, only to be chased back into the ring. When it came time for the kill, the crowd yelled in protest. The bull, exhausted from its high-jumping activities, stood, legs wobbly, looking at the matador as if pleading for him to end it all. It still took the clumsy bugger eight thrusts of his sword to finish the job as the fans whistled, jeered, and threw cushions and wine bottles at him.

Still, it was bullfighting and I had been bitten years before one unforgettable afternoon in Acapulco. It had now become almost a ritual for the gang to gather at my house for a pre-fight party in my courtyard. It wasn't that I was particularly popular, but the whisky was free. We would entertain up to 50 guests—300 one night for a party after the fights—and, after two hours of drinking, I would give each person a bag containing a hunk of cheese and a half-litre of red wine. The parties became so popular even the matadors sometimes showed up. One of my neighbours was Manuel, the shoemaker down the street who also played lead trumpet in the band. He spoke no English but he would come through the door with a big smile and head for one of the bars to sample the tequila. He would take out his trumpet, insist I play the set of drums I had taken to Mexico and give him a swing beat. He tried every Sunday to play what apparently was supposed to be the theme from the film, The Man with the Golden Arm, but he never got it.

At 3:30 p.m. sharp, we would leave the house and stroll up the hilly, cobblestone streets, Manuel leading with his trumpet, and make our way merrily to the bullring. But, alas, one day Manuel became even drunker than usual and, as we entered the ring, he fell down the steps and broke his leg. No problem—his fellow musicians merely strolled down, surrounded their fallen colleague where he lay and played from there all afternoon. Some say it is the best they ever heard Manuel play. He did not feel any pain until the next day.

Sunday after Sunday I would go down to see the matadors to ask if anyone knew Fabian Ruiz. Some did but only casually and they couldn't give me any news.

"Ahhh, Favian . . . ," a matador said one afternoon, his eyes lighting up.

"Yes, yes," I said excitedly to a friend acting as an interpreter, "what does he know about him?"

"He never heard of him," my friend said.

I got all of the other bullfight news. Manolo Martinez was still numero uno, Eloy Cavazos was still a medium headliner, and the new sensation was young Curro Rivera. There was also sad news. Dashing Haime Bravo, an experienced matador I had met during the Olympics and a friend of Fabian, had been killed two years before. He had escaped death every Sunday afternoon in the bullring only to meet it on the highway while driving his car.

And then one day there was great excitement in San Miguel. Bullfight posters had been pasted up all over town announcing a very special corrida: Curro Rivera was coming to town and good bulls would be brought in for him. He was indeed a magnificent matador and, after his performance, he and his manager showed up at my home for the party. Certainly he knew of Fabian Ruiz, Curro said. Fabian was still fighting bulls. But, he had been injured many times. Serious injuries that had slowed him down and forced him away from the major rings. He was still fighting bulls in the small towns.

It hurt me to think of the proud, young matador I had once known. It hurt to visualize him, still a young man but with a patched-up body, fighting bad bulls in small, dusty bullrings. Was he still proud? Did he still have a dream? Did he still look at you with those burning eyes, suddenly smile, and say: "I love my bulls."

Dr. Espinosa's prophecy had been very accurate. I guess Fabian had been in too much of a hurry, too excitable and the bulls had made him pay for it. I stopped looking for him. I didn't want to see him in a third-rate ring like the one in San Miguel. I wanted to remember the boy I had watched in a mano-a-mano against the great Manolo Martinez in Acapulco. It had been a triumph for young Fabian and yet he had thrown himself across his bed after the fight and cried because he felt he had not done well enough.

I did not stop looking for Enrique Lutteroth. After my six-month sojourn in San Miguel de Allende, I returned on three separate occasions over the next four years. And each time I tried that number in Mexico City. Same maid. Same problem.

Dammit Enrique, wherever you are, please ask your father to hire at least one bilingual servant.

BY CONCENTRATING ON some lesser known sports, little did I realize that I was preparing myself for yet another short-lived career—that as a television pitchman for beer. I received a call one day from Caledon Advertising in Toronto asking if I would consider appearing in a commercial for O'Keefe Ale, one of Carling O'Keefe's many products.

"Sure," I said. "When would you like to meet?"

"How about one hour from now," said John Robertson of the agency.

That was a Friday afternoon. On Monday morning, I was in Wellesley, Ontario, a sleepy, little farming community near Kitchener, at the home of my old pal Elmer Hohl with an entire television crew.

Chances are that you have never heard of Elmer Hohl despite the fact he is one of the world's outstanding athletes. He is a big, rawboned farmer who, without ever practicing, just happens to be the greatest horseshoe pitcher who has ever lived.

The ad people had all been gathered in a board room on the Friday afternoon along with the brewery's marketing men. I had no idea that a hidden camera had been filming me during our two-hour conversation. I was wearing jeans and had left my thirteen-year-old daughter waiting in the reception area, for what I thought would only be a few minutes, while I met with John Robertson and his colleagues. They had an idea that I could make some commercials by telling stories of people I had written about. I suggested we involve real people.

"For instance," I said, "I happen to know this guy, Elmer Hohl, who can throw a horseshoe around a bottle of beer without breaking it."

"You do!" they said in unison, leaning forward with interest.

Frankly, I had no idea if Elmer could do it or not, but it sounded good at the time.

That evening producer Bob Schulz was sent down to the Saphire Tavern where I was playing drums and, as I later found out, he was watching me while we talked to see if he thought I could go on film without too much editing and makeup. A meeting was scheduled for Saturday morning at his apartment and, while we were talking, Schulz asked me to call Elmer Hohl to ask if he would be available Monday for us to shoot a pilot.

"By the way, Elmer," I said on the phone, "could you throw a horseshoe around a bottle of beer without breaking it?"

"Wal, now, I don't think that I ever tried," big Elmer drawled. "I think maybe I'd rather drink it."

So there we were that Monday morning, without a script, at a homemade horseshoe pitch on Elmer's farm. The neighbors had no idea what was going on, all of those long-haired city slickers hauling in camera equipment and lights. Big pigs kept rooting in the mud and lazy cows watched without interest while chewing their cud.

Elmer was one of my heroes, as honest a guy as you could ever meet and extremely humble for a man who was an almost perennial world champion. To give you some idea of his expertise, he once threw 69 successive ringers in world championship play. Elmer did some carpentry work, ran his farm, and lived the good life over there in Wellesley. I had written newspaper columns about him, interviewed him once for a national television show and, finally, did a full magazine piece on him for *The Canadian*. Now we were going to try to sell beer.

"Listen Elmer," I said, pulling him aside. "I've told these people you can throw a horseshoe around a bottle of beer. Do it and it'll be worth a minimum of $3000 to you."

"Wal," he said in his deliberate way, "I shure as heck will try. Don't seem too difficult to me."

"But Paul," said Elmer's wife, who was bustling around watching the crew at work, "does it have to be beer? Couldn't Elmer do this for Pepsi or somebody else?"

"Don't worry about anythin,'" Elmer said quietly.

I think he heard me when I said $3000.

After about an hour the cameras were set up to record Elmer's attempt. Nobody but me believed he could do it and, frankly, I was starting to have doubts. In case of a miracle, the crew decided to shoot Elmer's throw in slow motion, following the horseshoe from his hand until it landed so that nobody could accuse us of faking the shot. They had three cameras set up and enough film to record more than 20 attempts.

A bottle of O'Keefe Ale was set in the dirt, label to the camera, just in front of the peg in one pit. Elmer looked at it thoughtfully, walked back to the other pit, and turned to face the bottle. He held the horseshoe up, taking aim with his throwing arm which after years in the game, is about three inches longer than his other one.

"The arm's a little bit crooked, too," he told me once. "I figure that was from pitchin' softball."

Elmer went into his first backswing and there wasn't a sound other than an old cow who shifted her weight to another foot. Big Elmer let go with his famous delivery and the horseshoe arced gracefully in the air, doing its perfect one and a half turns, dropping towards the beer bottle with its toes open . . . Kerplunk!

There was a cheer as the dust cleared to show the horseshoe clearly around the bottle. It hadn't even touched it! It sent a shiver through me like the time I listened on the radio when Bobby Thomson hit his famous home run in 1951! Bob Schulz and Don Riches, the creative director of Caledon Advertising, were ecstatic, hardly able to believe their eyes.

"The only thing that could make it more perfect," quipped Riches, "is if there wasn't dirt on the label."

I decided to put Elmer on.

"Elmer," I said when I walked back down to where he was standing. "They say you put dirt on the label."

"Oh, gawsh," he said seriously. "I'm sorry. But, nobody told me about that."

Just for the heck of it, they decided to let Elmer try again. He concentrated even harder and—would you believe it—he made the shot that was eventually used in the commercial, without spraying dirt on the label! On his first two tries he had put the horseshoe around the bottle without breaking it or even touching it!

We shot film all day and, when we finally left, Schulz and Riches figured that not only had it been an excellent pilot, it might just be a finished commercial. Both Elmer and I were rookies in the commercial field and neither of us could believe just how much work went into something that, when aired, was only sixty seconds long.

I went on to appear in more than thirty commercials for O'Keefe Ale but nothing was as exciting, or as good, as that pilot with big Elmer on his farm. Not only did it appear on the air but that commercial took me to Hollywood in 1974 where it won a Spike Award as one of the world's best television commercials of the year in an annual competition sponsored by the Society of Hollywood Radio and Television Artists.

Elmer, let me thank you again. It meant more than $3000 to me. It gave me four years of exposure and financial gain that I never expected. Unfortunately, it also meant eventual trouble with the income tax people, but that's another story.

Elmer displays his championship form ▶

Our next effort for O'Keefe was a commercial featuring Diane Warriner, Canada's top woman softball pitcher who had played with the U.S. champion Raybestos Brakettes. She had no trouble at all striking me out. I used to tell them at banquets that she wasn't the only girl I had struck out with.

Our third commercial was with Cliff Thorburn, Canada's snooker champion who, in 1980 at the tender age of 32, astounded the world of pool by winning the world professional snooker championship in Sheffield, England. Pool, of course, is one of my favorite pastimes and I pulled another Elmer Hohl on Schulz and Riches, two guys for whom I was quickly gaining a great deal of respect and who became two of my best friends.

"I know this guy," I said, "who can curve a pool ball around a bottle of O'Keefe Ale to make his final ball in a corner pocket."

"You do!" they again said in unison.

Now I had to convince Cliff and explain the key shot to him. Again, this was not done until we were on location, the cameras were set up and we were wearing makeup. The location I should explain, was rather elegant—the home of the late Colonel Sam McLaughlin, millionaire-founder of General Motors in Canada, in Oshawa, Ontario, about thirty miles east of Toronto.

Colonel Sam's palatial estate is open for public tours and, in one wing, he had a magnificent pool room, complete with carved mahogany walls, a huge fireplace, and a unique snooker table with huge, carved feet on its legs. People have asked me what I meant in the commercial's final scene when I turned to Cliff and said, "Nice place you've got here." Cliff doubled over in laughter because neither of us could afford the public tour. Colonel Sam, incidentally, also had his own bowling lane, complete with an automatic pinsetter, and a huge, marble, indoor swimming pool.

Before the first take I took Cliff aside and whispered to him what I had planned. The cue ball would be tight against one of the end rails and his final ball would be down the rail, dead in front of the pocket. A very simple shot, until I reached down and placed my bottle of O'Keefe Ale between them, flush to the cue ball so that it was touching.

"What!" said Cliff.

"It will be very easy for a player of your calibre," I said, "to put one helluva lot of juice on the cueball and shoot it out and in the opposite direction from the other ball. The cue ball will then stop, reverse direction and roll back to the other pocket and make the ball."

"You're kidding," he said.

"Oh, and the cue ball must have enough stuff on it to stop on impact so it doesn't follow the other ball into the pocket."

Cliff raised his eyebrows and looked away as if I was nuts. To his credit, though, he agreed to try. To make this shot, he would have to stand right over the cue ball, hold his cue straight in the air, and stroke the ball without being able to even touch the table for support with his bridge hand. Thorburn tried it twenty-two times without success. Schulz and Riches started to look worried. But, Cliff kept getting closer. On his twenty-third attempt he made what I feel is the greatest shot ever filmed and he made it four times in a row.

The advertising people decided to enter the Hohl-Warriner-Thorburn commercials in the Spike Award competition in the most difficult category of all—a series of three commercials, any product, with each commercial sixty seconds in length. It would have been much simpler to enter a single-commercial category for beverages. But, surprise of surprises, we got a wire saying our commercials had won an award by finishing among the ten finalists in this largest of categories. We were invited to the awards dinner at the mammoth Century Plaza Hotel in Los Angeles—in the same room they once used to present the Academy Awards.

The agency sent Don Riches and me and, because we were going to the land of show business, we went to my pal Nick the Needle and rented two powder blue tuxedoes for the occasion.

It was a memorable trip that was almost marred by Gene Taylor, a television host from Toronto, who had arranged to have me hit in the face with a pie. He arranged the hit through a Los Angeles firm called Pie Face International and, it would have been made except for a long distance call I received from one of my readers warning me about it.

"I am a photographer from Toronto," I lied to the hit man. "If you can tell me exactly when and where this will take place, I'll get a picture of it for Taylor."

The sucker told me everything, I avoided it and they say it is the first time that Pie Face International ever missed a hit. Meanwhile, I called my pal Johnny McNamara in Toronto and, when Taylor went on television the next day, Johnny Mac hit him square in the face with a pie. Unfortunately, Johnny slipped as he made the hit and almost broke Taylor's nose.

The night of the awards presentation was a magnificent evening. Les Brown and His Band of Renown were there, along with many big network television stars who, just like at the Academy Awards show, tore open envelopes and announced the winners.

We didn't expect to win and so we weren't disappointed when the final, big category came up and the envelope contained the names of an English agency and production company that had produced a series advocating the use of safety belts in cars. But, we didn't realize just how close we must have come to winning until after the dinner when the head judge, slightly tipsy, recognized me from the commercials and approached us in the lobby.

"You guys were robbed," he said. "But, you'll never beat safety belts with beer."

We packed up our powder blues and prepared to head home when one of us had this bright idea of stopping in Las Vegas on the way, seeing as how neither of us had ever been there. I recall us missing eight planes while we sat in the L.A. airport drinking with some guy who went around buying commercial airliners that had crashed so he could sell the parts.

We arrived in Las Vegas late that night and got a couple of rooms at the Holiday Inn on the strip where the casino resembles an old riverboat. I had only $50 left and wired my bank for an additional $500.

I sat down at a blackjack table at 10 o'clock the next morning, and, one hour later, was convinced that I had discovered paradise. It seemed that I couldn't lose, not even when I stayed on twelves. In addition to my increasing pile of chips, I just loved those free drinks they delivered to the players. I was half corked by early afternoon but, I sat at that table until 6 a.m. the following day—twenty consecutive hours.

Riches figured I was up about $14 000 at one point, my pockets bulging with $100 chips. The pit boss and floor manager kept giving me their business cards as the shifts changed and telling me I could return as their guest any time I wanted. By golly, I was a high roller!

The rest of the story you have heard many times before. Riches was practically on his knees pleading with me to cash in. I looked at him through eyes glazed by scotch on the rocks and with this sudden feeling of confidence, power and incredible wealth.

Poor Don kept after me all evening and into the wee hours of the morning before he finally gave up. My chips had started to disappear. The hotel had their best and most experienced croupiers working my table. Others stood behind me and watched, just like in the movies. I loved the attention. I even started using the high-roller slang I was picking up, even though I had not the faintest idea what I was doing. One pocket was soon empty. Then another pocket was empty. . . .

"Are you satisfied now?" demanded Riches when my chips had vanished.

"I've had a helluva time," I slurred. "Oops, I missed a few. There are still some chips in my back pocket."

He pulled me over to the cashier and, despite the fact that most of my chips were gone, I still had fourteen $100 chips in that one pocket. The cashier gave me fourteen $100 bills.

"I'll just try this game a couple of times and then we'll go to bed," I mumbled, heading for a roulette table. It was 6 a.m., I guess I was very drunk, and I peeled off one of the bills, plopped it down on the table and said to the young lady croupier, "Even."

The casino was practically empty, no one else was at the table and suddenly an older gentleman, obviously more experienced, tapped the girl on the shoulder and said he would handle the wheel. I am not suggesting there was anything dishonest, but do you know that I bet even fourteen times and the number came up odd fourteen times in a row? If that man did not have an intimate relationship with that wheel, he certainly was very lucky. Riches, meanwhile, walked away after my sixth consecutive loss, unable to watch. He still looked sick after we had managed to get some sleep and were leaving the hotel for the airport. He was absolutely disgusted with me.

"Just think," I said. "I had all of that fun for $50. I haven't picked up my money from home yet. I wonder if anybody will believe what happened?"

"I still don't believe it," he said. "But I saw it happen."

Since that time, I have gotten to know Las Vegas quite well. And in fact I can honestly say that I have left there several times with money in my pocket—not anything near $14 000, but enough to have gone home happy. I love the action, love the shows and, used to love the drinks.

Riches, Schulz, and I continued making commercials and continued winning awards. In 1976, we won The Gold Bessy, the highest honor in Canada, which is awarded to the single best commercial, any category, of the year. This was for a commercial we called Party Tricks. It showed a group of us sitting around a bar room table, playing tricks with coins, bottles, and glasses. The waitress Hilda (Canadian actress Barbara Hamilton) ended our games by pulling the table cloth out from under our drinks without spilling a drop or knocking anything over. That commercial and one we called The Beaver River Rat Race also won top awards in the U.S. Television Commercial Festival which we accepted at a luncheon in Chicago.

We made commercials about sports no one had ever seen before and travelled halfway around the world filming them. There was one in Stockholm about a game called varpa, where the object is to hurl a heavy, discus-like stone on something resembling a horseshoe pit to see who can land nearest to the stake.

In Czechoslovakia, I was filmed playing a game called legball where two teams play with a soccer ball, using only their feet and heads in something resembling volleyball. We couldn't understand a word of each other's language but we still filmed a drinking scene with good old O'Keefe Ale and I taught the guys to face the camera, smile, raise their bottles, and say my closing line: "Here's to you with O'Keefe!"

A commercial from Finland showed me playing a game that sounds like "base-a-bollo" with two girls' teams. They wear baseball uniforms, and funny little catching gloves. The pitcher stands right beside the hitter and throws a hard rubber ball in the air. The batter must hit it as it falls. It's a helluva game, complete with baserunning, a lot of hitting and fielding and, if anyone ever decides to start a league in North America I'd certainly try to buy a franchise. It would be sure box office.

Back home in Canada, we made commercials featuring such sports as croquet, a greased pole climb, cutting horses, and a ridiculous game called underwater hockey.

Sometimes it wasn't all fun. We shot the cutting horse commercial on the ranch of singer Ian Tyson who first gained fame paired with his folk-singing wife Sylvia. Tyson also happens to be one of the top cutting horse riders in the country. Cutting horses are finely tuned animals, well trained to move carefully into a herd of calves, select one and bring it out, supposedly for branding. As the calf tries desperately to get back to the herd, it is poetry in motion as the horse and rider move in unison to block its path, almost as graceful as ballet.

My problem that day was that my back was out. It happens occasionally and they tried to massage me into shape as I lay in pain on a wagon.

"Schultzy," I growled at producer Bob Schulz, who had escaped from Hungary after the 1956 revolution, "if I break my back on this horse you are going to think 1956 was a picnic."

That, incidentally, was the first beer commercial where, in the final drinking scene, one of the cowboys declined my offer of an O'Keefe replying, "No thanks. I don't drink." Sadly, that same cowboy drowned only weeks later in a boating accident. He had been one of the country's top cutting horse riders.

M y most dangerous experiences were while we made the Beaver River Rat Race and underwater hockey commercials. I almost drowned during both of them. The Beaver River Rat Race is a wacky event held each spring in ski country north of Toronto for which the prime requisite seems to be that the entrants must be drunk. The race begins in the hamlet of Thornbury and is designed for homemade rafts over a seven-mile stretch of the churning Beaver River. There are two waterfalls along the way that end the race for many of the rafts, their occupants thrashing for shore wearing wet suits in the icy water. Crowds of more than 20 000 brave the cold to watch gaily costumed sailors, flushed with drink, pour over those falls in rafts of every shape and size and made from everything imaginable—styrofoam, inflated inner tubes, plywood, and fiberglass.

A big guy named Chip Climo built our four-man raft and we even had an old-fashioned square sail. The name, of course, was The Good Ship O'Keefe. I wore an admiral's hat fashioned from a football helmet. Chip assumed a position in the back along with Phil Styles, bar-owner, production manager, experienced sailor, and bon vivant. I was joined on the bow by Freddie (The Flashbulb) Ross, my old photographer pal and co-owner of Annabelle the Wonder Horse.

Everything went smoothly as we coasted along, sipping from plastic spray bottles of scotch that each of us had tied to the deck in front of us—until we rounded a bend and hit white water. The Good Ship O'Keefe was swept away like a cork, heading straight for a cliff on the other side and directly at a protruding tree stump in the water. Freddie the Flashbulb tried to break our impact against the stump by using his paddle to veer us away.

He missed, brought it back for a second attempt and, in so doing, hit me square in the chest with his elbow and knocked me overboard.

I was swept 100 yards down the foaming river in what seemed only a matter of seconds, until I was hurled up against the side of the cliff and managed to grab a branch. It was just like in the movie *Deliverance*. Suddenly, however, I was pulled from my safe spot by a huge arm around my neck. Good old Chip. He was saving me. Saving me? Hell, now we were both being washed down the river and, as he grasped for branches with one arm, he was holding my head underwater with the other. I was fighting for air and thought I was a goner until he finally pulled me up.

"Sorry about that," he said, puffing and red in the face. I was gasping and choking. But, do you think anybody cared? Hell, the sound man on the job started yelling at me because I had lost the remote microphone he had taped to my wet suit!

They tell me it cost more than $50 000 to film that one-minute spot, including underwater cameras, motorcycle messengers along the course, and a cameraman shooting from above in a plane. That cost, I can assure you, would have been considerably higher if Chip had held me underwater just a few seconds longer.

As if I hadn't learned anything from my ride along the river, I agreed to do a commercial about underwater hockey. This placed me in absolutely the most ridiculous position of my life and came infinitely closer to ending my life than the Beaver River Rat Race.

U nderwater hockey is, at best, an obscure sport played by scuba divers in a swimming pool. I had never heard of it before and haven't heard of it since. It is played by two teams wearing diving outfits, complete with fins and snorkels. There is a goal marked out underwater at each end of the pool and the players use metal hockey sticks that are carried in one hand. Each stick has a pipe-like handle on the end of which is a U-shaped blade. The puck is made of heavy metal and slides along the bottom of the pool.

This was the setting and then they decided to film the commercial as a farce. The first scene showed me sitting on top of a curved slide beside a pool in someone's backyard wearing a complete ice hockey uniform: helmet, shoulder pads, elbow pads, gloves, pants, shinpads, skates, and holding a real wooden hockey stick. My line, as I started sliding toward the water, was: "Some of the guys invited me over for a game of hockey. But, what they didn't tell me is, it's underwater hockey! Glug, glug, glug. . . ."

Schultzy and Riches wanted me to go to the bottom of the pool and stand there for a second on my skates, my stick down in front of me as if I was preparing to take a faceoff. An underwater camera would shoot me in that position before I started back to the surface.

Everybody, including me, was very surprised when, seconds after I hit the water, I bobbed back to the top and just floated there because of the bouyant material in my hockey pads. It was absolutely impossible for me to get to the bottom. But, there was an immediate solution. One of the divers climbed the ladder to the top of the slide before our next take and strapped a belt of lead weights around my waist. They weighed thirty-six pounds and he slipped them around so they were at my back and therefore wouldn't be seen by the camera. My hockey sweater was then pulled over the belt to cover it.

◀The Good Ship O'Keefe and her crew at the Beaver River Rat Race.

"This is very simple," explained the diver. "You just pull this clasp on the front of the belt and it will fall free so that you can come up again. Do it as soon as they get the picture of you standing on the bottom."

We tried it a couple of times while I sat on the slide and the belt worked perfectly. Then I slipped my hockey gloves on again, picked up my stick, and faced the camera.

"Roll!" Bob Schulz yelled, holding up his arm.

"Underwater hockey! Take seven!" barked one of the crew, clapping the board in front of me.

"Action!" yelled Schultzie.

"Some of the guys invited me over . . .," I began as I started down the slide.

Well, we had overlooked a few things. First of all, by saying my lines before I hit the water, I was already a little short of breath by the time I got there. The weights were all on my back, which pulled me down into a prone position on the slide and that's the way I hit the water, going straight to the bottom where I stayed, flat on my back, unable to get up, even to a sitting position.

Finally, we forgot that it was absolutely impossible for me to raise my wet hockey sweater to spring the release clasp on my belt while wearing cumbersome hockey gloves. I lay on the bottom of the pool, almost in a panic, short of breath, unable to move, unable to get at the belt. . . .

If it had not been for the quick thinking of the underwater cameraman, who suddenly realized my predicament, I would have left this world then and there, while about thirty people above wondered what was happening. The cameraman dropped his equipment, swam to me, tore at my sweater, released the weighted belt, and then tried to pull me to the top. I looked up and saw light but it seemed miles away. I was now gripped by complete panic, thrashing with my hockey skates, grabbing at the cameraman, fighting this tremendous urge to try to breathe. I now understand how a drowning person feels. I realize why a person drowns. You can't stop your body from taking that final gasp, even when you know there is no air. It is an automatic reaction. There is nothing else to do. You can't help but suck water into your lungs. Goodbye Louie. . . .

I almost did that twice on the way up. And I know I couldn't have stopped myself again. I suspect I was just a moment away from sucking water into my lungs. I hadn't taken a breath since I started talking on top of that slide. When I finally reached the surface, I almost blacked out. I was so weak I was barely able to hold onto the side of the pool.

"Okay, okay!" Bob Schulz was ordering. "Everybody back to their positions. Let's do it again!"

The cameraman explained what had happened. I couldn't talk. The crew had no idea. They didn't even believe the story until we watched the rushes later that week and realized just how long I had been underwater.

I now also realize something about a man's last thoughts before he dies. They say your life flashes past your eyes in those final seconds. That didn't happen to me but I did have this crazy thought. Realizing my situation and how close I was to dying, I saw this vivid scene while I was underwater.

Another kid is asking my daughter: "How did your father die?"

"Lying on the bottom of a swimming pool with thirty-six pounds of lead weights around his waist," she replied. "There were about thirty people around the pool, television cameras, lights, and a whole bunch of scuba divers. He was wearing a full hockey uniform, skates and everything. It was just a little swimming pool in someone's backyard. It was all very sad. Everyone was quite surprised." Honestly, that would have been my last thought.

This all started because I once did a magazine story about a guy named Elmer Hohl. We had fun making those commercials, worked hard, won awards, and I learned a lot from guys like Schultzie, Don Riches and Geoffrey Smyth, the man in charge of marketing for Carling-O'Keefe. Eventually, however, Smyth left the company and the experiment came to an end. We had one problem, despite our awards, production expertise, and originality.

We didn't sell enough beer. ●

The goal that death was watching

prologue *Once in a while during your life you meet someone that you consider to be a special person. Bruce Draper was that kind of a guy.*

I first heard his story from Toronto sportscaster Pat Marsden, a longtime friend of the Draper family when he lived in Ottawa, and Pat arranged our interview.

Bruce Draper's story had been a well-kept secret and he had to give it considerable thought for a few weeks before consenting to tell it. I received more mail about this story than any I had written before.

○ ○ ○

MARCH 4, 1967—It was 7:30 p.m. on Wednesday, January 11, and in a few minutes the Hershey Bears would skate out on the ice to warm up for their game against the Providence Reds.

They sat there now waiting, shifting uneasily as the tension built. Coach Frank Mathers paced nervously, wondering, perhaps, if he had made the right decision.

The game itself wasn't worrying them. The Bears, storming along in first place in the American Hockey League's Eastern Division,

didn't figure to have much trouble with the last-place Reds.

Yet, even the hardest veteran felt soft inside. Some of them said a prayer in the silence.

"Hey, you guys!" boomed Bruce Cline, an assistant captain, "Looks like we got a rookie with us tonight."

Bruce Draper, wearing number 21, smiled, embarrassed, as his teammates laughed with the release of tension.

It was a preview to one of the most dramatic moments I have ever seen in sport—the night

Bruce Draper came back. It is a story of courage and a young man's faith in God.

There were only 3400 fans in the 7000-seat Hershey Sports Arena that night as number 21 stepped onto the ice, and only a handful realized the significance of the moment

Bruce had called me in Toronto at noon that day to tell me he would be playing his first game since February 9, 1966—almost a year.

"I didn't sleep all night," he had said. "But you'd better get here early. I'm not sure how long the legs will hold out. I may have to score on the first shift."

Draper skated easily now in the warmup, his head down as if in deep thought. The game started, and when he skated out to center between wingers Gary Dornhoefer and Myron Stankiewicz, there was a polite smattering of applause from the couple of dozen fans who knew his story.

What the others didn't know was that underneath his Hershey jersey, Bruce Draper carried an ugly scar from the base of his abdomen to his chest.

The announcement a year ago was brief. It said that Bruce Draper had left the Bears to have an operation for " a glandular condition." It was a routine announcement and had received little attention back in Canada, where many fans remembered the famous Draper brothers who played for St. Mikes. Bruce, now 26, played on a line with Dave, his identical twin, when St. Mikes won the Memorial Cup in 1961.

At one point in their career, an older brother, Mike, was on their line and often they were mistaken for triplets. Newspapers kept getting their names wrong in captions under their pictures and sportswriters were always writing stories about how Father David Bauer, their coach, couldn't tell them apart.

Anyway, Bruce has been knocking around in the minors, though he played briefly in one game with the Toronto Maple Leafs four seasons ago.

He has played in every minor pro league, first with Rochester, then Sudbury and Denver. Two seasons ago, Bruce and Gene Ubriaco, who had been on the St. Mikes team with him, were traded to Hershey.

This is where Bruce Draper's story begins.

He missed half the season with a cracked kneecap, returned to the lineup and, just before leaving for his Ottawa home for the summer, noticed a small cyst on his lower abdomen. The team doctor told him to see his doctor in Ottawa to have it removed.

But he kept putting it off, and finally it was too late to get a hospital bed. His Ottawa doctor, however, assured him it wouldn't do him any harm if he continued playing. So he returned to training camp without having the cyst removed.

That was last season and Bruce got off to the best start of his career.

"I was starting to pop a few," he smiles. "Finally I was going to prove to people that I could play pro hockey."

On February 9, 1966, the Cleveland Barons were in town. So were Mrs. Jack Draper, to see her son play for the first time in three years, and Mrs. Ben Villeneuve from Aylmer, Quebec, near Ottawa, mother of Bruce's pretty wife, Judy.

Bruce didn't disappoint his mother and mother-in-law. He scored two goals and had two assists to bring his total to 14 goals and 21 assists in 41 games.

But he had been having pains in his stomach for about two weeks and he saw the team doctor that night, fearing he might have a hernia or pulled stomach muscle. The doctor had forgotten about the cyst, thinking Bruce had had it removed. It was larger now and he sent Bruce to Dr. Josiah Reed, a urologist at the Polyclinic Hospital in Harrisburg, 22 miles from Hershey.

Dr. Reed admitted Bruce to the hospital the next day, a Thursday, and removed the cyst Friday. Bruce figured he would be away for a week to 10 days.

In medical terms, they call it a testicular tumor and Bruce remembers vividly coming out of the anesthetic briefly when they took him back to his room.

Dr. Reed looked at him and said: "Bruce . . . it was malignant."

"That was the hardest check I ever took," says Bruce. "I was so mad I was going to rip my bed apart, but I fell back and went under again. All I could think of was Murray Balfour."

Balfour, his linemate the previous season and a former Chicago Black Hawk and Boston Bruin, had died eight months before—May 30, 1965—of lung cancer. Bruce remembered how Balfour coughed so hard on the bench that the other players told him to tell the management he was too ill to play.

Bruce and Gene Ubriaco had a few beers with Balfour, a non-drinker, the night he was to leave for his home in Regina when the season ended.

"So long, Bruce," said Balfour. "Have a good summer, I'll see you at training camp in the fall."

"That was really sad," Bruce recalls. "Both Uby and I knew how serious it was. We knew he wouldn't be there. But little did I know at the time, that I had the same thing."

The difference was that Balfour's condition was too advanced for anything to be done about it. Dr. Reed told Bruce, when he awakened that day, that he felt he could arrest his.

When Bruce went back to sleep that day, Dr. Reed phoned his home in Hershey and asked to speak to his mother. Judy was expecting a second child in June and Debra Lynn was one and a half years old at the time.

"He told Mrs. Draper not to tell me what he had found because it might upset me," Bruce's wife remembers. "But when she put the phone down, she started to cry and I made her tell me."

"They were both with me when I woke up that night," says Bruce. "Dr. Reed told me they were going to operate again on Monday. I remember they sent for my dad and told me on Sunday that I could see my little girl if I wanted to. I knew it was serious, but those two things really shook me up."

H is father's plane was grounded by bad weather at Baltimore and he had to continue by bus, arriving at Harrisburg early Monday morning, just in time to see his son being wheeled into the operating room.

"My father is a big, strong man," says Bruce, "and he always made us stronger somehow. I know it did me a lot of good to see him that morning."

"He was on the operating table four and a half hours," says Dr. Reed. "The seed of the disease had spread to the lymph nodes of the retroperitoneal space up as far as the kidneys. We removed this from his abdomen and chest."

Bruce weighed 174 pounds when he entered the hospital and left two weeks later, pale, weak and weighing only 155.

"He would sit on the chesterfield for about five minutes and it would tire him out so much he would have to go and lie down," says Judy. "He looked terrible and his clothes didn't fit him."

"My wife was fantastic through it all," says Bruce. "She stood up like a rock and this was a great inspiration."

But what Judy didn't tell him at the time was that she went to see the Bears play the night after Bruce went into the hospital, and broke down when she met Frank Mathers. On another occasion, she didn't feel as if she could visit him without crying, so she asked his mother to go alone.

"She never let me see her like that," says Bruce. "And my family was tremendous. I know it must have shocked the hell out of them as much as it did out of me. Father Bauer called me from Montreal when the Canadian team came back from the world tournament. I knew I had a lot of good people praying for me.

"It never entered my mind that I wasn't going to make it. I made up my mind that I was going to beat this thing."

He spent a lot of sleepless nights, though, worrying about his growing family and what would happen if anything did go wrong.

"I think he kept fighting for us," says Judy, who now has a second daughter, Kimberly Ann, eight months old. "If he had been single, I don't know if he would have made it."

Dr. Reed told Judy not to cater to Bruce after he left the hospital and to see that he did a lot of walking. He walked around the house at first, built himself up so that he could make it around the block, and kept extending his walks each day.

After two weeks, they started the cobalt treatments. Bruce was scheduled to take 10 weeks of treatments, 2½ minutes each day—one day on his stomach, the next on his back.

"We treated his entire lymph drainage area, from the groin to the neck," says Dr. Reed. "We x-rayed the entire spine. These treatments were so powerful that bone marrow would be partially destroyed and he had the chronic weakness of severe anemia to overcome.

"The tissues in the spine would have turned to scar tissue had he not exercised. And I know that exercising sometimes hurts like hell."

With grim determination, Bruce kept working. In April, only two months after his operation, he astounded Dr. Reed by asking if he could play golf.

"I went out and tried to swing a club, but it hurt like hell," he says. "I rested a couple more weeks and tried it again. By June, I was playing 27 holes a day and carrying my own bag."

After eight weeks, his blood count became too low for the cobalt treatments to be continued, so Bruce and his family went back to Ottawa for the summer.

Before they left, however, his teammates surprised him. A couple of them, including Gene Ubriaco, drove him to Harrisburg for his treatment one day, then went back to the Drapers' apartment where their wives had gathered.

"Uby asked me to go upstairs and when we were going through our living room, there was a color television set," Bruce recalls. "I thought they'd rented it for the day for some special program, but the guys on the team had chipped in to buy it for us. It was a nice feeling."

At a players' meeting the next afternoon, Bruce—who is an excellent and witty public speaker—became nervous as he tried to thank his teammates.

"This is the nicest thing that has happened to me in pro hockey," he said. "You hear of other players having special nights and things, but you don't ever think it will happen to you."

The players ended his embarrassment with applause and wished him the best of luck during the summer.

Soon after returning to Ottawa, Bruce—who had gained a few pounds—discovered a couple of lumps on the left side of his neck. He went to his family doctor, who had his full history from Harrisburg, and had the lumps removed under a local anesthetic.

That was Monday, June 27, 1966. On Tuesday, Kimberly Ann was born. On Friday that same week, the doctor called him. Familiar words: "Bruce . . . they were malignant."

"It was as if someone had hit me over the head with a hammer," says Bruce. "I really blew up. I thought it was the end of the world."

Three more weeks of cobalt treatments followed at Ottawa's Civic Hospital, where he made quite an impression on Dr. Gordon Edgar Catton, a therapeutic radiologist.

"There is no doubt," says Dr. Catton, "that Bruce is all desire. He showed an unusual response to cobalt treatments. Nine of 10 tumors as advanced as his was when discovered wouldn't have responded to treatment as well."

In August, the professional hockey players around Ottawa, including the Draper brothers, rented the arena at Hull each night to start preparing for their respective training camps. Bruce asked Dr. Catton if he could try skating.

"I encouraged him" says Dr. Catton, "and he encouraged me with his spirit."

Earlier in the summer, Bruce realized that if he ever played hockey again, it would have to be with Hershey. The Bears put him in something called the reverse draft, which means any other team could have claimed him. No team did, though—obviously because nobody wanted to take a chance on his health.

A healthy Bruce Draper, as coach Mathers says, likely would be drafted when the new National Hockey League teams stock up for expansion.

At this time, however, Bruce had a long, long way to go.

"I couldn't skate very well," says Bruce, "so I sort of hung back on the defence."

Some of the players he worked out with each night were Ralph Backstrom and Claude Larose of Montreal Canadiens, minor leaguers Brian Smith and Terry Clancey, and, of course, his brothers—Dave, Mike and Pat.

"I drove my brothers crazy," Bruce says. "I'd keep feeling myself to see if there were any more lumps, which, I guess, is natural. Anyway, I'd feel something on my arm and I'd keep going over and feeling their arms to see if they had the same thing."

Twin brother Dave had diagrams of the isometric exercises his teams used at Michigan Tech and he encouraged Bruce to use them regularly.

"I think they helped me more than anything," says Bruce. "We also went to the YMCA each day for steam baths and bike riding and we ran a lot."

Hershey invited him to attend training camp and Bruce, though barely able to skate the length of the ice and back, headed south with his family.

His muscles were beginning to harden again. After his first stay in the hospital in Harrisburg, he'd lost almost all his strength, including the leg muscles.

"But something happened during that car ride to Hershey," Judy says. "Bruce seemed to get new strength and a new outlook."

"That's right," says Bruce. "When I got to camp, I was able to do most of the skating drills and took part in scrimmages. I felt great. But, after a week, I stopped a shot on my ankle and had to miss another five days which put me even further behind."

It was obvious at the end of training that Bruce was not strong enough to make the starting lineup. But general manager Lloyd Blinco gave him a contract which would run until November 30, giving him two more months to make it.

There were only four days left when I visited him on November 26. Bruce still hadn't been told if he would be kept. He felt he was playing reasonably well in practices, but he hadn't been in a game. He wondered how they would be able to make a decision without seeing him in action. He was in the unfortunate position of trying to crack a lineup that had put the Bears in first place.

Bruce made up his mind to wait until the Friday to see if he would get a pay cheque. The cheque was there, and so were subsequent cheques, though nothing was said.

Bruce continued to work out alone while the team was on the road. Then, in early December, they took him on a road trip. He called me and he was obviously excited. But he didn't dress for any games and still nothing was said.

I kept in touch with Bruce and on January 10, called Frank Mathers.

"It's funny. I was sitting here now thinking about Bruce," said Mathers. "I may play him tomorrow night. But I'm not thinking of it just to give him a chance. He's up to 170 now and he looks good in workouts. He might be able to help us.

"Playing him out of sympathy would prove nothing. It wouldn't be fair to the team and it wouldn't be fair to him."

Mathers knew, as anyone in hockey knows, that even a man in perfect health, if he's been away from hockey for a year, finds it extremely difficult to come back. You just don't get enough work in a practice to condition you for a game.

Mathers, watching Draper now as referee Bruce Hood prepared to drop the puck, had had to make a big decision.

Above, sitting with other players' wives, Judy Draper bit her fingernails, every muscle tense.

The players on both benches leaned forward, showing sudden interest in number 21.

I sat beside goaltender John Henderson, who was dressed but sitting out tonight, and noticed that we, too, had edged to the front of our rinkside seats.

I looked up to where Judy Draper was sitting, wondering if the young fellows sitting behind her tonight were the same ones who hadn't recognized her as they talked during a game last season.

"Draper?" one said to the other. "Naw, he won't be back. He won't live until he's 26."

Judy had told him about it that same night, after the game.

"I knew then," said Bruce, "that I was going

165

to have to expect these things and learn to live with it."

I looked up to the walkway around the rink, where Bruce had stood, watching, during his absence. Human nature hadn't disappointed him. The word had got around and people stared.

"It got so bad," he said, "that I was going to paint 'I'm fine, thank you' on my forehead."

The puck was dropped and the Bears forged into the Providence zone. Bruce Draper, number 21, made a deft pass. He got the puck again, cut in on goaltender Ross Brooks' left, and shot. Brooks made the save. The whistle blew and a Hershey player was penalized. Draper's first shift lasted less than 30 seconds. The penalty-killers came out.

At the nine-minute mark, still no score and the Dornhoefer-Draper-Stankiewicz line made its second appearance. Gary Dornhoefer went up the right side and shovelled the puck toward center as he crossed the blueline. Stankiewicz made a move as if to pick it up, left it instead and charged in. Draper picked it up. He took two strides, hesitated, then fired a hard, true shot to the upper left side to Brooks' right. The puck whipped over Brooks' shoulder into the net and the red light went on.

Bruce stood there for a moment, staring in disbelief.

Every Hershey player on the ice jumped in the air, every man on the bench stood and screamed his approval, including coach Mathers. John Henderson jumped and almost took my toes off when he landed on his skates beside me.

Judy Draper squealed, jumped up and down, and slapped the other wives on the back. His teammates mobbed Bruce as if he had just won a decisive playoff game in overtime. He smiled shyly and skated back with his head down. The fans wondered what all the fuss was about.

"Get here early," he had quipped at noon that day. "I may have to score on my first shift."

◀Bruce is congratulated for his goal by linemates Gary Dornhoefer and Myron Stankiewicz.

It was, without a doubt, the most dramatic goal I have ever seen.

"Damn it!" I remember John Henderson saying. "I've been around hockey all my life and this is the first time I ever got goose pimples all over when somebody scored a goal."

"No goal ever gave me a nicer feeling," grinned Mathers after the game.

"It was the nicest thing that ever happened to me," said a flushed Mrs. Bruce Draper.

"Me?" grinned Bruce, "I almost went straight up in the air, right out of my uniform."

It would be nice to finish this off by saying Bruce Draper won back his spot on the team and became an all-star in the second half of the season. But this isn't a fairy tale, it's life.

The fact is that Mathers decided to replace him after two games because he felt Bruce wasn't strong enough to help the team.

"I have to think of winning," he said, almost apologetically.

Bruce, bitterly disappointed, was low in spirits for a couple of days, then said: "This means I have to try harder."

But, if Bruce Draper never plays another game, he made a magnificent comeback on the night of January 11, as far as his friends, teammates and doctors are concerned.

"I knew he'd do it or kill himself trying," said Dr. Reed.

Whatever fate has decided for Bruce Draper, at least he'll take a strong body into his battle against his disease. And the opposition in that game is far greater than anything he faced playing hockey.

"Eighty percent of the people who have malignant testicular tumors die within a two-year period," said Dr. Reed."Ninety-five percent of those who make it past the two-year period have it beaten. In Bruce's case, we have been making regular checks and so far it looks good. He has a year under his belt now."

Bruce knows the odds and he's realistic. He's also a devout Roman Catholic who feels his fate is in the hands of God.

"Naturally I want to play hockey again," he says, "but more than that, I want to lead a normal life with my wife and two kids. Hockey is secondary, I've said it right from the start.

"First, I want to live."

EPILOGUE   *There is no happy ending.*
Bruce played only two games with the Hershey Bears and that single goal on January 11, 1967, was his only statistic, proof of his unbelievable comeback. He finished the season with Hershey, played golf all summer, and was in great shape. Unfortunately, Hershey decided he did not fit into their plans for the following season and gave him his release so that he could try out with another club.

In September, Bruce went to training camp with the Baltimore Clippers of the same league and was on their roster when the season opened. He kept driving himself, eager to prove he could still play but, his real motivation wasn't to be known until a few months later. He didn't make it with Baltimore and, in November 1967, walked into the manager's office and told him his experiment was over, he was going home to Ottawa.

Later, long after he died, somebody noticed the date of his retirement and realized that Bruce Draper had pushed himself to stay in hockey to the exact date that made him eligible for a modest pension for his family. Actually, I suspect he knew the ending of his story all along. When we discussed doing it, he asked for $500. It was the only time I was ever involved with a payment to a story subject and, while it wasn't much, Bruce explained he wanted it for his family. He knew he wouldn't be around long.

As soon as he returned to Ottawa, that fall in 1967, Bruce saw his doctors and was admitted to the hospital. He was hospitalized on and off for the next month, over the Christmas season and then, in January, 1968, he went in for the last time.

His wife, parents, and brothers had to watch his rapid deterioration day after day on their regular visits. And, even though Bruce, now just a shadow of his former self, realized what was happening, he didn't lose his sense of humor. He tried to make it easier for everyone.

It took only a few weeks and he was gone.

I visited the family at their Ottawa home about a month after Bruce's death, planning to write a follow-up story in the magazine. But, I couldn't do it. It was too negative and everybody who knew Bruce had the same feeling: "Why him?"

Judy Draper has since remarried to Butch Barber, one of Bruce's teammates at Hershey, and they live with their family in Montana. Bruce and Judy Draper had two daughters, Debra Lynn who was two and a half when it was discovered that Bruce had cancer and Kimmy, who was born later that summer. Debbie is 15 now and Kim 13.

I remember visiting his father's home after Bruce's death. Jack Draper was treated as one of the boys by his sons and knew as much about hockey and other sports as they did. We sat around, talking over a drink and the two little kids were there. Debbie was about three and a half and Kim was just a baby.

Judy was talking about little Debbie and how difficult it was to explain things to her. Bruce used to call home every evening when the team was on the road and Debbie would wait anxiously for his calls and answer the phone herself.

"She still answers the phone all the time," Judy said. "She keeps expecting his call. I've tried to explain to her that Daddy won't be calling anymore because he's up in heaven with God."

The toughest incident had occurred a few days before. She saw little Debbie go over and lift the receiver off the phone.

"What are you doing?" she asked Debbie.

"Calling Daddy," she said.

"But I told you," said her mother, "Daddy's with God now."

"I know Mommy," Debbie said with that little-girl innocence. "But maybe God has a phone."

"It was hard to keep the tears back that night," Judy said.

After interviewing Bruce, I put the tapes away, thinking the little girls might appreciate hearing their father's voice when they were older. They weren't edited tapes, just conversations with Bruce talking about his problem and how much, he said, he wanted to live. The tapes are stored somewhere in a barn and I am hoping they haven't been damaged over the years. The girls are old enough now. There has been enough time.

MINNESOTA
FATS

"The greatest hustler on this here whole entire earth"

prologue If anybody asked me what sport I played best when I was young, I'd have to say pool. I was never really good at it, but I could beat most Sunday players when I was on and I spent more time at pool than any other sport.

My introduction to the game occurred when I was about six years old and our parish priest, Father Brennan, put a pool table in the basement of Our Lady of Perpetual Help Church. That was in Sudbury, the nickel-mining town in Northern Ontario where I was born. We played pool every Saturday afternoon in the church basement, ripping the cloth on the table, chipping the balls, and busting the tips off the cues.

Some years later, when I was 17 and sort of on the loose in Toronto, I hung around a poolroom over the old Town Tavern, a local jazz joint, and got to know all the best pool hustlers in town. I practically lived there, playing for a quarter a game while the big money games went on around me. I was certainly no hustler, Hell, I froze even for a quarter and, if it hadn't been for a kindly player named Cal Kirsh, I probably would have starved to death. When Cal, who eventually became Toronto's snooker champion, noticed I looked especially haggard, he would slip me twenty-five cents to buy a hotdog and Coke upstairs in the bowling alley.

I was also what they called a mark, a guy who could be suckered in on anything. The other hustlers were street-wise city kids and I was fresh from the sticks, willing to learn but unaware of how long it would take to complete the course. Geez, I was so dumb it embarrasses me just to think about it.

This is how bad I was. There were two brothers from the west, Marty and Arto, who were not just pool hustlers but also petty thieves. I played against Marty one day and beat him for five bucks but he didn't have it.

"Tell you what," he said, "I'll give you this watch instead." It was a beautiful watch to look at. I couldn't wait to show it to Cal.

"Hell," he said in disgust, "that's a gaff watch. Won't you ever learn?"

A gaff watch is one that a guy buys for two dollars and then, wearing a long face and with a well-rehearsed hard luck story, heads for the nearest train or bus station. His father is dying, he needs money to get home and all he has is this watch . . . "Please mister." The watches would bring in as much as $25 and each one was guaranteed to run for at least half an hour. When the sucker's new watch stopped and he opened it to discover it had no insides, the youth who had sold it to him was long gone.

"Just go out on the street and sell it," Marty said when I confronted him. "You'll make more than the five bucks I owe you." Well sir, I might have been a lot of things, but, I was no crook. I refused.

"Okay, okay," Marty grumbled. "C'mon with me. I'll sell it and we'll split what I get for it."

That was better than nothing. We went around the corner and Marty told me to wait at the front door of a bar while he went inside to make the sale. I might still be standing there if I hadn't gone looking for him half an hour later. Marty had merely slipped out of the back door. First he paid his five-dollar debt with a gaff watch and then he stole the watch back from me.

"I do not," Cal Kirsh said wisely, "think that you were cut out for this kind of life."

I put my trusty cue up on the rack, took his advice and stepped into the world to make something of myself. I was a busboy, an usher in a burlesque joint, a Fuller Brush Man . . . . But, I never lost my love for pool and, from watching Cal Kirsh in the big games, I learned the value of concentration— total concentration—and the importance of controlling the cue ball. Cal also had great discipline and would never try a shot unless he felt certain he was going to make it. Otherwise, he would play his opponent safe.

Years later, when I was travelling around as a writer, my favorite way to kill an evening was to find a roadside bar with a pool table where the customers played one another for drinks. Actually, Cal would have been proud of me. I patterned my game after his and won more than I lost. By golly, Cal Kirsh was my hero.

Eventually, I even had my own pool table at home and today I have two of them, one for regular pool and a bumper table. With this interest and education in the game's fundamentals, it was inevitable that I would one day seek out and write about Minnesota Fats, a character made famous in The Hustler. *We met thirteen years ago and, at that time, Fatty hadn't had much national television exposure and people didn't realize that he really existed. I am here to tell you that he does, larger than life and definitely one of the most unforgettable characters you could ever meet.*

o o o

OCTOBER 21, 1967—The switchboard operator at Chicago's Lakeside Inn said she was sorry but she didn't have anyone registered by the name of Rudolf Wanderone.

"Uh, did you ever hear of a guy named Minnesota Fats?"

"Fatty! Of course," she cooed. "Why didn't you say so in the first place? One moment please."

The Fat Man doesn't use his right name any more, especially since Jackie Gleason and Paul Newman made that movie, The Hustler. In fact, Rudolph Wanderone's social security card is even made out to Minnesota Fats.

"Yeah!" demanded his piercing, high-pitched voice. "Magazine story? You want to write about the greatest hustler who ever lived on this here whole entire earth, right? Okay. Fly to St. Louis. Y'unerstand? Get a car there, y'hear, an' drive on up to Dowell ... yah, Dowell. Know what I mean? You'll know the place. There'll be a big Lincoln and a gold Cadillac parked out front. An' lotsa dogs and cats and things around. Y'unerstand? See ya tomorra."

Southern Illinois is peppered with insignificant little towns and the sign on the road informs you that 400 people reside in Dowell. You turn off the highway, thump down a dusty, dirt road and finally you come upon a neat, medium-sized, white bungalow. The Fat Man's big cars are parked outside. Across the road is a field of corn.

Most people don't realize there really is a Minnesota Fats. They think he was merely a movie character portrayed by Gleason. Well, to be honest, Fats was known as New York and Chicago Fats before the movie, but he was also known as Minnesota, so he sued the movie company, trying to get his hands on some of the cash.

Things have been good since that movie. The Fat Man had been in Chicago for his weekly television show, Minnesota Fats Hustles The Pros.

His opponents each week are some of his old hustler pals such as Cornbread Red, Daddy Warbucks, Fast Eddie, Tuscaloosa Squirrel, Cicero Murphy, Champagne Eddie, Texas Badman, Cowboy Moore, Jersey Red and The Knoxville Bear.

And now they have captured him in color, in a network series, Celebrity Billiards, from Hollywood. In this one, Fats will play them all, from Liz Taylor to Willie Mays, and including Gleason and Newman.

And two years ago, this guy calls from Chicago and asks Fats if he wants to go into the home billiard table business, using his name. A job? Fats had never worked a day in his life—had never held a social security card.

"I told him the only way anybody'd get me to work is to make the hours from one to two with an hour off for lunch," says The Fat Man. "They did, an' they laid this company on me and made me president. I couldn't get out of it. Y'unerstand?"

The result is that Fats is a rich man today, no longer dependent on hustling.

He was at the door now, resplendent in a pair of startling green golf slacks which hung magnificently from his jiggling, 50-inch waist, and a golf shirt.

"Where you been?" he demanded. "Thought you was lost."

The first thing you notice about Fats—five feet, eight inches, 265 pounds—is that he can't stand still. He led the way into a bright kitchen, pointed to a lady there and said it was his wife Eva-leen (Evelyn) and kept stalking around in nervous little circles.

His right shoulder twitches continuously. He keeps whipping out his handkerchief to wipe his brow, he scratches himself, his head bobs as he talks—and he never stops talking.

He asks your name, then forgets it forever and twice during the first five minutes he disappeared from the kitchen, shouting all the while, and walked back in through another door.

Eva-leen, a handsome woman who looked as if she just stepped out of the beauty parlor, smiles politely, but says nothing.

The Fat Man met her 27 years ago. He had made a killing in Chicago and was driving to St. Louis with his old pal, the late gambler, Nick The Greek, when his car hit a mailbox on a post.

Fats and the Greek holed up in DuQuoin,

five miles from Dowell, and spent their time hustling some of the locals while the car was being repaired.

The Greek got into a big poker game and asked Fats to take home this girl Evelyn he had met. So Fats swiped the Greek's girl friend. He married her, and now, when people ask her why a pretty girl like her married a fat guy like Fats, she answers: "The power of conversation can do anything."

He was thrashing through the house now, loading the table-top in the kitchen with press clippings, advertising posters and anything else he could find with his name on it.

"I'll tell ya somethin' you didn't ever know before in your whole entire life," he says. "I led the biggest parade they ever seen in the whole world in this state. An' next week up in Springfield they're givin' me a great, big, fantastic ovation.

"**Y**'see, I revived the game. I upped it up—the pool. Me, the Fat Man. Know what I mean?"

He was in the living room now, where a prim little lady sat, reading a newspaper.

"That's Eva-leen's maw," blurted Fats and the little lady smiled politely.

"She teaches Sunday School," he said, in disgust.

In the centre of the table sat a large basket of southern fried chicken legs and, the way Fats looked at them, you expected to see drool form on his huge jowls.

Eva-leen's maw started to say grace and Fats, his eyes glued on the chicken, fidgeted nervously in his chair. He rattled his fork on the table as she sat with head bowed and he kept dabbing at the perspiration on his forehead with his napkin.

At the exact second she finished, a blur shot across the table—Fats' finely-manicured, pudgy right hand reaching for a leg of chicken. It is not exaggerating to say that Fats had finished eating the leg, stripped it bare, before anyone else had taken a second bite.

Then he jumped up, turned three tight little circles, whipped off his golf shirt and sat down again, his flabby chest, arms and shoulders, covered with hair, jiggling as he ate.

He smacked his lips, grunted and burped and washed it all down with iced tea, his favorite drink next to Coke.

Fats' best-known boast is that he will play pool against anybody, anywhere for anything. He will also do the same in an eating contest.

"Onct," he said between slurps, "I was eatin' against this guy—he weighed 450 pounds—an' I grab a ham and swallow it before we got started. Told him I wouldn't count it, y'understand? He took one look and quit right there.

"**I** can out-eat anybody who ever lived on this whole entire earth. But most of the guys who challenge me, they wanta play on their own table, like spaghetti or bananas. Know what I mean? I avoid those guys."

The Fat Man uses his patter to psyche out pool opponents, too.

Like the time Weenie Beanie challenged him. Weenie's real name is Bill Staton and he owns a string of hot-dog stands in Washington, D.C., which is how he got his nickname.

"There now, Weenie, there you go," said Fats as he chalked up his cue. "You just weren't happy makin' all that money, were you? Tell you what I'm going to do.

"They say you got eight of those hotdog joints up there. I want all eight of them. I figure there is one dingy old place that's hot and greasy. That's where I'll put you to work after I win them.

"You'll be the short-order cook in the dingiest and greasiest one of them all. And after you been workin' one day during the summer for about 10 hours and figure it is time for you to go home for the day, I'm goin' to come in and order 250 fried eggs over light. Yeah, 250 of 'em.

"I'll say, 'I don't want nobody cookin' those eggs but Weenie Beenie himself, the egg-cookin' champion.' Then, as you cook them, I'll eat them, one by one—I'll eat all 250 of 'em.

"And, my boy, I will get up and walk out and not leave you one red cent tip."

Naturally, Weenie Beenie didn't have a chance. Fats stalked the table while he talked, dropping ball after ball. Fortunately for Weenie, they played for cash instead of his hotdog stands.

Now, with the chicken all gone, Fats went to the telephone to call his pal George Jansco over in Johnston City, where they were setting up the tables in one of George's saloons for the upcoming world pocket billiards championships.

"George!" he yelled on the phone, fidgeting with the cord. "Well, where is he? Huh? Where? Look, how's the tables coming, I wanna come over and shoot some balls.

"I got a Canadian writer here. He's doin' a whole magazine thing, color pictures an' everything. I'm takin' him over there so you can cut in on the thing, y'unerstand? George tole me that table would be ready. What's the matter with him? Huh . . . ?"

"Fatty doesn't like telephones much," explained Eva-leen. "He's got claustrophobia or something. The longer he's on the phone, the louder he yells. And he wants the phone out in the open somewhere.

"He's been a rounder in his day, y'know. He could be a big bookie with his connections. He would be, too, but it would mean talking on the phone a lot. He can't stand the phone."

Fats burst into the kitchen again, his arms swinging wildly as he told about George not having the table up. Then he swooped down with one arm and picked up Fuzzy Cat, his little mongrel dog who makes all road trips with him. They are inseparable pals and Fuzzy Cat is the reason Fats drives on most of his trips, so he won't have to crate his dog for plane travel.

Outside, he opened the trunk of the Lincoln and got some more press clippings, all folded neatly in flat boxes, and opened a case to display an ivory-handled, specially-made cue which is very nice, but not the one he plays with.

"A guy made me one onct out of solid silver," he said. "But it was too heavy."

Back in the living room, Fats was talking about the movie.

"I knew Gleason when he was just a cheap hustler around the pool rooms in New York," he said. "He plays a little bit, but not very good, know what I mean? Anyway, he played me just like I am except for two things—I don't ever drink, y'unerstand? But Gleason, he can't do nothin', not even make a movie, without he's

gotta have a shot.

"An' they let Newman beat me at the end. I never lost no game for cash. But that's okay, I guess. It made me a rich man, the movie.

"I got more money than I can ever spend in my whole entire life. I got two Cadillacs and two Lincolns—two here and two in Chicago so I got somethin' to drive when I'm there."

Fats couldn't sit still any longer so Eva-leen took his place.

"The first time I ever watched Fats play was in Detroit when we were first married," she said. "The game lasted 24 hours. But I never minded sitting in on games. Because I knew he wouldn't lose and the next morning I could go to the bank."

The Fat Man reappeared, still stripped to the waist, jiggling as he wiped himself off with a towel.

"Eva-leen, we gotta feed the dogs an' cats," he said. "We got about 40 of them around here, y'know. Stray ones. This is the dumping-off place for the strays. They know they can get a square meal here anytime."

In the backyard, they have a 30-unit birdhouse and, although Eva-leen hoped for martins (who eat mosquitoes), they wound up with swallows.

"Look in here," Fats said, peering into a window in a small, concrete enclosure at the end of his carport. "It's full of cats an' kittens."

Fats was ready to go to Johnston City now and he said he'd lead the way over the 30 miles in his Lincoln.

"I'm just gonna knock a few around, know what I mean? I don't practice no more. I wouldn't give a quarter to play for nothing. When I play pool, it's for $500-$1000 a pop and up. Y'unerstand?"

Fats spun out of his driveway and burst down the dirt road, sending up a shower of small stones. When he got to Du-Quoin, five miles from Dowell, he suddenly made a left turn—after having turned on his right turn signal—into the parking lot of a bar.

"Want'cha to meet my pal Muzz," he said, going in through the back door. He stopped on the way to talk to a waitress in the dining room, his high-pitched voice announcing immediately who had come in.

"Muzz, you're too fat," he said to the proprietor. "This man here, he's gonna write a big story on me, color pictures, everything. He's gonna stay a coupla days, the man."

"See me sometime," said Muzz as Fats wandered off to the kitchen looking for more food. "I can't tell as many lies as him, but I can tell a few."

"C'mon," said Fats impatiently. "Let's go to Johnston City."

And off he drove, 80-90-95 miles an hour, fidgeting in the driver's seat, floating over to the wrong side of the road on turns.

Over the Little Muddy River, over the Big Muddy River and, just past Mulkytown, the big Lincoln screeched to a stop.

Minnesota Fats—the greatest hustler on this here whole entire earth, ruthless when money is on the line—sat there patiently, waiting for a big blackbird to walk safely across the highway.

We arrived at the outskirts of Johnston City and Fats pulled in at the J and J, a small truck stop and bar run by his pal George Jansco.

Now it is dark, the only bright light hanging over a miniature pool table, the kind that you put a quarter into to get the balls.

"A stinger, please."

"What!" says George, a former minor pro baseball player, now in his fifties, who's built like a truck. "We don't serve them fancy drinks in here. They're at the other place."

The other place is Jansco's Showbar, at the other end of the town. It's a more impressive establishment, catering to the shirt-and-tie trade. George's brother, Pauly, runs it, but George is the boss.

Directly behind the J and J Ranch, not visible from the road, is a small, box-like building made of cement blocks. On the front is a sign: "Big League Billiards—Private Club, Members Only." Inside, two worn chesterfields sit, edge-to-edge, on a raised platform overlooking a pool table. Bugs fly around the single fluorescent light, and in the back is where George Jansco sometimes sleeps.

This is where Minnesota Fats plays most of his pool. The only practice Fats gets now is when he and his old buddy George play four best-of-seven series of one-pocket for $20. One-

pocket is the game Fats usually plays. It's the hustlers' game.

Fats will modestly admit that "I've broke every hustler who ever lived on this whole entire earth at one-pocket."

But, Fats hadn't touched a cue for almost six years before the movie came out. He had run out of opponents and was concentrating on cards.

"I'll tell you something you didn't ever know before in your life," he says. "I'm known as the greatest short-card player on this whole entire earth."

George is executive secretary of the Billiard Players' Association. He also is a gambler and very big in politics in his area. In fact, he admits that is why all the hustlers come to his little pool room behind the Ranch. They know the police will never bother them at George Jansco's place.

So, the biggest money games in the U.S. have been played at the Ranch. They might meet in Miami, or Chicago, or Frisco, and find well-heeled backers ready for action, then the party will catch a plane and head for Johnston City, where George Jansco runs things.

Now, once a year, the All-Round Pocket Billiards World Championships are staged at the Showbar. The champion must prove himself at one-pocket, nine-ball and straight pool. There is a removable bar in one of the big rooms, the floor is collapsible and there are removable bleachers. Two tables are placed in this room for the important matches of the day and another seven tables are used in a special building behind the Showbar.

George and Fats have also branched out with another tournament, the annual Stardust Open in Las Vegas. They are on a first-name basis with all of the celebrities out there. George usually finds a little action at a golf course and he plays for big money.

Whenever a hustler runs out of money on the road, he sends a telegram to George, and George wires the guy enough to get him going again. Fats is a soft touch for the hustlers, too.

But George has them all tied up. When they drift into Johnston City—population 4000—for the tournament, they go to George. The

tournament is actually just a front. The money games in that room behind the Showbar are the main attraction.

In fact, George says he had to make a rule that no money games were to be played while a tournament match was in progress, because everybody would leave the tournament to watch the hustling. So they play at night, while the rest of the world sleeps.

"We gotta be careful, though," explains George. "Hustlers play only for cash, y'see, and we can't have all that cash floating around. First thing we know, a machine-gun mob will be here and clean us out."

So George devised a system whereby he becomes a sort of banker.

"When they come in, they come to me and deposit their money," he says. "One guy'll give me a grand; another one two grand. I put it all in the bank and OK their credit for whatever they have on deposit."

Fats doesn't play in the tournament any more. Usually he acts as master of ceremonies, does an exhibition, then hangs around and waits for the winner, hoping to play him a match for his prize money. And he has to pick his spots now because, the fact is, the Fat Man no longer plays as well as he used to.

Mostly, Fats restricts his pool to exhibitions, television matches and friendly games, such as the one he showed up for on this night with George.

"Hey, Fatty, come for some pool?" Jansco asked, as Fats walked into the Ranch. "Say, a couple kids were in here today from Connecticut. Came all the way down here, on a pilgrimage sorta, to see the place where the pool is played. I told them you might be in tonight and they stayed over for three days to see you."

Fatty stalked around the little room, his right shoulder twitching as it always does, gripping a Coke in one pudgy hand. He sat at the bar for a few minutes, got up and went over to a table, returned to the bar and then walked out to the kitchen to grab a bite to eat.

That's why his wife Eva-leen doesn't go with him to Johnston City.

"Fatty won't sit still for five minutes," she had said earlier that day. "He's here, he's there, and I'm left alone. Besides, he says I always drink too much."

George said he was going to have a shower before playing—he'd been working outside building a golf course during the day—and he left, his legs very prominent because he was wearing shorts. The calves on George's legs are like two large pumpkins and he always wears shorts so people can see them.

The boys from Bristol, Connecticut—Jay Bourbeau, 18, and his pal Don Kincaid, 21, both of whom fancy themselves as pool players back home—showed up and were invited to watch.

"Okay, Georgie boy," said Fats, starting the familiar banter that would continue until the final ball was shot. "You are facing the world's greatest player. Are you ready?"

The Fat Man did a couple of trick shots to warm up and the boys from Connecticut were suitably impressed.

"I ain't ever missed a shot like this," said Fats, making a long bank into a corner pocket. He continued to shoot them off and George lost the first game.

But George was no slouch and the first match went the full seven games before Fats won.

The door opened and in walked a funny-looking little man with large round-rimmed glasses, carrying a leather cue case. It was Cosmo The Great—funny, stuttering little Tom Cosmo, former vaudeville dancer and comedian who bills himself as The World's Craziest Pool Player.

Cosmo, who remembers playing the old vaudeville houses in Canada (he would go to a pool hall and hustle between performances) is now a full-time hustler who does an act combining his pool and dancing abilities. The huge glasses were designed especially for pool, so the rims wouldn't bother his vision when he looked down a cue.

"Why, if it ain't old Cosmo," said Fats. "Lookit them feet on Cosmo, them great big feet. You got no business bein' in a pool room, Cosmo. You should be up north stampin' out them forest fires."

George explained that Cosmo had been short of cash, so he and his brother Pauly gave him a job at the Showbar, painting, cleaning up and doing a little carpentry.

"But he's mad today," said George "We had him paint the women's and men's rooms, and he feels it wasn't very fitting for one of the world's great hustlers and entertainers."

"Watch this shot, Georgie," said Fats, and the two boys from Connecticut leaned forward. He missed.

"Amazing, absolutely amazing," said Fats. "Why don't you get this table fixed, George? Hell, it ain't *possible* to miss that shot."

It isn't hard to see how Fats wins some of his games. As soon as it was George's turn to shoot, Fats would turn around and start telling a story. People would laugh and George would miss.

Cosmo started talking about his prowess as a pool player, saying he would play anybody for anything.

"Y'know, Coz," said Fats dryly, "I gotta feeling you ain't going to have any trouble gettin' a game."

Cosmo, his dignity bruised, starting rhyming off names of good players he had beaten.

"Yeah," scoffed the Fat Man, "an' how did you make out with Minny-Haw-Haw Fats? Huh?"

"Well," said Cosmo, "Guess I always come out second best."

"Some guys ain't even that lucky," the Fat Man shot back.

He took George in the final game and a young man who had come in late, with his cue under his arm, spoke up.

"Fatty, I'll play you for $50," he said.

"Look kid, I'm tired, beat," said Fats. "Besides, save your money."

The young man, a truck driver from DuQuoin who did a little hustling on the side, stayed after everyone had left to do some practicing.

"I couldn't afford to lose the $50," he said, "but the only way to learn is to play the good ones, and they won't play for fun."

"Imagine," Fats was saying later over a heaping plate of ravioli at the Showbar, "that kid wants to play me for $50. Hell, I don't want his money."

Fatty came back with Eva-leen the next

night, this time wearing bright green shorts—a magnificent sight. The kids from Connecticut came back, too, and so did Cosmo, with three young suspects who looked as if they had stepped out of a police lineup, in tow.

"I tole them maybe they could get a pitcher taken with you," explained Cosmo, holding up a cheap little camera. "Whaddya say, Fats?"

The sleaziest-looking of the three was either completely stoned or else he regarded Fats as the god of pool. He stood there, his eyes squinty, mouth agape, not saying a word. Fats posed, Cosmo took aim and the flash didn't work. The camera failed twice more and Fats said to forget it; he had to get on with the game of pool. The young men were dejected, but finally left with Cosmo.

Fats laughed. "How about that?" he said. "Probably charged those kids something to get a picture with me."

On this night, George wasn't fooling around. Fats grumbling and blaming the table, was behind. There was a sudden change in his personality. He was downcast. George swept the first two matches to take the series and the $20.

Fats was rubbing his right shoulder. "I been sleeping on it a lot lately," he said to no one in particular. "Bothered my stroke."

He obviously was sulking, and when George and Eva-leen asked him to go to the Showbar for a drink and some food, he looked at the ground.

"Naw, I'm going home," he said surprising them both. "I'm tired."

Later, when Fats had gone, George questioned his wisdom in defeating the Fat Man.

"He's mad," he said. "He's mad because he lost while a story was being done on him. It's not good for his reputation. He's gotta be careful. It's bad for me, too. I don't want people to know I shoot that well. I like to do a little hustling myself. I never play in the tournaments."

Then George started talking about Fats' TV series in Chicago, in which he plays a different hustler each week.

"I wanted Fatty to win all of the matches," said George. "I could have selected opponents he was sure to beat. But no, Fatty, he's too honest. He wants all the matches on the square. So he loses a couple."

Later that night, or early the next morning, Cosmo was back at the Showbar, entertaining the customers by dancing around the bar stools.

Suddenly he looked up into the little crowd that had gathered and yelled: "Danny! Handsome Danny Jones!"

Handsome Danny and his travelling companion, Little Titanic, had just blown in from Canada. They explained that their tour had taken them to Montreal and Toronto and they had returned with $3000 in their pockets. Little Titanic handed over a Canadian $100 bill as proof, calling it "funny money."

"We dropped in on our way out west hoping to get some of the Fat Man's money," said Little Titanic. "There'll be a game between him and Danny if they know I'm in town. They know I carry cash."

Fats heard about it the next morning and came into Johnston City the following night. But there was no game.

"They ain't got a cent," George explained. "Like I said, no hustler has money."

Handsome Danny, a quiet, good-looking guy from Columbus, Ohio, explained it another way.

"You gotta understand," he said. "We all like Fats. We respect him. He's one of the greatest who ever lived. You don't challenge the Fat Man. He'll let you know if he wants to play.

"I think I can take him, even at one-pocket, his game. But I don't know if I'd want to. Look, why don't you go over to the Ranch—he's there now—and tell him Danny Jones says he isn't coming over because he knows he can't win. It'll make Fats feel good."

Cosmo? Well, Cosmo was prancing around telling people he'd play anybody for $100.

And Fats? Well, it was only a few weeks until the big tournament and he had all these television commitments.

"An' y'know, they might even make another big movie about me and have me play my own part," he said. "Know what I mean? From my book, y'unerstand? It's the biggest thing ever hit the whole entire book business. Can't buy it. Amazing. That means more money."

They could do worse than make Fats a movie star. Naturally, though, he'd have to beat out a guy named Gleason.

But maybe Fats could do it. A conversation earlier that week came to mind. Fats was asked if the doctors ever worried about that 50-inch waistline and those 265 pounds on his five-foot, eight-inch frame.

"Never," he retorted. "I can stay up for nine days in a row and sleep for eight. They checked me all over and they ain't ever seen anything like me in their whole entire life."

"Neither have I," sighed Eva-leen. "Neither have I."●

epilogue *Minnesota Fats died six years ago.*

"Yeah, not once but twice," he bellowed into the phone when I contacted him. "They pronounced me dead twice and I woke up both times. I had this prostate trouble, see, and I couldn't pass my water. So they gave me an operation and I died on the table. Two times I died. Six months later I'm okay. Playin' pool every day."

Fatty is still going strong and is even more famous today than he was when I first met him because of his numerous television appearances in exhibitions filmed in Las Vegas and on the West Coast.

"Yeah, they give me $75 000 cash in Las Vegas for two days' work," Fats said. "I work only 90 minutes playin' pool and then they give me a whole week of vacation for free. I could live in Las Vegas for the rest of my life for nothin'."

Fats, however, does not want to live anywhere but in the sleepy little town of Dowell, in his little house with his wife Eva-leen and all their stray dogs and cats.

"I could work anywhere I want," he said, talking even faster than I had remembered. "I'm the highest paid entertainer on this here whole entire earth. Augie Busch (the beer baron) bought me for six million dollars and all I gotta do is be the front man for these pool players who go around playin' and doin' all the work while I get all the money. I got nothin' but money—a whole fleet of limousines and this tremendous big Lincoln Continental that Augie give me with two big signs that say: 'Minnesota Fats, The King of Pool.' I got so much money that they beat me in my own company for 700 and some million dollars in 1979 alone. Yeah, more than 700 million. I was chairman of the board and I didn't go to enough meetin's. . . ."

Things have changed somewhat in Dowell but Fats is the same. His pal George Jansco who owned the J and J Ranch in Johnston City is gone. He was working on the golf course behind his little bar one day, went into the house, had a stroke, and died. But, George, unlike Fats, didn't wake up. That was only two years after I had met George and the little concrete building with his pool table is still out in the back. Fats wanted to buy it but George's wife keeps it to remember George.

Actually, Fats was not in a good mood the day I talked to him. He has continued to pick up stray dogs and cats and was seething because he had found two dogs almost dead from heat exhaustion in a pen near his home. The couple who owned them had left town and abandoned their dogs without food or water.

"You shoulda seen them dogs," Fatty fumed. "They was weak and unbelievable dirty. Those two creeps! She had like nineteen husbands and the one she was with is a crumb outta this world. I'm gonna have them extradited back here from Chicago and charge them."

Fats has more than one hundred dogs and cats now in his back yard and has built special kennels for them. People keep dropping by with another stray and, because of his work in this area, Minnesota Fats was named Humanitarian of the Year in 1979 by the humane society in St. Louis.

"There was 2500 humanitarians there from all over the world to see me get my plaque at the dinner," Fats says proudly. "I look after them animals good. Two days ago I bought two hundred pounds of fried chicken and I got only twenty pounds left. They get steak, too, and then some dog food so it ain't so rich."

Yes, Minnesota Fats is alive and well in Dowell. He could be with us forever. It's no mystery how he woke up those two times he died. Fatty simply can't stop talking long enough to go along with foolishness like that.

TORONTO, July 11, 1980—This has been fun, looking back, and remembering some good times.

It's funny how we change, how we all go our separate ways. Perhaps we don't think of one another often, but, we never forget.

For instance, as soon as this book is published, I intend to hold a reunion party of our old gang at *The Canadian*. I'll have them all over to the house one night and give them copies of the book in appreciation for their friendship during those years. The guest list would be endless. There would be Denny Harvey, Mike Hanlon, John Miller, Dick Brown, Mike Carmichael, Ken Rodmell, Jim Ireland, Tom Alderman, Helen Meyer, Barry Conn Hughes, David Cobb, Paul King, Paul Grescoe, Terry Hancey, Ken Elliott, Don Newlands, Jorgen Halling, and maybe our two publishers, Ross Munro and Eddie Mannion, and Jan and Prue who edited my copy.

I'd better be careful, though, because I notice in my contract that I get only six free copies.

You would hardly recognize Denny Harvey now. He left to go to *The Montreal Gazette* as editor, then to a top-level position with the Canadian Broadcasting Corporation and now is editorial director of *The Toronto Star*. I remember his sandy hair and boyish face. He now has a full beard and it has turned gray.

I have always admired Harvey as an editor and will never forget one experience I had while working for him. Although I was a sportswriter, I asked if I could do a piece on Louis Armstrong on what turned out to be his last trip to Toronto. Satchmo was playing at a place called The Embassy and, after spending some time with him, I just couldn't write the story.

"What's wrong?" Harvey demanded.

"I just can't write it, Denny," I said. "Louie is senile. He's not even a good shadow of his former self. It would be unfair to write that."

Harvey stood, his back to me, looking out his window. I stood, nervous and embarrassed.

"Don't write it," he said. "That's what makes you a good writer. You have a conscience. Don't ever lose it."

We became pretty good friends. I will never forget the night that Ken Rodmell and I were at Denny's house and the three of us were pretty well into our cups. Rodmell told about this psychological experiment being conducted at a California university. Three people who know each other very well sit down together and open their hearts and minds. A tells B and C exactly what he thinks of them, and then B and C do the same thing. Whew! We all learned a lot that night and, surprisingly, were still friends the next day.

Harvey was a good athlete and we had the usual softball and hockey teams in the Press League. Denny was a great catcher and I was a so-so pitcher. I remember one game when he shot out of his catching position as if fired from a cannon to catch three bunts before they could land in fair territory. We were all younger then but not as young as we thought. I remember one gruelling game on a hot day that put our battery out of commission—forever. Denny put his back out so badly he had to go to a hospital for spinal fusion surgery. I tore the cartilage in my right knee and was supposed to have it fixed but it's still there, aching from time to time.

We had a lousy but enthusiastic hockey team and, a couple of times, I invited them out to my twelve acres in Pickering where I had a two-acre pond which froze over in the winter. In the summer, it was a great fishing hole.

I would stay up half the night, clearing snow to make a skating rink. That is one of the great joys of a Canadian winter. The sky seems to have dropped, stars look to be no higher than a ten-storey building. The snow squeaks when you walk. The moon is a huge, Sunkist orange. . . .

The team would come out the next afternoon and we would be little boys again, skating and tripping over huge cracks in the ice, chasing the elusive black puck, searching for it when it became buried in a snowbank. We all laughed as little icicles formed and hung from Ken Rodmell's walrus moustache. You'll never forget the feeling if you get hit across a cold shinbone with a hockey stick, or, if you fall and hit your head on the solid ice. Often, in the evenings, I would invite them to skating parties. I had colored lights strung around the rink and a huge spotlight to illuminate it. I would take a barbecue set out, load it with coals and make up a steaming pot of half vodka, half apple juice and float cinnamon sticks on top of it. Year after year I would leave that barbecue set there too long, until the ice melted and it fell through. . . .

Somehow, things don't seem to be as much fun today. Mind you, we took our sports seriously. I remember being in Phoenix, Arizona, to do two stories, one on cowboy Marty Wood and the second on baseball's Willy Mays. The San Francisco Giants were training in nearby Scottsdale and I had made arrangements with Willy to interview him on the bus the next day when the Giants were going to Tucson for an exhibition game. A telegram arrived—phone Harvey in Toronto.

"What's up, Denny?" I asked.

"I want you to come home tomorrow," he said.

"Geez, Denny," I said, "I'm interviewing Willy Mays tomorrow."

"The hell with Mays," said Harvey. "We've got a hockey game in Maple Leaf Gardens Sunday afternoon against the *Toronto Star*. We need you."

That's the kind of boss he was. I loved it.

There were a lot of other stories, a lot of unfiled expense accounts and a staggering number of bar bills. I wrote more than 150 magazine stories for *The Canadian* and only nine are in this book. I have fond memories of other story subjects including baseball's Maury Wills, Bo Belinsky, Denny McLain and Ron Taylor, football's Bud Grant, Joe Kapp, Bobby Taylor and Cookie Gilchrist, and hockey's Gordie Howe, Bobby Orr, Bobby Hull, Jean Beliveau, Eddie Shack. . . .

L ooking back, I had a great system. Harvey let me pick my own story subjects and I made sure I was travelling in the south during the winter, the north in the summer and so on. My toughest interview, I guess, was Leo Durocher when he was managing the Chicago Cubs.

"Sorry," said The Cubs' public relations man, "but Leo refuses to talk to other than the reporters who travel with his team."

I decided to gamble. The Cubs were tied for the National League lead at the time with the Philadelphia Phillies and I arrived at Chicago's Wrigley Field just as they were beginning a showdown series. The Phillies swept the doubleheader. No sense trying Leo after that one. They lost again the next day, and the next. . . .

Hell, I had been in Chicago for five days and still hadn't even approached Durocher. I went to the park early the next day and Leo was sitting in a small canvas chair in left field, glowering at his slumping team as it went through its paces. Summoning as much courage as possible, I walked out to left field slowly, wondering if this was such a good idea.

"Sorry to bother you, Leo," I started, scraping one foot nervously along the ground, "but, I've been sent here by *The Canadian Magazine* which has a circulation of more than 2 000 000. They wanted me to try to get a story about you and how you'll probably be named manager-of-the-year this season. . . ."

"What the hell do they want a story about me for?" he grunted, not taking his eyes from the playing field.

"Well, you're big news," I said. "But, I've been here for five days waiting for you to win so I could at least ask you."

"What's the matter, you afraid of me?" he barked, still not looking at me.

"Nope," I said. "Frankly, I think your bark is worse than your bite. I don't give a damn if I do the story or not."

"What's your name?" he demanded, suddenly looking at me.

"Paul Rimstead," I said. "And all I know about you is that a mutual friend warned me not to play pool with you for money."

That was my ace. Good old Minnesota Fats. Fatty told me that Leo was the best of the celebrity pool shooters and had been a legitimate entry years before in the world championships.

"Ah well, seeing as how you come all that way, drop into my office tomorrow morning at 10," he said. "Bark's worse than my bite, huh?"

The next day he pretended he had never met me.

"Hell," I said, suddenly miffed, "I waited here another twenty-four hours because you told me to be here. I've got better things to do with my time. You're not that important to me!"

"Take it easy, take it easy," Durocher smiled. "Okay, what do you want to know?"

He gave me about twenty minutes and told me to see him again the next day. That's the way it went for the next five days. Fifteen or twenty minutes at a time. But, I had the only magazine story on Durocher in several years. He's an ornery cuss when he wants to be, but, most of it is pure show business.

Ken Elliott, our intrepid British photographer, arrived in Chicago and started recording Durocher's antics during a game. Leo screamed. He told the umpire that Elliott had to get off the field. He was bothering him. Elliott moved to an empty seat, high above the Cubs' dugout and continued shooting with a telephoto lense. Would you believe that Durocher spotted him in a crowd of 44 000 fans, called time, went to the head umpire, pointed at Elliott, and the ump had to squint to see? Anyway, Elliott had his pictures and we ran it as a cover story.

One of my biggest expense accounts was worth the story I did on the use of anabolic steroids by Olympic athletes. It was the first story of steroid use ever substantiated and was quoted the world over during the 1968 Olympics in Mexico City. I travelled far and wide in kooky California and was aided tremendously by Hal and Olga Connolly, two former gold medalists in the field events. My original source was Canadian shotputter Dave Steen and two other Canadian athletes, shotputter Mike Mercer and javelin-football star Zenon Andrushyshyn, also played major roles.

We visited doctors in small towns who had administered steroids to athletes, talked to scores of world-class performers and, suddenly, I had enough to break the story. Anabolic steroids are usually given to weakened patients recovering from surgery, especially to women after a mastectomy. European and Asian officials discovered, however, that used in heavy doses, steroids would help weight-event athletes gain tremendous amounts of weight and drastically increase muscle development. There were bizzare stories of side effects, such as women suddenly growing whiskers. Eventually, the practice swept the world and it was almost impossible to find a weight-event athlete who didn't use them.

It took about two weeks to research and I was staying in the expensive Century Plaza Hotel, in Los Angeles, the same hotel I would visit some years later to accept an award for television commercials. Mike Mercer weighed about 275 pounds, Zenon about 220. They were with me every day and I cringed as I watched my restaurant and bar tabs grow. When I was ready to leave, I had to wire for more money. Still, I was proud of the story. *Sports Illustrated,* for instance, had a team working on it and couldn't find enough proof to run the story. Shortly after, amateur sports bodies throughout the world made the use of steroids illegal.

My exotic trips are now things of the past. I write my daily column for *The Toronto Sun* and its two sister papers, the *Edmonton* and *Calgary Suns.* I live a triple life, spending time in all three cities with Toronto as my base. Years ago I slipped into a comfortable but lazy style of writing about myself and what I did yesterday. As you can imagine, a lot of those columns were from my favorite watering holes in the good old days. I more or less became a professional drunk. A young artist named Karl Mueller started a comic strip called Rimmer a few years ago and the main character, supposedly fashioned after me, walked about with spots around his head, obviously from too much booze. Poor Karl had to quit the strip shortly after I went on the wagon. The Rimmer character became Fuddy in a new, syndicated strip. Fuddy can drink. Rimmer couldn't anymore.

Come to think of it, it is exactly six months today since I had my last drink.

KARL MUELLER 80©

I magine, here I am, on the last chapter. Maybe, if I had stopped drinking ten years ago, I might have written that book in Mexico. Or the one at Stony Lake.

People keep looking at me in amazement. They have never before seen me so steady on my feet at midnight, a cup of coffee in my hand. Even Rusty Rita, my old Pontiac, is confused. She had more freedom in the old days as she found her own way home. Now I do the steering. There are also skeptics who are just waiting for me to go back to the booze.

I don't deserve to feel as well as I do. I feel so good, in fact, that if the doctors told me I could start drinking again tomorrow, I would have to give it serious second thoughts.

Now, though, I know what the late Oscar Levant meant when he said: "I only drink to make other people interesting." Heck, my old pals aren't nearly as funny as they used to be.

I still frequent the same bars, hang around with the same crowd, and enjoy myself almost as much—until about 11 o'clock at night. I find myself wishing the guys wouldn't order another round of doubles because I feel I'm losing their company. After one more drink they'll start laughing at little things I don't find funny and start to repeat themselves. That's the only part I miss. I miss being half in the tank the way they are. I used to shift gears myself at that stage of the evening. Now I feel uncomfortable, bored, and wish I was at home reading or watching a late movie.

What has happened is, I have become very dull. I don't wear lampshades at parties anymore. I don't even start arguments the way I used to late at nights. I have become very predictable. I even sleep well, a solid-six or easy-eight hours without waking once. Hell, I used to get up at least twice each night to go to the bathroom or get myself a cold drink. And now I sleep in bed. In the good old days, I could sleep anywhere. I'd often catch a nap at the Sai Woo Restaurant when the bars were closed. Garfield, one of the Chinese owners, would let me sleep until he was ready to close or I would wake up when my face fell into my fried rice.

When I finally got home in the middle of the night, I would catch another couple of hours while sitting on the toilet. I will never forget the night that I awakened in a panic. There had been these terrible pounding noises and it seemed as if I had flown through the air and bounced off something. I had fallen asleep on the toilet, tipped over and, fallen into the bathtub. I miss those good times.

And I miss stumbling to the refrigerator in the morning, groping for something wet and cold—orange pop, chocolate milk, tomato juice, fruit juices, or even a flat beer. They have not tasted nearly as good since I went on the wagon.

I started experimenting with substitutes for my scotch and Cointreau while I was in Hawaii, right after getting out of the hospital, I tried Virgin Marys—Bloody Marys without vodka. A friend says the real name should be Bloody Shames. That wasn't the answer. All I did was burp. Then, for a couple of months, I got hooked on Perrier water with fresh lime. All that did was make me go to the bathroom every ten minutes.

Now I have firmly established myself as a coffee freak. This happens to most drunks when they quit. But they drink it for the caffeine. I have one friend, a member of Alcoholics Anyonymous, who drinks about twenty cups at a sitting. Fortunately, I drink decaffeinated coffee and it doesn't bother me. My pal gets irritable and edgy. I know how he feels. If I go to a bar to hear some jazz and they don't have Sanka, I get higher than a kite on coffee and lie awake all night staring at the ceiling.

The biggest change is in my eating habits. I had stopped eating for about three years, just picking at my meals. I kept saying I drank Cointreau because it was made from oranges and was my source of vitamin C. It also was very sweet and killed whatever appetite I might have had. Now I am a glutton. Food tastes better than ever before. And then there is the sweet tooth. . . .

Holy smokes, do you ever crave sugar after you stop drinking, probably because you have to replace the sugar that you got from booze. Ask any reformed drunk. I have become a jellybean freak! I go around popping jellybeans, devour butter tarts and pies, fill myself on cookies (especially those chocolate ones with marshmallow in the center) and, whenever I see them, I buy bags and bags of Smarties and M & M's.

When I returned from Edmonton after my, uh, experience, I weighed only 159 pounds. That was in April. Miss C. Hinky, my lady friend (that is her nickname—she's Chinese), had ordered a three-piece tailored suit for my birthday from Nick the Needle. The Needle had my old measurements from the days he rented me formal wear from his Mister Tuxedo shop. When I went to pick up the suit, he turned white.

"Where did you go?" he cried. "What happened?"

I certainly had lost weight. Just before I left Edmonton I had walked through a bar and placekicker Dave Cutler of football's Edmonton Eskimos had yelled: "Hey Rimmer! I see you left your ass in your other pants!"

Poor Nick had to send the suit back to be recut and tailored all over again. I had lost six inches from my waist. While I was there, I ordered four new pairs of slacks and a camel hair jacket. I also got Nick to take in my old clothes so they would fit my new body.

My new clothes were ready a month later, including the re-done suit and Nick was grinning, until he saw me. . . .

"What are you doing to me?" he cried.

The chocolate cookies had increased my weight by fifteen pounds in two weeks. I still do not have my new suit. Nick has sent it back again.

Now it might be harder to beat the jellybean habit than it was to stop drinking. Frankly, though, I have not craved a drink since I stopped. I tell people I only miss the way it made me feel.

What bothers me most is when your old drinking pals try not to drink in front of you. I don't have to worry about that, thank goodness, in Edmonton. My buddies there, Wes Montgomery, Waldo Ranson, Peter Travis, Jackie Parker, and the rest have not slowed down a bit. I keep kidding them, telling them I am holding meetings in my basement every Monday night.

"We are not certain," said Montgomery one day, "if we care for you very much when you are sober. In fact, we are rather worried that you might become one of those reformed drunks."

Where I once was a professional drunk in my column, I am now a professional abstainer of sorts. There is added pressure on me to stay dry because, as my mail and doctors tell me, a lot of people quit when I did. Mind you, as I said at the beginning, if I am totally bored, I just might elect to drink it out.

I now realize what a large group I have joined. I get it from everybody. The barber, cutting my hair: "We, uh, have something in common," he whispers. Then he tells me a horror story of how he used to beat his wife, get drunk for weeks on end, and how Alcoholics Anonymous was the answer. Three waitresses came up to me at the racetrack one day and whispered that they, too, were AA members. Well sir, I have nothing against AA but, dammit, I am not a member and never will be a member. If I'm not strong enough to drop drinking by myself, there isn't enough to me that is worth trying to reform or save. Besides, I still insist I was an excessive drinker instead of a rolling, falling-down drunk.

I find it really embarrassing when someone comes up and tells me in a hushed and confidential voice how proud they are of my new look and life-style. I admire people, too, who stop drinking of their own accord because booze is ruining their family lives or jobs. But, hell, it isn't very difficult to stop drinking when you consider my alternative. As somebody once said, nothing is as bad as dying. I'm still against my abstinence. Nobody ever loved booze more than me. I still use a tone of reverence in my voice when I mention scotch, Cointreau, or any of those other joys of life.

One thing sobriety has not improved is my punctuality. As I sit here pecking at my typewriter, half a dozen people at Prentice-Hall are tearing at their hair. They keep telling me that a book must be out in time for Christmas and that I am about two months behind schedule. I keep shrugging my shoulders and telling them that I must wait until my creative juices begin to flow. Actually, I am just as lazy when sober as I was when I was drunk.

This, of course, is my first experience with a book and we all locked horns right off the bat. I wanted it to be a hard-cover book. They wanted it as it is, a deluxe paperback so that they could keep the price down. Our real battle was over the title. The original one we agreed on was: The Great Monopoly Caper and Other Stories by Paul Rimstead. The stuffed shirts at Parker Brothers turned us down flat. I went out and bought a game of Parcheesi.

Joerg Klauck, the editor, suggested Win, Place, or Rimstead! I told him I did not want my name in the title because nobody knows me. Then there was: Will the Real Paul Rimstead Please Sit Down!

They pacified me somewhat by using one of my title suggestions as a chapter heading: Top Hats and Tales of Woe. Editor-in-Chief Gerry Halpin seemed to have his heart set on Rambling with Rimstead.

"That," I bristled, "sounds like the name of a column in a smalltown newspaper."

Then I suggested Cocktails and Jockstraps.

"It must be decided by the quorum," said Halpin.

"But, don't you have a quorum?" I asked. "There's you, Janice Whitford, Joe Chin, Joerg. . . ."

"The Quorum," he said, "is in Vancouver on business."

Wally (The Quorum) Matheson returned the next day. The Quorum is the president of the company.

I lost the hard-cover but won the title. While awaiting their decisions, I agonized at home. Dick Duff, a former hockey great, was visiting.

"Duffy," I said, "if I was still drinking, I would have told them to shove this book long ago."

"If you were still drinking," said Duffy, "you wouldn't have written the book." ●